MW00806993

Crime and Circumstance

Crime and Circumstance

Investigating the History of Forensic Science

SUZANNE BELL

Westport, Connecticut
London

Library of Congress Cataloging-in-Publication Data

Bell, Suzanne.
   Crime and circumstance : investigating the history of forensic science / Suzanne Bell.
     p.   cm.
   Includes bibliographical references and index.
   ISBN 978–0–313–35386–4 (alk. paper)
1. Forensic sciences—History.   2. Criminal investigation—History.   I. Title.
HV8073.B424   2008
363.2509—dc22   2008008081

British Library Cataloguing in Publication Data is available.

Library of Congress Catalog Card Number: 2008008081
ISBN: 978–0–313–35386–4

First published in 2008

Praeger Publishers, 88 Post Road West, Westport, CT 06881
An imprint of Greenwood Publishing Group, Inc.
www.praeger.com

Printed in the United States of America

The paper used in this book complies with the
Permanent Paper Standard issued by the National
Information Standards Organization (Z39.48–1984).

10 9 8 7 6 5 4 3 2 1

To my colleagues past and present, and especially all the wonderful students I have met over the years. The future of forensic science is bright.

Contents

Figures

Preface

Forensic science became real to me some twenty years ago when I processed my first homicide scene. Although I had already spent six years studying the subject followed by months of an internship immersed in the laboratory, forensic science was not real to me until that day. It was only in hindsight that I understood what effect this early morning encounter had on me. A young woman (about twenty-seven, only four years older than me at that time) had been shot in the head at point blank range with a large caliber hunting rifle. It did unimaginable damage. Her husband had pulled the trigger while their young daughter lay sleeping in the next room. The legal issue was not whether he had caused his wife's death but rather the circumstances of that death. Accidental killing or homicide? That is what we were there to find out. Eventually, I testified in court to my findings, as did many of my lab colleagues.

Forensic scientists are archaeologists of the recent past. We recover artifacts from a place, carefully recording their context. That place is usually a crime scene that imprisons the echoes of a frozen moment in time. The information recorded in that moment begins to decay the second it is created. We use our expertise to evaluate and interpret crime scene artifacts to recreate the likeliest scenario to explain what we found, where we found it, and in what condition. By doing so, we help sort out conflicting versions of what happened and why. In this homicide case, I was asked to estimate the angle of the rifle barrel relative to the bed when it was fired. This one piece of scientific data was the heart of the case. If the angle of the gun barrel relative to the bed was close to perpendicular, the gun was pointing nearly straight downward, as it would have to be if the victim was laying down. Such evidence would support a version of the story in which the woman was killed in her sleep. If the barrel was closer to parallel to the bed, the victim could have been sitting upright. This supported a version of events in which she was awake and sitting up, possibly struggling, and conceivably causing an accidental discharge.

There was other evidence to interpret such as bloodstain patterns, but the tale hung on the question of the angle, a question I was not qualified to answer. My training and experience at that time was in crime scene processing and forensic chemistry, not firearms analysis. I was perfectly qualified to go to a scene, document it, and decide what evidence to collect. I also knew that collection is one thing, analysis and interpretation something else entirely. Forensic reality differs from forensic fiction in this way. We took the photos needed for our firearms analyst to answer this question and delivered the blood-soaked mattress to the lab for him to study. When asked on the stand what the angle was, I declined to answer.

This crime scene taught me that, largely, forensic science is the science of circumstance. It is not about solving cases as much as it is about applying typical science to atypical and often ugly and tragic situations. This process yields scientific evidence, the majority of which is circumstantial. Contrary to popular misconception, circumstantial evidence is not weak evidence. Hard science applied through forensic methods produces hard evidence; the challenge is interpretation. Therein lies the challenge, excitement, and rewards of forensic science.

I stayed on as a forensic analyst for a couple more years after that homicide scene before my interests turned toward research and education. I left the forensic laboratory to move first to a national laboratory (Los Alamos) and later to one dedicated to research. After a few more years, I made the daring leap onto the ivory tower, although my "tower" was an unimposing brick building. I have come full circle, returning to forensic science as a professor, author, researcher, and consultant. To teach forensic science, I have spent time studying its history, and the fascination born of that work motivated me to write this book.

Good forensic science can implicate the guilty, but also and just as importantly, it can exonerate the innocent. It has taken many years to get to this point. False prophets, fools, and self-proclaimed experts marred early forensic science, often dazzling courts with salesmanship over expertise. Pseudoscience still knocks on courtroom doors and sometimes manages to slip in. In the worst case, scientific evidence can become so complex that juries simply ignore it. Scientific analysis appears so convoluted and technical that a clever attorney can easily raise a reasonable doubt to prevent a conviction. If this trend continues, courts will fumble complex cases, and public trust, the blood currency of the justice system, will be lost.

As an educator, I believe that knowledge is the cure. If society can integrate science and technology, then so can the courts. The legal system adapted to the industrial age; the same will be true of the technical one. The courts are as flexible and adaptable as they are slow and deliberate. Indeed, to do the job right, the process must be meticulous and methodical. To incorporate scientific learning and expertise, the courtroom must become a place of education that includes all participants, from the jury to the judge. If we understand where forensic science came from and how it evolved, we are much better equipped to evaluate and apply it in the future.

When I ask my students how long forensic science has been around, predictably I get a range of responses—from twenty years (an eternity to one the same age) to a thousand years. In truth, we do not know who first applied what could be called science to what could be called crime. The definition of those two ideas has only recently crystallized into something generally agreed upon. We know that the Chinese used fingerprints for identification, but we do not know if that included criminal identification. We also know that the Chinese were the first to record information about how to tell whether someone had died of strangulation or some other less nefarious method. Yet as scientists are fond of noting, absence of evidence is not evidence of absence. Based on what we know of human nature, we can surmise that crime predated fire, stone knives, and bearskin rugs. Forensic science was likely born the day after the first crime was committed. This book will examine the earliest documented uses of forensic science with the understanding that it existed long before them. I often imagine what the Sherlock Holmes of ancient Egypt or China was like, but I never doubt if he or she existed.

As to that first homicide scene, I do not know the outcome of the trial. I rarely think about it, even though the memories of the images, and especially of the smell, remain vivid. When I do recollect it, I wonder how that little girl, now a young woman, has managed. I do not know if the court ruled her mother's death an accident or a murder, nor do I know what fate befell the husband. That was for the court to decide, because it had the totality of the evidence. I testified and left, and that was the end of the case for me.

Unlike most fictional portrayals, forensic scientists must keep their distance to protect their objectivity. Some mistake this detachment for indifference or even callous denial, but nothing could be farther from the truth. The good forensic scientists, and there are thousands of them, care passionately or they would not be where they are. The profession does not pay well, the hours can be long, and the off days are often at the whim of the courts. Anyone who enters a study of forensic science based on what he or she has seen on TV rarely gets past the first year of chemistry, biology, calculus, and physics. Forensic science is science first; *forensic* is easy, *science* is hard. The dedicated people who make it through a demanding curriculum and a competitive job market rarely care about money, fame, or the perceived glamor of the field. Rather, bench forensic scientists care about making a difference every day and live for the endless variety of cases that come through their doors. Theirs is a history thousands of years in the making.

As I became more interested in that history, I began to search out resources and references to study. I quickly found that conspicuously missing from the forensic library is a timely and accessible history that approaches its subject as a history of science rather than a history of crime and detection. It was that discovery that led to this project. Through the story of its early practitioners, this book will tell the intriguing tale of how an ancient and obscure offshoot of medicine matured into forensic science. The story encompasses law, culture, and science because forensic science does the same. In this way, it is one of the most uniquely human sciences.

Acknowledgments

This project came together thanks to the efforts of Suzanne I. Staszk-Silva of the Greenwood Publishing Group. I am also indebted to Ms. Jodie Rhodes, literary agent and career mentor. It is not easy to find agents to represent scholarly work and texts, and without her this proposal would have never gone out, much less become a book. Finally, I wish to acknowledge as a group my wonderful forensic science students, colleagues, and mentors. I have found my professional home among them and am constantly amazed and heartened by their passion and dedication.

Introduction

I approached this subject through the lens of the three sciences (medicine, chemistry, and biology) from which forensic science emerged. History of law and society weaves through the narrative to highlight their overlaps and divergences. The emphasis is on personalities, historical trends, and the threads that link the ancient to the modern practice of forensic science. I relate selected cases, but those seeking true crime and lurid details will be disappointed. By all means, please purchase and read the book, but realize that the cases related are illustrative sidelines. Still, fans of true crime will find much to like here. If you are interested in true crime, this is as true as it gets.

The treatment of individual forensic disciplines is purposely broad and integrative. Death investigation was the spark that led to forensic science, and it involves medicine, chemistry, and biology. Forensic toxicology was the first to emerge from the medical umbrella, yet it never strayed far from those roots. The first distinctive forensic biology was not DNA but rather fingerprints and biological measurements. The forensic areas the public is most familiar with, such as crime scene investigation, are ultimately derivative and integrative, bringing together fundamental scientific tools and knowledge but applying them in unique ways. Thus, the story touches familiar areas such as crime scenes, questioned documents, and firearms, but this treatment is not meant to be a definitive history of those individual disciplines. I intend no slight to my forensic friends and colleagues in forensic engineering, tool marks, or anthropology. I have simply selected to paint the picture using a bigger brush.

The book opens in the present to set the stage. From there, it leaps back to ancient times and follows a roughly historical order until reaching the medieval era. The paths of medicine and chemistry start to diverge there, and so does the narrative. Chemistry and death investigation is emphasized until we reach the 1800s, when forensic science finally sets as a profession. The story branches to follow several paths, ending with the biological advances that are currently having such a great impact on forensic science and the rules of admissibility that govern it.

Although I am familiar with aspects of the law and am a historian by avocation, I am neither a lawyer nor a historian. My approach emphasizes science and how it has overlapped with the law as seen through my scientist's eyes. I have not delved much into recent controversies of and related to forensic science principally because this is a history. Many cases familiar to general readers, such as the O.J. Simpson trial, are mentioned peripherally because either their impact on forensic science was not significant or they are too recent to judge the impact. I also have purposely avoided recent controversial cases for the same reason.

Where to start this journey? The beginning lies with the beginning of civilization, but before venturing back, we need to ground ourselves in a common definition of forensic science. That is best accomplished in the present day.

1

Sexy Science?

Criminalistics (forensic science) "is concerned with the unlikely and the unusual. Other sciences are concerned primarily with the likely and the usual. The derivation of equations, formulas, and generalizations summarizing the normal behavior of any system in the universe is a major goal of the established sciences. It is not normal to be murdered, and most persons never experience this unlikely event. Yet, when a murder occurs, some combination of circumstances suddenly alters the situation from unlikely to certain."
—Paul L. Kirk, American criminalist (forensic scientist)[1]

Forensic science is sexy. It thrives by embracing human intrigue and frailties, great mysteries and tragedies, and scientific triumphs and disgraces. Add in a dash of sex, drugs, crime, and murder, and the lure is irresistible. Paul Leland Kirk (1902–1970), a central figure in American forensic science, understood that forensic science is intriguing because it is unusual. The response of the forensic science community to newfound fame is a predictable mix of excitement and dismay. It is fun to be at the center of attention, but at the same time being the subject of books, movies, and television shows inevitably leads to false impressions and unrealistic expectations.

Beyond being intriguing and unusual, what is forensic science? Because the label *forensic* has become fashionable, it is being used in new, creative, and often inappropriate contexts. Ever heard of forensic seismology? How about forensic meteorology, forensic accounting, or nuclear forensics? Ten years ago, describing these procedures as forensic would have seemed a stretch, particularly to analysts who have been doing autopsies, testing fire debris, and plucking hair from underwear for decades. Investigators at crime scenes don jackets emblazoned with FORENSICS in huge letters. What do these people do? A strict definition of forensics has to do with formal oral argument, but these people are assuredly not the high school debate team. Rather, they are the team that collects, documents, and delivers evidence to a laboratory staffed by forensic scientists. Store shelves teem with T-shirts honoring and advertising television and movies with forensic themes (forensic entertainment) such that anyone can wear one. Therein lies the price of popularity. Everyone wants the forensic moniker and as a result, the definition of forensic science is so thin that its original shape is hard to imagine, let alone define. Pop the balloon, and it fragments into unrecognizable shreds.

The words *forensic* and *science* each relate to the common theme of truth, either speaking it or seeking it. Forensic arose from the Latin *forum* or "in the public." The definition roughly translates as, "to speak the truth in public." In the present case, this extends to speaking the truth in court, the modern forum. The definition is incomplete without considering science, a much harder word to define. And what about truth? Discretion being the better part of valor, an attempt to define that term will be left to scholars, philosophers, and to the tenth edition of *Merriam-Webster's Collegiate Dictionary*, which defines truth (as applicable here) as "sincerity in action, character, and utterance; the state of being the case: *fact*; the body of real things, events, and facts: *actuality* [emphasis added]." The role of science is to help society recognize fact; the role of forensic science is to help the legal system define it as it applies to the natural world.

Forensic science is often described as the application of scientific knowledge and techniques to legal matters, but this fails to define what distinguishes forensic science from any other science. Two of the first forensic scientists, Paul Kirk and the Frenchman Edmund Locard (1877–1966), considered forensic science to be the science of comparison. If a tiny red spot is found clinging to a suspect's shirt, simple chemical tests can determine if it is blood that can then be compared to a blood sample from a murder victim. The science used to perform the comparison, Kirk or Locard would argue, is not forensic science. Rather, it is the *comparison* itself and the interpretation of the results that defines the science used as forensic science. The best forensic scientists must have a breadth of knowledge across the sciences coupled with the ability to use that knowledge to make meaningful comparisons and draw defensible conclusions.

Forensic comparisons require successive classification. An analyst might first test the red stain found on the shirt with a chemical reagent such as luminol. The results classify the stain into one of two groups: probably blood or probably not blood. Before DNA typing was available, the analyst would next classify the blood as human or animal. If human, the next classification according to the ABO grouping would further narrow the population size. Each categorization places the questioned stain in a successively smaller group. The smaller the size of the group, the more meaningful it is to place the stain in that group. Finding a bloodstain with the blood type AB makes it easier than finding type O because the number of people with AB blood is much smaller (about 4 percent of the U.S. population) than in other groups such as type O (about 45 percent).

In forensic comparison and classification, smaller groups are better; groups with one member are the best. The goal is always to analyze and successively categorize evidence until it belongs to a group consisting of one. With proper caveats, fingerprints and DNA evidence can fall within this ideal; for any fingerprint, there is one and only one possible source. Most forensic comparisons are less definitive. Frequently, even the most exhaustive testing leads to a seemingly tepid conclusion of exclusion or inclusion. A trace evidence specialist compares a fiber found on a murder victim to fibers collected from a carpet in the trunk of a car, for example. Testing may prove that both are black nylon fibers with a hollowed-out design. For all the time and effort extended, all the analyst can say with certainty is that the fiber found on the victim could have come from a jacket. This is *inclusive evidence*. Put another way, the jacket cannot be excluded as a possible source of the fiber. The value of such findings depends on the context of the investigation. The Wayne Williams case, described in Chapter 13, depended almost exclusively on fiber evidence. In many other cases, fiber evidence may be peripheral or of no use; it all depends on the circumstances of that unique case. Regardless of its weight, the evidentiary value arises from comparison and classification. This is the process of forensic science.

Paul Kirk and others of his generation described the comparison process as *criminalistics*, first coined by Hans Gross (1847–1915), an Austrian magistrate turned forensic scientist. Gross assumed that since *criminology* is the application of social sciences to crime, *criminalistics* is a reasonable description of natural science similarly applied. The elegant symmetry never stuck, and the confusion created lingers to this day. Criminology and criminalistics are not the same; never have been, and never will be. Further confusing the nomenclature is the description of forensic science as *police science*. True, in early forensic laboratories, many of the analysts were active or retired police officers, and so logically, the term *police science* described the science performed by police. This muddied the picture because police science included everything from fingerprinting and photography to criminal law and interrogation techniques. The term became hopelessly vague and outdated. Since the 1980s, the more inclusive and accurate *forensic science* description has caught on, but the other terms still appear.

Even forensic scientists struggle to agree on the best description for what they do. One of the professional bodies that oversees certification of forensic scientists is the American Board of Criminalistics, while the largest professional society in the field is the American Academy of Forensic Sciences. The inability to settle on a description is more a symptom of youth than confusion. Among the modern sciences, forensic science is the screaming newborn of medicine, chemistry, and biology.

HISTORY OF A HISTORICAL SCIENCE

Forensic scientists are the archaeologists of the near past who use scientific comparison to recreate plausible scenarios and dismiss implausible ones. When a forensic team processes a crime scene, they act as field archaeologists, retrieving artifacts and recording their contexts. One without the other is useless. A bloody knife found in a butcher shop means something different from a bloody knife found at a homicide scene. A properly processed scene unfolds as a choreographed ballet of excavation, documentation, and collection. Knowing what to leave is as important as knowing what to take; too much irrelevant information drowns the relevant in a sea of noise.

Forensic science is historical in practice as well as in philosophy. Many modern laboratory protocols recreate history with each rendition. A forensic analyst faced with a red stain on a shirt must first determine if the substance is blood. This requires a presumptive test that produces a color change if positive. These tests first appeared in the late 1800s. Determining the species and type of the blood requires techniques refined before the Great Depression. DNA analysis spilled out of molecular biology and into the forensic world in the 1980s. History and precedent lie at the heart of science, just as they do at the heart of the law. Forensic science lives where the two overlap.

Science and the law are not the compatible bedfellows people often assume they are. Both seek to investigate events based on available evidence, articulate presumptions based on probability, and use those presumptions to arrive at the most likely interpretation of events. The more probable a presumption becomes, the closer it approaches fact. The law and science differ dramatically in their goals and methods. The goal of science is to describe the workings of the natural world, while the goal of the law is to settle disputes. Science relies on the scientific method of hypothesis, experiment and observation, and refinement to validate ideas and presumptions. The law relies on the adversarial system and argument to determine how best to resolve conflict. Theoretically and in simplistic terms, whoever makes the better argument wins in an adversarial system.

In such a design, the crucible of truth is argument. In science, that crucible is observation and experiment. The test of truth in science is not always valid in a legal setting and vice versa. In both science and law, finding the truth, be it through the scientific method or argument,

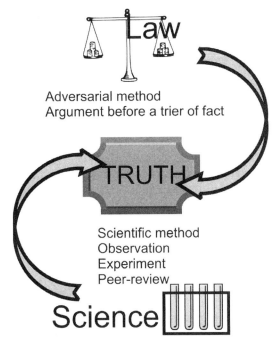

Figure 1.1 Science and the law both seek the truth, but using different methods.

is singularly useful in achieving a goal; however, truth is not the only or even the primary goal of either process. Understanding the differences between law and science is as vital as understanding the similarities. The history of forensic science rings hollow without it.

In keeping with its uncommon lineage, the central characters of this forensic tale are, with few exceptions, not forensic scientists. Indeed, until recently there was no such thing. Many scientists played a peripheral and unintentional role in the creation of forensic sciences and few would ever have labeled themselves as such. The playbill includes: several Nobel Laureates; alchemists such as Jabir (~700), Paracelsus[2] (1493–1541), Albertus Magnus (1193–1280), Robert Boyle (1627–1691), and Isaac Newton (1627–1727); chemists such as Wilhelm Bunsen (1811–1899), Eduard Buchner (1860–1917), and Johann Adolf von Baeyer (1835–1917); biologists such as Gregor Mendel (1822–1884), Charles Darwin (1809–1882) and his cousin Sir Francis Galton (1822–1911), Joseph Lister (1827–1912), and Karl Landsteiner (1868–1943); forensic practitioners such as M.J.B. Orfila (1787–1853), Kirk, Milton Helpern (1902–1977), and Bernard Spilsbury (1877–1947); and the occasional odd historical figure such as Alfred Nobel (1833–1896), Oliver Wendell Holmes (1809–1894), several members of the Du Pont family, Sigmund Freud (1856–1939), and King Louis XIV (1638–1715). The story is multidisciplinary, cross-cultural, and driven by human personality as much as by human ingenuity.

Because forensic science arises from such diverse and nontraditional historical treads, traditional timelines are not terribly useful. However, comparing the flow of events in the maturing of judicial practices with acts of scientific advances can act as the framework for the history of forensic science. The precepts of law such as taxes, torture, and death investigation were well established by the end of the Roman Empire, as was trial by jury. The interesting aspect from the forensic perspective is how the rules of evidence changed, eventually leading to the appearance of expert witnesses in the 1600s. From there, the leap to forensic expert witnesses was easy, but not quick.

Science as relevant to the forensic story arose from ancient medicine and medicinal treatments based principally on plants. Since many plants contain poisonous substances, criminal poisoning was known, understood, and feared by 2000 years B.C.E. Medical and biological sciences continued on parallel paths until the Renaissance when biology (and many other sciences) became specialized and distinct from the amorphous *science*. Chemistry took a slightly different path because there was an ancient need for chemical technologies, notably in metallurgy and making of alcoholic beverages. Following the events along these separated paths sets the stage for the emergence of forensic science from the indistinct mass of medicine, biology, and chemistry.

To tell such an unusual tale, unusual tactics are called for. The history of forensic science begins at the scene—how it exists frozen in the moment, the evidence present, and its context. From there, careful analysis, classification, and interpretation are used to recreate the events and characters that defined this history.

2

The Scene of the Catastrophe

MASS DISASTER AND THE NEW CRIME SCENE

For many Americans, the year 2005 is associated with one word—
Katrina—and the year 2001 with one day—September 11. In between came
the D.C. snipers, a Christmas tsunami in south Asia in 2004, and the
London and Madrid terrorist bombings (in 2005 and 2004, respectively). A
year after *Katrina* came a near miss: a disrupted plot to blow up airliners
over the Atlantic in late 2006, near the five-year anniversary of September 11. The plotters planned to smuggle the ingredients of explosives
aboard planes and synthesize and detonate them en route. For the forensic
community, these dates were mileposts rather than turning points. These
crimes and disasters represented the culmination of the slow evolution
of microtragedy that was always the forensic scientist's stock and trade.
Before September 11, a mass disaster was a plane crash or railroad accident with casualties in the hundreds. Agencies and first responders prepared for worst-case scenarios involving 500 deaths.[1] After the attacks,
crime scenes were measured in miles and debris in tons; casualties were
numbered in thousands or tens of thousands. The public face of forensic
science became less associated with crime and evidence and more closely
associated with recovery and identification of the dead. Forensic scientists
did what they have always done. In the new century, they have emphasized scaling up to fundamental change.

SCALE AND SCOPE

September 11, 2001 was a day of cheerless milestones. It marked the largest deployment to date of the Federal Emergency Management Agency's (FEMA's) Disaster Mortuary Response Team (DMORT) to the largest single crime scene ever created. Thousands of pieces of scattered and shattered human remains awaited recovery and identification. Multiple federal, state, and local agencies learned on the fly how to coordinate efforts on an unprecedented scale. A few weeks after the air assault, a still-unidentified person sent anthrax bacteria through the mail killing five, infecting seventeen, and forcing 30,000 people to take antibiotics. The dispersed but deadly trail of evidence stretched up the East Coast from Florida to Connecticut. In less than two months, these two terrorist incidents upended the very definition of the term *crime scene*. What was once limited to a room, house, or a body dumpsite now crossed state boundaries. Still, the dead held center stage.

The National Funeral Directors Association conceived DMORT in the 1980s. At the time, there were no uniform processes for handling mass disasters, nor was there a mechanism for local authorities to request assistance. The beginnings of DMORT were portable morgue units and teams of professionals trained to manage mass casualty incidents. The identification tools available to DMORT include visual identification of a body by relatives, use of personal effects like drivers' licenses, tattoos and other markings, fingerprinting, comparison of antemortem (before death) and postmortem X-rays, dental work, fingerprints, and DNA analysis. The combination of techniques proved invaluable when what little remained of a person or people was damaged, separated, burned, commingled with others, and unrecognizable as human, let alone as something that was once living.

The DMORT autopsy emphasizes identification rather than cause of death, since the latter is usually obvious. The first DMORT deployed in 1993, and the system now operates under the National Disaster Medical System (NDMS), a part of the Federal Emergency Management Agency (FEMA). Each team consists of doctors, dentists, X-ray technicians, anthropologists, and support staff, and each team brings with it a complete portable morgue, including refrigerated storage units. Four DMORT teams responded to New York City on September 11, the largest deployment in its history until August 2005, when all ten DMORT teams responded to *Katrina*.

Identification of remains from the September 11 attacks in New York and Washington relied principally on DNA technology because the remains were fragmented, badly damaged, and removed from any useful context such as airplane seat number. The obliterated planes fused with the structures and remains of passengers mingled with those of building occupants. The collapse of the towers destroyed any sense of relative location (floor of the building or office number) that could have been helpful in associating a bone chip or tissue fragment with a small pool of likely victims. Rescue efforts yielded 287 intact bodies out of nearly 3,000 victims. Four years after the attacks, recovery efforts yielded approximately 20,000 separate samples from the site that have been documented, cataloged, and analyzed to the extent current technology allows. This number does not include comparison samples collected from relatives and family members. As of November 2005, DNA techniques have successfully identified 850 victims from the World Trade Center attacks out of the 2,749 listed as missing. When combined with other means such as fingerprints and dental records, nearly 1,600 individuals have been identified.

DNA typing methods, similar or identical to those used in forensic labs, produced the majority of the identifications. Some new technology and software emerged to address problems associated with damaged and degraded samples. One of the greatest challenge to forensic scientists was not scientific; it was organizational—developing a system to catalog each item, labeling and storing it, keeping track of results as they became available, and linking similar samples. All samples had to be linked to one of the missing to provide conclusive identification. The comparison samples came from families and included toothbrushes and hairbrushes used by the victims, as well as cheek swab samples from relatives. Unlike most forensic cases, many of the matches were made indirectly using DNA types of relatives rather than by simple comparison of a known and questioned sample. Development of this next-of-kin software was indispensable to the identification efforts. Collection kits and methods developed in the wake of September 11 were distributed to other agencies and countries, and the lessons already applied in the 2004 tsunami and the 2005 hurricanes.

The 972 deaths so far associated with *Katrina* presented a different identification challenge. Most bodies were intact and found in context such as in a home or hospital bed. Trauma from fire and collapse was absent, but severe decomposition arising from prolonged immersion in warm, swampy, and animal-infested water was typical. Much to the surprise of the forensic community and state officials, knowledge gained from September 11 was of limited use in the Gulf Coast. Despite a smaller death toll and intact bodies, identifications were proving problematic.

In the immediate aftermath of the storms, efforts focused on rescue before turning to recovery. In the hot and humid conditions, this delay allowed rapid decomposition that quickly made bodies unrecognizable even to the victim's closest family and friends. A week or so in the water causes skin shedding and the loss of useable fingerprints. The storm's fury exhumed the long-buried dead, adding several hundred additional bodies to those killed by the hurricane. Soon after the storm, when dire predictions of thousands of deaths were the norm, the Federal Emergency

Management Agency, part of the new Department of Homeland Security formed in the aftermath of September 11, began planning construction and deployment of a morgue facility that could handle 150 bodies a week.

Utilization of postmortem records like dental X-rays for identification requires the existence of antemortem data. Unfortunately, the generalized destruction destroyed dental and medical offices and storage sites and contaminated sample sources like toothbrushes and hairbrushes that were so useful after September 11. Many victims were poor and had few medical or dental records to begin with, adding to the challenge. With personal possessions destroyed and relatives dispersed, collection of comparison samples was difficult.

The scope of the disaster magnified problems. On September 11, the three attack sites were each located within a single local jurisdictional area. The hurricanes struck across city, county, and state lines. Death investigation in most areas is the responsibility of local coroners rather than forensic pathologists and medical examiners, the latter of which are often too expensive for poorer jurisdictions. Whether this had a direct impact on the recovery and identification process is not yet clear, but certainly, it did not help. A few weeks after the storms, the projected death toll fell to 1,000–2,000, and much of the initial work was completed. By February 2006, over 900 bodies had been identified, leaving fewer than 100. Most of the autopsies were completed before the FEMA morgue opened. The facility closed in February 2006, shortly after the last body was recovered.

As bad as *Katrina* was, the worst mass disaster of the young century occurred in December 2004 when a massive tsunami inundated thousands of miles of southeastern Asia. Estimates of the dead range from 150,000 to 220,000, but the final toll remains elusive. The disaster struck isolated islands and coastlines in an area far poorer and less developed than the U.S. Gulf coast. The wave devastated tourist areas, killing hundreds of Europeans, Americans, and other visitors. The wave swept thousands irretrievably out to sea, never to return. Others were washed ashore miles away or in different countries. Survivors buried countless bodies to stave off disease. As would occur with *Katrina*, heat and humidity accelerated decomposition, and there was little if any access to refrigerated storage areas.

Because so many foreigners died in tourist areas, the government of Thailand coordinated with the Interpol to form the Thai Tsunami Victim Identification (TTVI) operation. Forensic professionals from Europe, Canada, the United States, and other countries arrived within days of the disaster and began to assist in recovery and identification. Eventually, forensic practitioners from twenty-nine countries were involved in the tsunami identification efforts. Compared to identification work after September 11, DNA had not been used extensively. As of late 2005, dental identification accounted for about 48 percent of the identifications, finger-prints for 34 percent, and DNA for about 17 percent. Approximately 3,000 victims had been identified, leaving about 750 in the system unidentified. Tens of thousands still remain missing.

Bracketed by September 11 and *Katrina*, Europe endured two bomb-ing attacks, one in Madrid, Spain, on March 11, 2004, and one in London on July 7, 2005. The attack in Madrid targeted four commuter trains and killed 191 people. Two thousand were injured. The bombs utilized stolen commercial explosives detonated by cell phones, and the perpetrators later blew themselves up to avoid capture. The London attack targeted the underground subway system and involved three bombs that went off deep in the tunnels within less than a minute. A fourth bomb went off nearly an hour later, perhaps by mistake or by mishandling. In contrast to Madrid, the London bombings were suicide attacks. Some of the re-covery workers who endured the heat of the underground tunnels were veterans of tsunami recovery efforts. The Madrid attacks spawned an in-ternational controversy over a mistaken fingerprint match and wrongful arrest of a Muslim lawyer in Portland, Oregon, a story that will unfold in a later chapter.

Recovery and identification of the dead has become the most visible forensic response and responsibility. Also new are the scope of these events and the resulting globalization of forensic science. Teams moved from New York to Madrid to Thailand to London, carrying new knowl-edge and hard-learned lessons to each new site only to find that what worked before was not entirely suitable for what was happening now. The definition of a crime scene, both the crime and the scene elements, has be-come fuzzy and indistinct. Was September 11 an act of war or a criminal one? From the forensic perspective, the line became vague and irrelevant. New Orleans and south Asia were not crime scenes, but they were def-initely forensic scenes. In the new century, crime is no longer a forensic prerequisite.

PREMONITIONS

If 2001 marked the culmination of transition in forensic science, where and when did it begin? Some early hints came in 1982 in Chicago. That year, a still anonymous killer took bottles containing Tylenol off store shelves and replaced the contents of some capsules with sodium cyanide. Seven people died, and whether the killer had a specific target in mind is unknown. Within days of the poisonings, forensic labs across the country dealt with an influx of pharmaceuticals and other materials suspected of containing cyanide at a time when rapid, reliable, and inexpensive chemi-cal screening tests were not widely available for that deadly species. In the wake of the poisonings, product tampering became a federal offense, and manufacturers developed tamper-proof containers and seals to prevent a recurrence.

This incident was a small but significant dress rehearsal for the anthrax mailings nineteen years later. Both cases created trails of evidence and victims dispersed over a wide area. Both required the rapid development and dissemination of fast and reliable screening tests for deadly materials. Both flooded local authorities with requests for analysis of suspicious materials that would not have raised an eyebrow before the incidents. Both created, if not panic, certainly anxiety and doubt about law enforcement's and forensic science's ability to respond quickly and effectively to such incidents. Finally, both forced alliances across agencies and jurisdictions never before envisioned, and both generated systematic changes in basic products and services and in the way people live and use those products and services.

As the Tylenol poisonings presaged the anthrax case, the first bombing of the World Trade Center in 1993 and the 1995 bombing of the Alfred P. Murrah Federal Building in Oklahoma City played out as dry runs for the attacks on the twin towers and the Pentagon. Both of these earlier bombings used simple explosives made from easily obtainable materials. Both blasts created massive crime scenes and the need for extensive engineering analysis and reporting. The collapses of the World Trade Center twin towers caught many by surprise, leading to extensive engineering analysis. The same teams that combed the ruins of the Murrah Federal Building are studying the death of the twin towers and the injuries to the Pentagon, and their findings will reveal underlying pathology in the construction that contributed to the collapse. From this study, recommendations have already emerged, such as improving the fireproofing applied to steel girders. Forensic skills were used again in 2005 as engineers studied the failure of the New Orleans levy system.

A pivotal and final omen of the coming change in forensic science came in 1996 with the crash of TWA Flight 800 off the coast of Long Island. The incident encapsulated the fundamental role of circumstance in forensic investigation. Was the crash an accident or purposeful? If intentional, was it an act of terrorism? The circumstance would dictate the response. The interplay of science and engineering, the handling of massive casualties, and the identification of hundreds of bits of fragmented remains were all encountered in an atmosphere in which it was unknown if the incident was a crime or a horrible accident. The flight departed the John F. Kennedy International Airport in New York at 8:00 P.M. on July 17, 1996, for Paris. At 8:31 P.M., the plane exploded as it climbed through 13,000 feet and rained down in a flaming trail of debris littering twelve square miles off the Long Island coast. Two hundred and three people died. The spectacular demise of the huge Boeing 747 lit up the sky before hundreds of witnesses on the ground, in the water, and in the air. Fearing the worst, the Federal Bureau of Investigation (FBI) geared up for what would become its largest and most complex investigation up to that time.

Numerous eyewitness accounts of fiery streaks heading upward led credence to theory that a shoulder-launched missile had brought down the huge plane. Discovery of traces of high explosives on parts of the recovered wreckage (later discounted) supported the theory of a missile or a bomb. Despite the preponderance of early evidence pointing toward a criminal act, investigators from the National Transportation Safety Board (NTSB) converged on the site to investigate the possibility of an accident. If so, the task of the NTSB was to determine what caused it and how to apply the findings to preventing future accidents. It would take months of painstaking examination by the FBI, the NTSB, the Federal Aviation Administration (FAA), and many other state and federal agencies to determine that the crash was most likely due to an accidental explosion of the center fuel tank. What malfunction or problem sparked the explosion remains a mystery.

The accident scattered debris over several square miles of ocean with a depth of 120 feet. As salvage crews and divers recovered the wreckage and delivered it to a rented hangar, forensic chemists from the FBI and the Bureau of Alcohol, Tobacco, and Firearms combed the pieces for any traces of explosives using dogs and portable equipment. At the same time, the NTSB conducted numerous engineering and flight tests and computer models to reconstruct the last moments of the flight. Extensive tests were conducted on wiring, fuel, fuel vapors, fuel probes, and potential electromagnetic interferences from personal electronic devices and other electrical components. After months of investigation and scientific and engineering analysis, the investigators found no convincing chemical or structural evidence of a missile or bomb. This, coupled with other evidence and the flammability of the vapors in the center tank, led to the investigations closing within a few months. The NTSB listed the probable cause as ignition of these vapors, but even after months of work, it was not able to pinpoint the source of the spark or flame that ignited them.

CHICKEN OR THE EGG?

Public interest in forensic science, real and fictional, has reached a near frenzy, but this popularity is nothing new or unique. Sir Arthur Conan Doyle's Sherlock Holmes stories were the first medium to bring scientific detection to the public's attention, but it took modern American pop culture to enshrine, embellish, and mythologize it. Television shows such as *Quincy, M.E.* (during the 1970s) and *CSI* (2000 and beyond) depict forensic science as it never was or could be. Movies such as *The Silence of the Lambs*, *The Bone Collector*, and *Kiss the Girls* (all based on best-selling novels) blithely sidestep the realities of forensic psychiatry, forensic investigation, and forensic psychology in the name of fictional license. This is not a crime (pun intended); all are marketed as fiction. The danger is that the audience, bombarded with the triumphs of forensic fiction, grows to expect the same feats from the real thing. Few reading science fiction mistake it for reality, but forensic science fiction is often interpreted as fact.

Forensic science professionals respond differently to this affection. Some embrace it, welcoming the scientist-as-hero portrayals. Youth growing up watching *CSI* and other media become interested in science and may decide to pursue it as a career, bringing fresh blood and new ideas into the forensic system. Less-enthused practitioners argue that unrealistic publicity bring false expectations that come to rest squarely at the laboratory doorstep. A few forensic scientists have embraced popularity by writing novels. Fewer still have exploited it for fame and financial gain.

Although it may seem like a modern phenomena, these happenings are nothing new and the pattern of popularity is more a continuation than a revolution. A century ago, the "*CSI* effect" was called the "Sherlock Holmes effect." The few universities and medical schools that taught forensic specialties were besieged with applicants. The same occurs today. Has the popularity of forensic science driven entertainment, or has entertainment driven the popularity? Both. A great writer, such as Conan Doyle, senses what will capture imaginations, but that is only part of the formula. A foundation in reality is essential for the reader to suspend disbelief long enough to be drawn into that fictional world. Doyle was in the right place at the right time, but even he had historical precedents. Chinese readers in the Middle Ages delighted in detective fiction with death investigators as heroes and victims dispatched by nails through the head. Now, as it was in ancient China and Victorian England, when the real world comes knocking, the unrealistic and unrealized expectations of forensic science are easily miscast as failure. This can lead to cynicism and a loss of faith in the justice system as well as in science. It is in this charged and complex atmosphere that forensic science must function today.

AN AUTOPSY OF HISTORY

As any science, forensic science advances at a pace dictated by a thousand variables, important among them being personalities, technologies, and societies. Its history, like forensic science itself, is all about circumstance. Forensic science is a derivative and exquisitely interdependent science that was not born but rather coalesced as a distinct profession in the 1800s. As such, there is no explicit timeline on which to drape a description of its history. The precursors, law and science, followed separate paths for much of recorded history, and those practicing them needed or had little interaction with each other. This narrative will emphasize the science aspect because it reflects the proper emphasis in light of how modern forensic scientists work—as scientists (first and foremost) operating in a judicial, legal, and law enforcement context.

3

Uniquely Human

Science as a profession and a practice is a newcomer to the human repertoire, yet it is fundamental in defining us as human. It relies on symbolic thought and language and is part of culture. The scientific method begins with an idea or hypothesis that explains an observation or experimental result. The hypothesis is tested and revised until results of experiments and observations unfailingly fit the hypothesis. Generally, such a proven hypothesis progresses to theory, and if it survives more scrutiny, it becomes accepted as a scientific law or fact. This does not mean that a law is unalterable in the face of new results, but it does mean that the fact has survived challenge and is as reliable as the current state of human knowledge and experience can make it.

The roots of science (though not the method itself) are older than civilization. Early humans understood how to make tools, how to cook food, which plants were edible and which were not, and how to make rudimentary paints. This knowledge was technical and not based on any underlying unifying principles. The core of these behaviors is the drive to learn, which as a survival strategy was invaluable to humans. Through learning, humans learned to cope with different environments and conditions and to eventually develop a system called science to assist in that process. Eventually, the information encoded in human DNA gave us the ability to learn how to analyze, classify, and type that very same DNA.

Science as a way of thinking traces back to the ancient Greeks, who were the first to impose systematic thought and analysis to observations. This occurred around 500 B.C.E. Prior to that, knowledge resided with priests or other spiritual figures. Understanding of how the world worked arose from experience (i.e., trial and error) and was passed on by apprenticeship. The Greeks organized ideas about the natural world and were able to conceive of advanced concepts. They postulated the atom (from the Greek *atomos*) as the fundamental unit of all matter. Indeed, Archimedes, a Greek mathematician, was one of the most brilliant thinkers of his or any day. Aristotle (384–322 B.C.E.) embraced the forensic concept of categorization. He was the first to record an attempt at classification of biological organisms. He also studied reproduction and heredity, the ancient forerunners of genetic marker testing such as DNA typing. The Greeks were also among the first to study anatomy, medicine, and physiology in a systematic way and did us the favor of leaving extensive written records of their work.

The core tenet of science is an idea or hypothesis stated in such a way that it can be tested and verified by experiments, observations, or both. The results of these observations and experiments lead to refinement of an idea, restatement, or, in the extreme, rejection of it. The experimenter or observer is (ideally) independent and objective. Absence of neutrality or an unwillingness to accept results at odds with existing ideas discounts the observation or results. Of course, if humans are involved, some level of subjectivity is inescapable, but science admits this danger and incorporates protections to prevent against them.

Another critical aspect of science that is particularly relevant to forensic science is the concept of *falsifiability*. A scientific fact or hypothesis is stated in such a way that it can be disproved. Often that statement is mathematical. For example, a fundamental physical law can be expressed as $F = ma$, or force is equal to mass times acceleration. This statement is unambiguous. As a result, it is easy to devise laboratory experiments to verify or disprove it. In forensic science, analysts' state results in such a manner that they can be tested and falsified. A toxicology report might state that a blood alcohol sample contained 0.12 percent alcohol. Another analyst can obtain a portion of the same sample and repeat the tests to verify or disprove the results. This is a reason why forensic analysts leave some portion of evidentiary sample for later testing. An irreproducible result represents a failure and a falsification of the original statement. The key to falsifiability is in the original statement itself, which must be clear, unambiguous, and quantitative. If it fails to meet these standards, it is not a scientific hypothesis.

Contrast a scientific statement such as $F = ma$ with a nonscientific statement such as: "the position of the stars at your birth determines your destiny." This statement is so general and vague it cannot be tested or verified; there are no objectively measurable criteria associated with it. There is nothing to find false in it, and if it is not falsifiable, it is not science. This is relevant to forensic science because pseudosciences such as astrology and graphology (divining personality traits from handwriting) still knock on courtroom doors.

Gravity is a scientific fact because all observations and experiments have supported the hypothesis. The concept has been refined as new data becomes available; the fundamental truth of gravity has never been disproved by observation or experiment. This reproducibility of results drives conversion of hypothesis to fact. A fact as defined here is not written in cosmic stone but rather represents the best explanation supported by the available evidence. In other words, a fact is the most probable explanation or expression of an idea based on all of the current data obtained by vetted scientific methods. As new tools and technologies arise and new data is created, the probability of one interpretation over another can change. Science welcomes new data as long as it was generated using the scientific criteria of falsifiability, objectivity, and reproducibility.

The scientific requirement that results be observer-independent creates interesting legal consequences. Eyewitness testimony, once considered nearly infallible, is proving less reliable than thought, as shown by recent conviction reversals based on DNA evidence. The science of DNA typing has survived legal and scientific scrutiny; accordingly, the results of properly conducted DNA testing are reliable to a reasonable degree of scientific certainty. The same qualifier applies to gravity. Indeed, DNA evidence is becoming one of the few trusted defenses against false witness, accidental or intentional. This is an example of the objective (science, DNA typing) triumphing over the subjective (human memory, cunning). That is forensic science's reason for being.

IS THAT A CRIME?

If there were no crime, there would be no forensic science. Interestingly, behavior that humans label criminal is common among other organisms and animals. Chimpanzees practice infanticide; baboons rape unwilling females; lemmings voluntarily (as far as one understands lemming motivation) leap off cliffs. Only humans define killing of other humans as homicide, appropriation of food as theft, unwanted sexual contact as rape, and purposeful killing of oneself as suicide. As social structure evolved from small isolated bands of hunter-gatherers to large concentrated populations, mutual dependency and safety of the group led humans to define crime and to label it as undesirable, something to be controlled and deterred by punishment or forced retribution.

In modern times, a crime is considered to be *malum in se* (in Latin, "evil in itself") or *malum prohibitum* (a prohibited evil), ideas that undoubtedly predated any formal definition. Breaking the speed limit is prohibited but not morally evil; rape or murder is evil in and of itself. Acts that are *malum in se* run against a deep and indefinable chord within the human psyche, the roots of which are biological as well as cultural. Crime has also always contained a moral element, much of which invoked and still invokes spiritual authority or a religious entity. Such *sinful* crimes traditionally result in punishment severer than crimes that are prohibitions. Speeding is not inherently evil but rather as behavior that endangers the driver and others. These distinctions remain important in modern law enforcement and courts. The killing of another person (homicide) is divided into categories of severity based on intent and premeditation. The question is not the killing but the circumstances surrounding it. These circumstances determine the moral weight of an act and its definition as inherently evil versus prohibited. Physical evidence and forensic analysis are pivotal in helping the legal system determine these circumstances.

To understand how this human characteristic of regulating behavior for the benefit of society evolved into codified law, it is necessary to examine the roots of both science and the law albeit in a broad and simplified way. Modern humans emerged around two million years ago, surviving in small bands of hunter-gatherers, most likely in groups representing extended families. In such groups, survival of the individual depended on the well-being of the tribe. A lone human being was vulnerable; a cohesive human band was formidable. Whatever systems evolved within these groups were probably tied primarily to the welfare of the pack. Written laws were unnecessary and impossible given that no known system of writing existed until around 5000 B.C.E. Customs and other unwritten traditions, coupled with some central authority, make possible administration of justice as defined within the small social unit. The definition of crime, determination of guilt, and administration of punishment were probably the responsibilities of one or a few tribal leaders. There was no need for consistency outside the tribe since interactions were limited; however, it is likely that concepts of justice, particularly in the case of crimes such as murder were compatible between human bands. These shared behavioral standards would facilitate melding small nomadic groups into a larger social organization.

The turning point came with agriculture, which is a form of biological science. Once people could grow food, they no longer needed to be nomadic. Food stocks became more stable and capable of sustaining larger groups. With the increasingly complex social structure came the need for social adaptations such as a legal system. Groups became so large that it was impossible for any one person to know all of the others. As a result, the scope of disputes exceeded the acquainted group. This development highlighted the need for a formalized system of litigation to resolve disputes. Another critical aspect of centralization was the need to collect some form of taxes to support developing services and governmental organizations; this necessitated systematic record keeping including a system of writing and a literate population that could read it. With these elements in place, the foundation of forensic science was laid.

Why did some form of taxes necessitate systemic record keeping including a system of writing?

4

Settlements and Civilization; Justice and Death

The first known permanent settlements appeared around 7000 B.C.E., and by 3500 B.C.E., agricultural settlements appeared in the valleys near the Tigris and Euphrates Rivers in a region called Sumer (the modern Iraq). City-states within the area are collectively referred to as ancient Sumeria (or Mesopotamia), and it was around 2000 B.C.E., that the Sumerian ruler Ur-Nammu created the first known set of codified laws. Not coincidentally, the Sumerians are credited with the earliest known system of writing, so it is likely that the first case of questioned documents (or in this case, questioned slabs) debuted in Sumeria. The Sumerians developed the concepts of personal property and its protection; items cannot be stolen if they belong to someone, and others recognize that ownership.

The Sumerians were keen on education and taught the students about mathematics, medicine, and astronomy. Basic pharmaceutical knowledge existed there by 3000 B.C.E. The appearance of medicinal skills and rudimentary knowledge of primitive drugs (usually obtained from plants) is central to forensic history. More than any other science, medicine is the direct precursor of forensic science; ancient palliatives and treatments were the precursor of medicine. The first record of a medical text was a tablet recovered in Sumeria dated 2100–2200 B.C.E. On the tablet, an anonymous physician had recorded a list of prescriptions along with instructions on how to prepare them from plant materials.

Sumerians were also skilled in metalwork and in pottery and ceramics, crafts that required an understanding of chemistry and physics. They maintained standards for weights and measures (a prerequisite for science) and developed a reliable calendar. Yet, at this early stage, knowledge was technical in nature and based on experience; the advent of science as a formal approach to knowledge had to await the Greeks. The Sumerian period ended around 2000 B.C.E., leading eventually to the rise of Babylon. The cultural influences of the Sumerians, including their approach to law and criminal justice, had a major impact on those to follow, including the Israelites. The latter influence in particular persists throughout the modern Western world.

Around the same time ancient Mesopotamia was flourishing, the nearby Nile River Valley hosted the birth of another civilization. The Egyptians developed a system of writing and codified laws with strong religious overtones. Broadly speaking, two tiers of justice existed there. The first was more informal and addressed private disputes between or among families. Social taboos, customs, and traditions comprised much of this system. The second tier of justice attended to crimes and issues of public concern that involved disputes between a person and the state.

This delineation between tradition and codified law was not unique to the Egyptians. Often, social customs rather than codified law served to deter or address criminal or undesirable behaviors. In Egypt, one such custom was to delay the delivery of the corpse of a beautiful woman to the embalmers long enough for decomposition to proceed. The goal was to discourage necrophilia. This undoubtedly effective deterrent did not require any law or formal regulation. Like the Sumerians, the Egyptians were excellent engineers and record keepers particularly in the area of financial matters and taxes. Between them, Egypt and Sumeria were surely the first civilizations to need forensic accountants.

The Egyptians also had extensive knowledge of plant-based medicines including opium and its derivatives. By 300 B.C.E., they were teaching classes in anatomy and performing the odd dissection on living criminals. They observed and documented the cooling (algor mortis) and stiffening of a body (rigor mortis) after death. By the second century C.E., they were performing expressly medicolegal work, defined as the application of medical knowledge to affairs of legal consequence. By 1300 C.E., their system incorporated clerks, agents, and even employees that acted as investigators. The concept of precedent played a central role in the workings of the system.

The Egyptians enjoyed alcoholic drinks, particularly beer and also wine. It is not clear how or if intoxication from alcohol had a social stigma or legal aspect as it does today; blood alcohol determinations (BACs) are a large part of the workload at many modern forensic toxicology labs. The Egyptians were also well aware of poisons, and during the final days of the Egyptian empire, Cleopatra reportedly committed suicide by allowing a poisonous snake to bite her. In life, she was purported to be a skilled poisoner and experimentalist. According to legend, she tested asp venom on slaves before selecting it for her own exit strategy.

Egyptians left, as did the Sumerians, written records of prescriptions and preparations used as drugs. Perhaps the most famous example is the

Ebers Papyrus, named for the Englishman who acquired it in 1862. It is 110 pages long and contains hundreds of drug formulations along with spells, incantations, and descriptions of diseases and conditions. It also included a reference to the use of the opium poppy. They were probably using hemp extracts (marijuana and hashish) as an anesthetic for primitive surgeries as well as for general pain relief. It may have been used to assist in childbirth, a use that persisted into the 1800s. Other ancient texts referenced henbane, a plant found to contain scopolamine (a barbiturate). The Egyptians were also aware of the poisonous nature of plants such as jimson weed, and they employed careful measurements in the preparation of their ancient prescriptions. They employed metal ores and minerals as cosmetics, some of which included heavy metal poisons like antimony (Sb).

Ancient Egyptian and Mesopotamian law shared a reliance on oral testimony supported by oath. When oral testimony was not sufficient to make a decision and supporting evidence was lacking, the other option was the ordeal in which the court deferred to God. Trial by ordeal in Mesopotamia involved such procedures as binding the accused and tossing him or her into the river. The ancients assumed that the guilty would sink while God would save the innocent. This was the opposite of the later ordeals used in Europe where the guilty floated and the innocent sank.

Other cultures were evolving around roughly the same time as Egypt. In the Yucatan peninsula region, the Aztecs left far fewer records but also had an understanding of herbal treatments. They also were the first to identify "peyotl," the cactus now known as peyote, a controlled substance. A potent hallucinogen, it remains legal for members of the Native American Church but illegal for everyone else. The Mesoamericans also thought of tobacco as a medicine even though nicotine is a poison. These beliefs filtered into European society as the two came in contact.

Ancient China also banded together into an empire where medicine and law developed. There is evidence of trade and thus shared knowledge between China and Mesopotamia, the Nile, and India. China had an extensive legal code that incorporated traditional elements as well as state-administered oversight and regulation. The rudiments of a legal system were in place as early as 700 B.C.E. and documents from that time recommended that executions occur in autumn, since this was the time of year associated with falling leaves and death. Criminal matters included homicide, assault (wounding), and theft. The Chinese also had an extensive knowledge of plant-based medicines including ephedrine, a substance they extracted from the plant *Ephedra sinica* and used to treat cold and allergy symptoms. Today, ephedrine is sold over the counter as a decongestant and is used illicitly as the key ingredient in making methamphetamine.

Like Sumeria and Egypt, China had a system of writing that allowed for dissemination of rules of law and for administering a large bureaucracy.

They were also well versed in medicinal chemistry and pharmacology, having addressed topics such as herbal medicines (including marijuana) and poisons as early as 2800 B.C.E. Records of caesarean sections existed by 300 C.E., and expert testimony by a physician named Wu P'u in medicolegal matters had been recorded. There are also indications that a text devoted to medicolegal matters was written in the sixth century by Hsu Chich-Ts'si. Authentic dated copies have not yet surfaced. It was not until 1247 C.E. that a surviving text on legal medicine appeared, this one by Sung Tz'u and entitled *Hsi Yüan Lu* (*The Washing Away of Wrongs*). Medicolegal investigators used this book into the twentieth century. It covered strangulation, drowning, wound characteristics, poisons, and even a dash of forensic dentistry. Characteristic changes that occur in a body after death (the postmortem interval or PMI) received detailed treatment because this information is vital to estimating the time of death. Despite the existence of this medical text, Chinese physicians played a limited role in death investigation. This pattern was repeated in the Western world and can still be seen in the coroner system still in use in parts of the United States.

Athens, a city-state similar to those that had existed in Sumeria, introduced concepts in the area of law and justice, particularly the emphasis on personal freedoms (except for slaves, of which the Athenians had many). The Greeks strongly influenced the Roman Empire to follow. As in other cultures of the time, evidence was principally testimonial, although some other methods were also recorded. One unique approach to search and seize used in Athens was called the platter and loincloth method. In cases of alleged theft, the aggrieved party could go through the suspect's house wearing nothing but a loincloth. This practice made it difficult for the accuser to plant evidence since a loincloth afforded precious few options for concealment. The premise behind the method was that stolen goods would somehow make themselves obvious.

As in Egypt, the responsibility for instigating legal matters lay with the aggrieved party. Court decisions were often made by more than one person, although the formal concept of jury trial was centuries away. In addition to their legal contributions, the Greeks formalized the concept of science and contributed the concept of autopsy (from the Greek *autopsia*, the act of seeing for oneself). The somewhat deceptive naming convention masked the understandable distaste for the procedure correctly called *human dissection* or *necropsy*. The latter term still describes the postmortem dissection of animals. The Greeks' interest in autopsy was more anatomical than forensic, and it was not until the 1600s that forensic autopsies occurred with any significant frequency.

The Greeks gave the world Hippocrates, the founder of medicine and the person after whom the Hippocratic oath taken by new physicians has been named. Around 400 B.C.E., he was writing extensively, including on topics of forensic and medicolegal importance. He discussed issues such as epilepsy, wounds, and medical fraud. In 130 C.E., a doctor testified concerning wound characteristics in a court, the first such record to come out of Greece. Similar progress occurred in India in this period, where surgeons trained using dissections. By the third century C.E., they had produced documents relating to the investigation of sudden and unexpected deaths.

Athens was also a center of legal development, and the city had a written code of law by 700 B.C.E. Although not the first to use juries, the Athenians relied on them largely as triers of fact. This enlightened approach allowed oral and written testimony but added a cruel twist to the concept of the ordeal. The Athenians believed that torture was a viable and trustworthy method of eliciting the truth and confirming oral testimony. The Romans absorbed and adopted many of the legal practices of the communities they conquered and had judges, juries, and advocates that were loosely analogous to modern defense and prosecution lawyers. By the fourth century B.C.E., Roman proceedings were giving more weight to documentary evidence, but oral testimony and evidence remained the primary type of evidence available to the triers of fact.

The Roman system absorbed many of the earlier Mediterranean cultures and was influenced by them. An incident in 331 B.C.E. led to the expression, "Live by the poison, die by the poison." A group of women convicted of mass poisoning were forced to drink the same brew they were accused of using for murder. It took a couple more centuries for the Romans to pass a law against poisoning (around 80 B.C.E.). By 200 B.C.E., the Empire had in place an extensive judicial system founded on concepts of citizenship and significant protection of citizens from overly powerful magistrates and other officials.

One of the earliest recorded expert testimonies was recorded in Rome. In 44 B.C.E., Julius Caesar died at the hands of a group of senators wielding daggers and knifes. A physician named Antistius examined the body to determine which wound was fatal. He found over twenty wounds and determined that the second one killed Caesar. The conspirators had apparently hoped that so many wounds precluded a definitive assignment of the fatal one. The practical Roman officials took the only sure route to punishing the true killer by putting all to death. Antistius' determination probably gave rise (directly or indirectly) to the term *forensic*, since he would have presented his findings in the *forum*.

Death investigation took on importance as society and governments advanced for many reasons, aside from the obvious one of detecting a murder. The manner of death (natural, accidental, suicidal, homicidal, or indeterminate) was crucial for matters of inheritance and taxes. Modern humans are hardly the first to face the dual certainties of death and taxes. As soon as people settled into permanent agricultural communities and created the concept of "my stuff" (material possessions), the concepts of theft of "my stuff," as well as the taxing of it by the governments, inevitably followed. Depending on how a person died, his or her property could become the property either of the family or of the state.

Time of death could also be critical in an era when death was frequent and complex inheritance rules were common. The difficulty in determining cause of death (other than in obvious cases involving a weapon) coupled with the advanced state of knowledge of drugs led to widespread poisoning. The Greeks were well aware of botanical poisonings and used compounds such as hemlock as a mode of execution, the case of Socrates being the most infamous. From Roman times to well into the Victorian era, poisoning was a recognized profession, and it was a logical choice for concealing murder. Often, the symptoms of a clever poisoning mimicked death by other common causes such as infections, typhus, and dysentery. Since there were no scientific tests for detecting most poisons, the evidence against the accused came from witnesses and accusers, a practice taken to its logical absurdity in witch trials, convictions, and executions. It was not until the 1740s that the first rudimentary tests for the presence of arsenic (the perennial favorite) appeared; another hundred years passed before those tests were applied to death investigation.

5

The Emerging Rules
of the Game

After the withering of the Roman Empire, Western law stagnated and predictably turned toward religion. The discipline of science, at least in the
West, followed much the same path. The Christian Church exerted its influence, resulting in an increasing reliance on validating testimony by ordeal and by oaths sworn before God. Of particular interest to our story
is English law, which served as a model for Western law in general. English law had at its foundation tribal and ancient practices tempered by
procedures brought to the island by the Romans. After the Roman influence waned, subsequent waves of invaders fine-tuned the system which
included juries, advocates, and, by the 1400s, recognition of law as a profession. The concept of sequestering of juries appeared in 1380, as did the
role of the government in bringing legal matters to courts (rather than just
individuals). English law codified terms such as manslaughter, lying in
wait, and malice aforethought.

Another key development of this era was the concept of the *rules of evidence*. Simply put, these are the rules used by a court to determine which
testimony and evidence should be heard by the trier of fact and which
should not. The goal of presenting evidence of any type is to reconstruct
the likeliest version of an event that is in dispute. Evidence is also used to
discredit reconstructions. How the rules of evidence evolved and, by extension, how the courts verified the reliability of evidence are fundamental
to the emergence of forensic science.

EVIDENCE AND THE RULES

To a forensic scientist, evidence is a tangible thing that can be tested and analyzed to derive facts about how it came into existence. Such an object, like a knife or an article of clothing, is *physical evidence*. Associated with physical evidence is an equally tangible written report describing the result of the analysis of that evidence. The report is a form of *testimonial evidence*. Throughout the history of law, and to some extent science, all evidence was and is either physical or testimonial. When evidence is brought before a court, it must first be decided if that evidence can or should be presented to the trier of fact. This leads to questions about the relevance and reliability of the evidence, be it physical or testimonial. Because scientific testing requires and creates both kinds of evidence, the emergence of the rules of evidence is integral to the history of forensic science.

 Aside from the divisions of physical and testimonial evidence, several other categories are of interest here:

- *Direct evidence:* Such evidence does not require any interpretation to reach a definitive conclusion, as opposed to circumstantial evidence. If a person's fingerprint is found on a gun, this finding is direct evidence that he or she touched it. Alone, it means nothing more or nothing less; the circumstances of how the print got there are deduced from other evidence.
- *Circumstantial evidence:* This type of evidence does not reflect directly on the question at hand but rather is evidence that is used to draw conclusions. Much of the evidence produced during forensic analyses is circumstantial evidence.
- *Exclusionary evidence:* This is evidence that excludes or eliminates a person or disproves a possible scenario. For example, if semen involved in a rape case is found to be of a type that does not match that of a suspect, it is considered exclusionary evidence since it eliminates that person as a possible source. If a bloodstain has a DNA type different from a suspect, the suspect is excluded as a source of that stain.
- *Inclusionary evidence:* Inclusionary evidence does not exclude a given possibility or disprove a given hypothesis. Inclusionary evidence is the opposite of exclusionary evidence. In the above example, if the stain does have the same DNA type as the suspect, the suspect is included in the small group of possible sources.

 From ancient to modern courts, such evidence is divided into three broad categories. First is oral (or written) testimony by a person under oath. The second type of evidence is documentation (or records) that corroborates or refutes oral testimony. The third type of evidence is physical evidence other than the documentation. Forensic analysis crosses all of the boundaries described above. A forensic scientist can analyze a physical object, generating a written report that results in oral testimony under oath before the trier of fact. A forensic scientist may also be asked to analyze documentation to assess whether it is genuine and reliable.

For most of history, oral testimony was the only viable evidence. Egyptian records from 2200 B.C.E. record the use of oaths made before God as evidence. The oath was the proof that the testimony was true. If the gods were watching while a person made a deceptive statement, the reasoning went, they would surely take action. The absence of any sign from the heavens constituted divine validation. Additional sworn testimony was used as supporting evidence to strengthen a case.

In situations where sworn testimony was hopelessly contradictory and no decision possible, the next step was usually an ordeal. The type and severity of the ordeal varied among cultures, but ordeals were used in Mesopotamian, Roman, Greek, Jewish, Chinese, Indian, and Islamic laws. The ordeal could be combat or a physical test that invoked God to act as referee. The verdict and sentence depended on the result of the ordeal.

Despite the superstitious aspects, ancient laws also recognized the importance of high standards of proof and evidence in criminal proceedings and particularly in capital cases. This precedent survives in modern law where criminal cases typically require proof of guilt beyond a reasonable doubt. To increase the reliability of evidence, ancient practices required more witnesses, more oaths, and additional ordeals. In some cases, the witnesses called were physicians or scientists of a sort, but their participation rarely had anything to do with their professional skills. As legal systems evolved across the ancient world, supporting and physical evidence came to play a larger role. This led to the formalization of procedures governing what the triers of fact would be able to consider and what they would not.

The rules of evidence are mostly exclusionary in that the court usually decides what to exclude rather than dictating what to include in a given proceeding. They act as information filters that can decide a case before it ever sees a courtroom. Ideally, the rules dictate what information is both reliable and useful (probative) without dictating how to interpret that information. From the earliest records of Mesopotamia and Egypt to the present, the best rules of evidence are those that incorporate common sense based on the shared human experience and standards of social norms. For the ancients, this was virgin territory since civilization itself was new. Settling disputes within an extended family or tribe is a different challenge than settling disputes between strangers living in large, anonymous settlements.

It did not take long to realize that the laws of evidence and science share a common thread woven into the larger concept of probability. When an event occurs that is subject to litigation, there are at least two conflicting versions and interpretations of that event. Which version is the most trustworthy and the closest to the truth? The job of the court has always been to determine which version is the most probable. The truth of a disputed event, as interpreted by human observers, will never be completely objective; the truth is never knowable. The court must reconstruct the most probable version of it, and, in so doing, decide how to settle the dispute in the most just way.

SUPPORTING EVIDENCE AND HALF TRUTHS

After direct oral testimony, legal systems adopted the concept of supporting evidence. Supporting evidence could be in the form of either sworn testimony or supporting documentation and records. The extent of its use varied among cultures, but by Roman times, the practice was widespread. Although this early form of supporting evidence did not include scientific evidence, accepting it was a prerequisite for the eventual acceptance of scientific analysis, testimony, and reports.

Analysis of documentary evidence was recorded during the Roman Empire, and by the thirteenth century, Italian courts were admitting the analysis of documentation, particularly handwriting. Comparisons of handwriting to distinguish genuine signatures from forgeries were reported. It is not known what techniques were used. However, in a case from 1150 C.E., the techniques described are remarkably similar to modern forensic questioned document examination. During the reign of Pope Innocent III (1198–1216), a number of what appeared to be forged papal letters surfaced. Because there was a market for such letters and other Church-related items and relics, genuine letters were quite valuable. The forgeries were uncovered by detecting erasures, writing added at a date later than the document was originally created, overwriting, a new wax seal that showed none of the expected weathering, incorrect images and seals, and inconsistent spacing of letters. Modern questioned document examiners utilize the same techniques.

The reign of this Pope was important in the history of forensic science and evidence in another way. Much of the Church's effort during those and subsequent years was devoted to rooting out heresy, a crime impossible to prove with any objectivity. Scientific and physical evidence rarely played a part in such proceedings but sadly, torture did. Equally sad, this was nothing new. As noted earlier, the Greeks considered torture to be the best method of validating oral testimony. The Inquisition made extensive use of torture for the same reason. Often torture came after conviction to elicit information for later investigations.

Ironically, the Church, an early and fervent adopter of torture, eventually grew uncomfortable with the concept of the ordeal, reasoning that it was immoral to tempt God. By the thirteenth century, ordeals had become uncommon and the courts returned to a reliance on sworn oral testimony as the best evidence. Ironically, this was a period when humans were considered to be innately sinful and untrustworthy. Partially in recognition of this tension, the concept of a "half-truth" appeared in the English law during the Middle Ages. Calling something a half-truth was not derogatory but rather indicated what value should be placed on that evidence. Alone, a half-truth was not enough to prove or disprove an issue, but it did have value in supporting one version of it over another. A half-truth in medieval law did not imply a purposeful omission of key information; rather it weighted the evidence as somewhat definitive and possibly useful.

Admission of supporting evidence and half-truths demonstrates a trend that would influence scientific and supporting evidence as much as it did oral testimony. By definition, the role of supporting evidence is to make a stronger case. With each piece of consistent supporting evidence, one version of events becomes the most trustworthy. The tipping point occurs when the probability of truth is sufficient. The concept of *sufficiency* underlies both science and law and, by extension, forensic science.

LOGIC, PROBABILITY, AND TRUTH

Since ancient times, two degrees of proof (i.e., probability of truth) have existed. First is the much higher standard required in capital and criminal cases, that of belief of guilt beyond a reasonable doubt. Jurors are often told that these levels of certainty correlate to a percentage such as 99 percent probability of guilt. The other standard, today applied in civil cases, is that of accepting the version that is likelier, the one supported by the preponderance of evidence, often cited as a 51 percent probability.

Science does not overtly divide the threshold; rather probability and acceptability of a given idea or theory falls along a gradient. Gravity is accepted as fact with perhaps 99.9 percent probability that the current theory and understanding is correct. The devil, as in the degree of doubt, lies in the detail. Many people jump off bridges, but not to test gravity. Barring a stunning and unexpected discovery, the model of gravity is true and will improve over time. The totality of the evidence proves that gravity is real beyond a reasonable doubt. Other scientific ideas start out with less general acceptance and a lower probability of truth. The Greeks proposed the atomic theory, but it was not until the Renaissance that the modern version began to take shape. It was only a few years ago that atoms were imaged and their existence confirmed.

The Greeks, particularly the mathematicians, used a system of thought called *deductive logic* to consider the natural world and weigh the most probable explanations for what they observed based on deductive logic.

Inductive logic was also used but to a lesser extent. Far from a historical asterisk, the difference between these thought models is important in modern science and forensic science.

Both deductive logic and inductive logic are part of science and are utilized in forensic work. In deductive reasoning, conclusions follow from established evidence and facts. The following is an example of deductive reasoning: All animals that have spines are vertebrates. Humans are vertebrates, so it follows that humans have spines. The other type of logic is inductive or inferential reasoning.

An inference is a conclusion, assumption, or deduction based on the existence of other facts. If a person leaves a fingerprint at a scene, it can be inferred that the person was present at the scene at some point. Inductive reasoning starts with a large body of evidence or data obtained by experiment or observation and extrapolates it to new situations. By the process of induction or inference, predictions about new situations are inferred or induced from the existing body of knowledge. In other words, an inference is a logically and scientifically defensible generalization.

Since inductive reasoning is part of the scientific method, it is also ingrained in forensic science. An example of an inference in forensic science is in the area of DNA typing. Only a small subset of the human population has been typed, yet based on knowledge of genetics and probability, the frequency of types within the entire population is known and accepted within a range of uncertainty. The distribution of types in the entire population is inferred from (and extrapolated to) the entire population based on observation, experiment, and accepted principles of genetics.

The idea of associating probability with science and litigation is founded on the idea that observed events and behaviors do not happen by chance. The Greeks were the first to enunciate this idea of *causality*, and since then, the concept has underlain science and justice. Different explanations can be postulated to understand the underlying order. Humans define the most probable one as truth. In the realm of science, an example is the observable behavior of the movement of the sun and stars across the sky. Since the movements show repeatable and predictable patterns, there exists some underlying explanation. Explanation one is biblical: the universe rotates around the Earth because God made it that way. Copernicus, Kepler, and Galileo argued for explanation two, that Earth rotates around the Sun. Which is the most probable explanation of these two? Certainty the second, but that certainty required knowledge unavailable before these men lived.

By definition, good science is self-correcting because such new knowledge constantly updates and refines theories and ideas. As such, scientists of all people should be the most capable of producing reliable and useful testimonial evidence. However, prior to the Renaissance, science lacked the tools, resources, and body of knowledge to make significant independent contributions to judicial proceedings. However, physicians had acquired centuries of data and experience. As such, they were the first protoscientists to cross the frontier in significant numbers.

ENTER THE EXPERT WITNESS

The concept of an expert witness traces to the early Middle Ages. Courts in Europe solicited and accepted expert testimony, principally from medical practitioners. These experts received payment for their services and submitted results in writing. Usually they escaped any cross-examination by opposing counsel, a luxury modern forensic scientists might envy. The need to determine cause of death drove much expert testimony. Other pressing issues, such as the physical resemblance of a child to the purported father or how long a pregnancy really lasted, frequently arose. Although law and science changed, human nature, it seems, did not.

Writings from seventeenth century Rome noted that medicolegal witnesses and proceedings were increasingly at odds with ecclesiastical-legal entities. Interestingly, these writings are among the first to verbalize the diverging paths of science and law and to note the similarity of roles of judges and physicians in elucidating truth. The same writings noted the different ways in which the two approached the task. None of these trends are coincidental; as science began a slow ascension in the legal system, inevitably the role of religion waned. Scientists and judges, rather than religious figures assumed increasing responsibility for reconstructing events, weighing evidence, and assigning probabilities of truth. As medical testimony became accepted and trusted, expert testimony in such areas as sexual conduct, mental illness, and faking the same was invited and accepted.

A medieval equivalent of a workman's compensation case illustrates the growing rift between law, science, and religion. In the early 1600s, a Spanish priest named Gomez claimed to be suffering from crushing headaches. He requested that his employer, the Church, provide him with an assistant or relieve him of his duties. A lower ecclesiastical authority granted the request, but higher Church authorities challenged it. A hearing before twelve judges resulted. The Church asserted that witnesses supporting the priest's claim were merely relating information given to them by Gomez himself. He said his head hurt; they believed him. The Church argued that there was no independent or medical basis for the claim of the headaches. The initial decision was overturned. Gomez promptly appealed.

During the appeal, the testimony of Gomez's doctor was accepted as that of an expert witness. The doctor stated that in the absence of obvious injury, the only way he or any physician can diagnose pain is by patient complaint. The fact that each person's pain tolerance was different and that people could lie about pain was no secret even in the 1600s. This behavior is called *malingering*, and it bedevils physicians, forensic psychologists, and forensic psychiatrists to this day. For Gomez, the legal proceedings themselves became a headache, spanning ten years and eventually resulting in the rejection of his request. The decision was based on the assumption that such severe pain, if real, should have been accompanied by other symptoms or signs such as fever that a trained physician would be able to detect.

This story is emblematic of the status of evidence and testimony as the Renaissance dawned. Science and the law progressed along separate paths, but they were beginning to cross with greater frequency. Science was emerging from the medieval doldrums and, by the 1600s, was advancing at an unprecedented pace. Still, two more centuries would pass before science and the law would intersect in such a way as to give birth to forensic science. First, science itself had to catch up.

6

Science and Biology; Alchemy and Chemistry

Although intertwined with medicine over the ages, chemistry is a separate and, for this story, critical discipline. The other foundational forensic science, biology, remained hidden under the coattails of medicine until the Renaissance. Chemistry itself arose from medicine, metallurgy, and alchemy, and it was not until the 1600s that the word *chemistry* was first used to describe the practices of the discipline.

The practices that would become chemistry preceded biology because there was an immediate need for applied chemical knowledge in early civilizations. The technology of chemistry existed long before the science did, mostly due to practical need. One of the first chemical technologies was brewing beer and making wine. The Egyptians and the Mesopotamians made beer and wine. The Nile Valley was home to many types of grapes, while the Mesopotamians were probably the better beer-makers. Production of fermented beverages required skills in distillation and chemical separations along with the ability to make specialized glassware and measurement equipment. Chemistry relies on such tools and techniques.

As a separate and definable discipline, chemistry began as the study of purity of precious metals such as gold and silver. Perhaps the oldest recognizable form of chemistry was analytical chemistry, and analytical chemistry remains at the heart of forensic chemistry today. Ancient forensic chemistry dealt with forgery and fakery. As an example, the King of Babylon wrote the following to the Egyptian Pharaoh around 1360 B.C.E.: "Your Majesty did not look at the gold which was sent to me last time, they were sealed only by a clerk, therefore after putting them into a furnace, this gold was less than its original weight."[1]

The only way the King could know he was being cheated was to have the gold analyzed by an unknown ancient chemist. The technique the analyst relied on to uncover the forgery was a fire assay.

Until the late 1700s, fire assays were about the only viable technique for analyzing metals because there were no other reliable methods to achieve chemical separations. To know how much junk is in the gold, it is first necessary to separate the gold from the junk. Pure gold survives the fire, but adulterants such as copper and other minerals do not. The Egyptians used heat in a similar vein and assumed that metal unchanged by heat was gold. If the material turned whiter, the sample likely contained silver, and if the mix hardened, it likely contained copper. This knowledge was gained by trial and error and did not indicate knowledge of the underlying chemistry of metals. Thus, fire assay was a technology with no scientific knowledge underlying it.

In a fire assay, heat drives off many, but not all, impurities. To determine the weight or percentage of gold in a sample, it was weighed before and after the trip to the furnace. A sample of pure gold lost no weight. Other terms used to describe fire assays are *pyrolysis* (fire cutting) or *pyrochemistry*. For centuries, chemists had no other tools that allowed for selective separation of metals from each other, let alone more complex separations. As such, methods for the forensic detection of metals and metal poisons like arsenic were limited. Investigators used pyrochemical methods to detect arsenic poisons well into the nineteenth century. It would not be until the 1600s that mineral acids such as hydrochloric, sulfuric, and phosphoric acids were first isolated and used for selective dissolution of metals.

Another ancient test for gold purity was the use of a *touchstone*, a special stone that would show a gold streak if pure gold were rubbed against it. The touchstone remained a tool of alchemists for centuries. They considered the touchstone a replacement for fire assay, and this glorified rock represented the first attempt at developing an analytical instrument. The ancient historian Pliny (23–79 C.E.) mentioned such a type of stone, as did Plato and Aristotle. The general idea behind the stone was simple—when touched or rubbed with the material in question, it would reveal through reaction if the sample was pure gold or not. A writer summed up the practical need for a touchstone: "[W]hen gold coins are assayed in the fire, of what use are they afterwards?"[2] In otherwords, once you put a gold coin through a furnance, it isn't useful as a coin anymore. A touchstone test was non-destructive. References describing the use of touchstones and touch needles appear into the sixteenth century as means for determining the purity of metals.

Pliny appears to have been an experimentalist with a notable lack of interest in theory. He reported tests for copper metals that contain iron compounds. One of those tests was the first record of a *spot test*. In forensic chemistry, a spot test, also called a presumptive or color test, involves testing a questioned substance with a specific chemical reagent and watching for color changes. Analysts use the same reagents and tests today for suspected drugs, gunshot residue, and explosives. The luminol and phenolphthalein tests for blood are spot tests that react with the hemoglobin in blood. Pliny described a test in which a strip of papyrus was soaked in the extract of pine gallnuts. If an extract of the suspected copper salt was placed on the test strip and a black color developed, it was assumed that the copper was contaminated with iron.

The word *adulteration* has different connotations than *contamination*. Gold must be extracted and refined to a pure state, and given the crude methods that the ancient metallurgists had at their disposal, there is no doubt that the gold was impure by modern standards. The crude tests could detect only significant contamination. Nevertheless, when detected, the contamination was usually assumed to have come from purposeful adulteration rather than inevitable or accidental contamination. The problem of contamination would play an important role in arsenic poisoning cases, described in Chapter 7.

As chemistry evolved, the ability of the science differentiate contamination from adulteration became more important. To understand the circumstances leading to one over the other, reliable measurements were needed. Natural contaminants are usually found in lower concentrations compared to those from purposeful adulteration. For example, arsenic, the king of ancient poisons, exists naturally in the body at very low levels. It also resides in soils. Because bodies are buried in soil, detecting purposeful arsenic poisoning is not as simple as it might seem, especially if a body has been buried in soil. These complications had to await better chemical techniques.

SEPARATION AND ADULTERATION

Alchemy is often categorized as a diversion from science, but alchemy *was* science for more than a millennium. Alchemists such as Paracelsus, Robert Boyle, and Sir Isaac Newton made discoveries and developed techniques still used in forensic laboratories. Alchemy was the earliest form of analytical chemistry, which is the separation of compounds and elements from each other and from the matrix they are found in. To determine the purity of gold, it is necessary to analyze the gold; to analyze gold, it is necessary to isolate the gold from any adulterants found in it.

Most ancient cultures that left records practiced alchemy, which grew out of mining, metallurgy, and medicine. The undercurrent, even though the ancients did not recognize it, was chemistry. Alchemy was an odd and interesting blend of science, art, and religion that focused on the concept of purification and of separating material that was considered "pure," such as gold, from the "impure" or whatever it was embedded in. An analytical chemist would call the gold the *analyte* and what it was embedded in the *matrix*. Analytical science depends on the ability to isolate one or more component from a matrix. Without access to even the simplest chemical tools such as acids and solvents like alcohol to dissolve and extract materials, the ancients used the most ancient of human technologies—fire. Using fire and heat, alchemists perfected three fundamental means of separation: sublimation, distillation, and pyrolysis. Without these, modern science, let alone forensic science, would never have evolved.

The first mentions of alchemy date to around 400 B.C.E. The Greeks had a word *chyma* that described processes of metalworking, and this might be one origin of the word, but the Chinese and Egyptians recorded similar words also related to metallurgy. All three cultures also practiced alchemy, and the "al" part appears to have come from Arabic, forming al-chemy or "the chemistry." Although analysis and transformation of gold and other materials was part of alchemy, from its inception there were strong religious, spiritual, and mystical aspects to it. It was only in the sixteenth and the seventeenth centuries that the mystical part of alchemy superseded the practical, corresponding with the eventual rise of chemistry as a science.

Some alchemists were also adulterers (in the chemical sense). Recovered writings included instructions for making copper appear like gold such that the "touchstone test" would fail to detect the alteration. To perform the touchstone test, the tester scratched the gold across the touchstone, observed any color change, and gauged the purity using a set of comparison standards. A touchstone is not the same as the mythical philosopher's stone, the famous alchemic idea of a stone that would turn base metals into gold. Because knowing how to make a touchstone and how to transmute matter were desirable and potentially dangerous skills, much of the early alchemists wrote formulas and notes in elaborate codes. This practice served two purposes: First, it insured that knowledge was passed on in person from master to apprentice rather than widely disseminated. The advantage of this practice is obvious in cases such as faking gold. Secondly, coding was a way to protect trade secrets.

Alchemists were technologists who learned by experience and passed on what they learned to a select few. It was not of particular interest to them why fire assay worked. It did, and that was good enough. As a result, innovation came slowly. From the forensic perspective, the key contribution of the ancient alchemists was in their interest in fire applied to metallurgy and the use of heat as a means of separating materials from one another. Pyrochemistry was to play a role in the first viable tests for arsenic.

The ancient era of alchemy ended with the decline of the Roman Empire. In the West, the Church was hostile to science (which it perceived as paganism) and particularly to alchemy and its magical connotations. The death of a woman named Hypatia (370–415 C.E.), a scholar based in Alexandria, Egypt, was emblematic of the end of the era. Hypatia's home was founded by Alexander the Great and had become a center of learning, nascent science, and philosophy. The city was also home to the fabled Great Library of Alexandria, a repository of ancient knowledge collected from all over the world. Hypatia studied and taught there and is the first woman known to practice and teach advanced mathematics. Statements that she reportedly made such as, "Reserve your right to think, for even to think wrongly is better than to not think at all," did little to ingratiate her to Roman authorities.

In 391 C.E., a campaign sanctioned by Rome and the bishop of Alexandria led to the destruction of the Library and rampant anti-Semitism. Authorities outlawed paganism, and Alexandria became a city wracked with religious and mob violence. In 415 C.E., a mob of Christians took Hypatia to her death by lynching, symbolically ending the progress of ancient science and driving alchemy underground in much of the world. It was not until the Arab conquests in the period of 600–800 C.E. that a semblance of order and stability returned to the region.

JABIR AND THE ACID TEST

The Western perspective labels the Dark Ages as a time of stagnation. Not all the world fell into such a sorry state. The Moslem Empire that emerged in the shadow of Rome was larger than the Roman Empire and Alexander's conquered territories combined. Its scientists and scholars kept the knowledge of the ancient world alive through transcription and dissemination. Although their contribution to biology was more preservation than innovation (no small feat), the Arabs made significant advances in chemistry. The empire also gave science some breathing room because Islamic philosophy was tolerant and considered both Christian and Jewish traditions to be part of their own. This tolerance faded as the empire matured, but for a time, science and culture thrived. During its zenith, from about 750 to 1150 C.E., knowledge moved freely with travelers that crisscrossed the known world from Sweden to China.

Arabs also were the first to delineate alchemy from what would become chemistry. They studied chemical reactions and attempted to classify them. A modern example would be classifying reactions as acid/base (dissolving metal in acids for example), oxidation/reduction (rust formation), combustion, and decomposition. They knew how to use nitric acid and studied medicines and pharmaceuticals extensively. Arab culture absorbed ideas from the conquered areas including what was left of Alexandria. They also had contact with the Chinese, from whom they adopted papermaking, allowing for much wider dissemination of knowledge in portable formats. The Arabs also absorbed ideas from the Greeks, and many accepted the idea of atoms, although they referred to them as *minima*, the smallest particle of a substance that retains the properties associated with it.

One of the most interesting characters from this period is the Arab alchemist known as Jabir ibn-Hayyan, also known as Jabir or Geber. Legend places his birth around 720 C.E. and his death by murder in 815 C.E., but to live so long in that age would have been remarkable. He was a member of a religious sect called the Hashashins, a radical group that would take part in political murders reportedly under the influence of hashish. Hashish is a potent hallucinogen derived from marijuana. Jabir's cult and its practices are thought responsible for the origin of the word *assassin*. Jabir has been credited with hundreds of publications, and that combined with the age has led historians to question if such a man actually existed or if the name represents collected works. Jabir made many noteworthy accomplishments including those related to dyes, inks, glass, metallurgy, and medicines. He probably was the first to isolate arsenic metal from arsenic mineral. Other Arab alchemists worked with acids such as vinegar and were the first to recognize that acids were a distinctive class of compounds. They also understood that some diseases were infectious, an idea well ahead of its time.

As the Arab Empire began to decline around 950 C.E., alchemy and science slowly migrated westward into areas of southern Europe. During the medieval period, little progress was made in science or chemistry, although artisans continued to try new ideas in painting, glassmaking, and metallurgy. Alchemy returned to its ancient roots of science, religion, and art, but made little forward progress. Expertise honed in glassmaking became critical for work with optics. This class of forensically important tools includes lenses, microscopes, and prisms. In addition, chemists need their glassware, and having the right tools is requisite for progress.

Other advances in this period include distillation, a fundamental chemical separation technique. The Arabs had isolated ethanol (the word alcohol is derived from the Arabic *al-kuhul*) during brewing and distilling. In addition to human consumption, alcohols are versatile solvents of organic material. Discovery of the mineral acids—hydrochloric, nitric, and sulfuric—and a combination of nitric and hydrochloric acids called aqua regia traces to the same time. This was important to the alchemists because aqua regia can dissolve gold. Once a substance can be dissolved into a solution, the analytical chemist has many options for separation and analysis. For example Nitric acid was widely used to detect counterfeit coins. When this acid is dropped on copper, the copper dissolves, a green color develops, and a brown fume is given off. When nitric acid is placed on pure gold, nothing happens. This practice may have been the origin of the phrase "the acid test."

Natural science reemerged, starting around 1200, still cloaked in the guise of alchemy. More emphasis was being placed on preparation, administration, and understanding of drugs. This period in chemical history is referred to as that of *iatrochemistry* or the application of chemistry to medicine and, by extension, to biology. During this period, metallurgy, which had been so closely linked to chemistry, began to diverge from medicinal work. In the early years of iatrochemistry, it and alchemy were closely related. Gradually, alchemy drifted toward more into the mystical practices. By the 1700s, alchemy was no longer relevant to forensic history.

"LESS TALENT THAN MY ASS"

The age of iatrochemistry ushered in much greater dissemination of work (ancient and current) via printed materials and the definition of experimental science by pioneers such Francis Bacon (1561–1626). Chemists turned their attention to medicines with an emphasis on fundamental understanding. A key figure whose work would directly affect forensic science was Paracelsus (1493–1541), an alchemist, philosopher, and writer with unconventional ideas and enormous experimental skills. He sought to understand why certain treatments worked so that existing medicines could be improved and new ones developed. An appropriate quote sums up his approach: "Without chemistry, we are trudging in darkness."[3]

Paracelsus was a colorful and controversial figure, born into a Swiss family and named Philipus Aureolus Theophrastus Bombastus von Hohenheim. The name *Bombastus* was appropriate. He modestly assumed the name Paracelsus, which means "greater than Celsus," a physician in Rome during the first century C.E. From his early teens, Paracelsus moved frequently between universities, gathering knowledge, and moving on, once remarking, "All the universities and all the ancient writers put together have less talent than my ass."[4]

Over the years, Paracelsus learned and practiced medicine, gaining respect despite his personality. Most of his ideas about healing and chemistry were wrong, but he managed to upset the rusted foundations of medicine and chemistry, which was still being taught based on Roman texts. The modern equivalent would be going to medical school and learning from a book published in 1000 C.E., before the plagues swept Europe. Science needed a good shaking up, and Paracelsus was the man to do it.

Paracelsus' work in medicinal chemistry led him to state, "What is there that is not poison? All things are poison and nothing (is) without poison. Solely the dose determines the thing that is not a poison."[5] Without a fundamental chemical understanding of medicines, there was no way to know what the appropriate dose was. Above a threshold, any therapeutic agent can become toxic and poisonous. For its time, this was a revolutionary idea and one that started a chain of events that led to effective tests for arsenic in the body. Paracelsus was one of the pioneers of experimental science when science was more philosophical than experimental.

Paracelsus cannot lay claim to being the father of forensic toxicology, but it is fair to call him its grandfather. He laid the groundwork for the broader field of toxicology both experimentally and philosophically. He wrote widely, and his works were popular and thus widely disseminated and studied. This is the first appearance of modern science. Existing understanding, even if faulty, formed the basis for the next round, leading (ideally) to a continually self-correcting and improving knowledge of the world.

BIOLOGY AND CHEMISTRY; HOOKE AND BOYLE

The metamorphosis of alchemy into chemistry falls somewhere around 1600. The lines between and among chemistry, alchemy, biology, and medicine remained ill-defined, although biology was clearly emerging as a separate science. As with chemistry, biology as a recognizable science traces back thousands of years. The ancient and Greco-Roman periods saw biology diversifying and specializing earlier than its chemical cousin. Aristotle was among the first to delve into systematic classification, the core science of the forensic scientist. He also championed the concept of spontaneous generation that held that small creatures such as insects arose spontaneously from putrefied organic material. In this sense, Aristotle was among the first to study decomposition, although his aims were not forensic. Aristotle had noticed that insects quickly attack decomposing or putrefied material, but he incorrectly assumed creation rather than attraction as the cause. The mistake is easy to understand; flies can find bodies within minutes of death, a process of attraction that remains a mystery. Aristotle was among the first to study a discipline now called *forensic entomology*, or the study of insects in the context of death investigation.

Three branches of biology relevant to forensic history survived the fall of Rome. The first was closely associated with medicine, pharmacology, and death investigation. Anatomy, studied through dissection and autopsy, had become an important established precursor to forensic medicine and biology. Among its most famous practitioners was Galen (125–216 C.E.), a Greek who served as a surgeon to the gladiators of Rome. He was able to study wound characteristics and practiced and wrote extensively on this and related subjects. His influence lasted well into the Renaissance.

As the Enlightenment began, chemistry and biology had developed into recognized, if still archaic, sciences. Given that the knowledge base in both was fairly small, many scientists of the early Enlightenment period practiced multiple disciplines, as had their ancient predecessors. From the forensic perspective, the most notable scientific development of the Renaissance was the slow death of alchemy and the corresponding birth of chemical science. Significant forensic aspects of biology appeared much later, well into the eighteenth century.

In 1597, Andreas Libavius (1540–1616) published one of the first textbooks to identify chemistry as separate from alchemy. For chemists, it is not an auspicious beginning. Libavius noted that chemistry was "a bilge-flood and chaos of impurity and human dregs and that chemists were the enemy of nature."[6] His ire targeted chemists themselves more than their vocation. Practitioners of that age were often forgers, fakers—the type of people that made copper that looked like gold and sold fake medicines and potions.

Libavius' book was meant as a strike against such deceit. In it, he described and classified reactions and lab procedures, the hallmark of modern chemistry. He just did not want to be a chemist (or at least called one in public). The first textbook to be used appeared, by a Frenchman Nicholas Lemery, who took the leap and used the word *chemistry* in its title, published in 1675 (*A Course of Chemistry*). The publication split the gap between alchemy and chemistry wide open.

Robert Boyle (1627–1691) is a man who would not have considered himself a forensic chemist. Yet, without his work, there would be no such discipline. Boyle began his career as an alchemist, but more than any other individual, he was responsible for extracting chemistry from alchemy. Born to privilege, he had an excellent education and made use of it. He was also devotedly religious and authored successful novels that today would be classified as Christian fiction. One of his many theological titles was *Free Discourse Against Customary Swearing*. It would have been interesting to put Boyle and Paracelsus in the same room.

Boyle found his way to London where his interest in chemistry blossomed. Eventually he found an assistant named Robert Hooke (1635–1703), now famous for many discoveries including significant work with microscopes, the first forensic instrument. Hooke was more of a generalist than Boyle, having dabbled in mechanics, physics, and biology as well as chemistry. The microscope served him well in all his pursuits.

The use of a lens to magnify images was known to the Egyptians and Greeks, perhaps first sparked by noting how a spherical drop of water can act as a magnifying lens. A natural extension would be to use a second magnifying glass to magnify the image produced by another. Simplified, that is what a microscope is—two magnifying glasses in series. The concept is easy to conceive and damnably difficult to execute. The Arab alchemists and others had learned to manipulate glass, but the technology to make lenses to exacting standards was not available until the Renaissance. Hooke was the right man in the right place at the right time, but he was hardly the first or only person to get there.

A father-son team whose specialty was making eyeglasses built the first recognizably modern microscopes. Hans (the elder) and his son Zacharias Janssen (1580–1638) built their device around 1595. It was simple but functional, something like a telescope with a tube enclosing lenses at opposite ends. The crude device could be used to magnify samples three to ten times (3–10×) their original size by sliding the tube and adjusting its length.

Another early adopter of microscopic technology was the Italian Marcello Malpighi (1628–1694) who in 1661 used a crude microscope to find blood in capillaries. He also is the namesake of the inner layer of skin called the *Malpighi layer* familiar to fingerprint analysts. Malpighi championed the spread of diagnostic microscopy into medical science. He also was one of the earliest to investigate fingerprinting, although his attention was more on fundamental anatomy rather than on criminal identification.

Perhaps the most famous early microscopist was the Dutch microbiologist Anton van Leeuwenhoek (1632–1723), a self-taught scientist and tinkerer in the Hooke tradition. He was adept at lens making and grinding and fashioned many magnification devices consisting of a single lens. From the 1670s on, he used his inventions to see bacteria scraped from teeth and microscopic life in pond water, sperm, and red blood cells, the latter two of which make up a large part of forensic science. His microscopes were capable of magnifying objects up to 300X. Hooke built on this previous work and produced the first true compound microscope, one that included a lamp as a light source. He published a book entitled *Micrographia* in 1665 and was the first to use the word "cell" to describe the fundamental biological unit. Leeuwenhoek had referred to them as "animalcules." Hooke was also the first to describe sperm cells, a task still accomplished using this method in modern forensic laboratories. From the middle of the 1600s on, the microscope's basic design has not changed, although some of the early ones were as much art as instrumentation. As a lab rat in the best sense of the term, Hooke would appreciate the description of a microscope as a work of art.

Apart from their individual contributions, the Hooke-Boyle partnership led to fundamental discoveries such as Boyle's law of gases. This law described the inversely proportional relationship of pressure and volume of gases; that is, as pressure goes up, volume goes down. Boyle realized the fundamental implication underlying this simple observation: air is not empty space or a vacuum; rather, it has to be made up of *something*. He christened these little somethings "corpuscles" that could crowd together as pressure increased and force the volume to decrease. Not exactly the atomic theory but close. From a forensic perspective, the discovery of the nature of gases was critical. Many chemists of the age, including Boyle, knew of arsenic poisoning and were trying to develop a reliable test for arsenic in human tissues. The first successful tests relied on converting solid arsenic compounds to gaseous ones before converting the arsenic from the gas phase into the metallic form. Heating (pyrochemistry) was used to force the arsenic compounds to decompose into the gaseous phase.

Other conceptual breakthroughs attributed to Boyle were the definition of what an element is: a substance that is not combined with anything else, or that cannot be further broken down into any other material. Consider arsenolite, As_2O_3. The Greeks thought that this white powdery mineral was elemental arsenic, but Boyle contradicted that in two ways. First, the arsenic is combined with something (oxygen), so the powder cannot be an element. How did he know this? By heating it, just as the ancients heated gold to drive off impurities.

Second, using heat, it is possible to generate gaseous arsenic from this material. If that is so, then the original substance itself cannot be a pure substance or element. The difference is subtle but a critical one. Metallic arsenic can be melted by heat, but it forms a puddle of arsenic that weighs the same as the original piece that was exposed to the heat. This does not happen with arsenic compounds or minerals. They decompose, giving off gases and leaving residuals that weigh less than the original sample. Boyle helped clarify the understanding of what gases were and how they behaved.

Boyle also studied acids and bases (then called alkaline materials), both fundamental to later forensic work. He devoted extensive efforts toward developing a test for arsenic based on sublimation, or the direct conversion of a solid to a gas. Solid carbon dioxide (dry ice) sublimes, as does solid iodine. Some of Boyle's tests relied on hydrogen sulfide gas (H_2S, which has the smell of rotten eggs), a technique adopted by later chemists. Unfortunately, Boyle was unable to generate reproducible and reliable results with the tools and reagents available. Finally, Boyle was also the first to advocate the use of solution chemistry over pyrolysis as a means of analysis. Because mineral acids and other methods of getting metals into solution were available during his time, significant progress was made in moving toward dissolution as a means of separation.

THE LAST OF THE ALCHEMISTS

Sir Isaac Newton (1642–1727) shared with Boyle an early interest in alchemy, and Boyle's work influenced much of Newton's work in the field. Aside from all of his other contributions, Newton was the first to realize that visible light literally contained more than met the eye, similar to Boyle's realization that air was made of invisible particles. Newton proved that white light consists of a combination of light of different colors. He did so by building the first prism, which took daylight and broke it into its components. Newton also worked extensively in the field of optics, essential for everything from microscopes to modern analytical instruments indispensable to forensic science. He gave a series of lectures at Trinity College in Cambridge entitled *Of Colours* during the years 1670–1672, and he published a book series called *Opticks* (1704). Newton believed that light, like air, was composed of corpuscles. This concept fits with the modern concept in several ways. Light shares the nature of both energy and particles called photons, which are discrete packets of electromagnetic energy loosely analogous to corpuscles. Interestingly, Newton was at odds for most of his career with Boyle and Hooke. The conflict deepened with Newton's often irrational and unreasonable responses to criticism and Hooke's insistence that Newton had in effect stolen some of his work.

Newton also described concepts such as chromatic aberration, familiar to microscopists and photographers. Because the refractive index of a material such as glass is a function of the wavelength, a glass lens will bend blue light more than it will bend red light. Indeed, this was the physical basis of how his prisms were able to break white light up into the colors of the rainbow. Lenses in microscopes, being curved, also cause light to break up to some extent, which can cause false coloring of samples viewed through them. When working on the small scale of a microscope, this difference can be significant, but it can also be exploited to aid in identification. Newton's work was fundamental in developing microscopy as well as a host of other analytical tools routinely used in forensic laboratories.

The deaths of Boyle in 1691 and Newton in 1727 marked the end of the age of alchemy as a viable part of natural science and paved the way for the birth of forensic science. This pivotal moment coincided with mounting pressure within the legal community to find something—*anything*—that could supplement oral testimony without returning to torture and ordeal. For the first time in human history, science had something of substance to offer to the legal system. Setting the stage had taken nearly 4,500 years; forensic science as a recognized discipline and an arm of the legal system emerged in less than 200.

Poisoning is the crime that drove it.

7

One Element's Story

Arsenic is the ideal murder weapon. Because it occurs in soil and minerals, it was easily available even in ancient times. In large doses, it kills quickly; in small doses, it kills insidiously. As a cumulative poison, small doses of arsenic accumulate gradually in the body, the only signs of impending death being symptoms that mimic food poisoning, dysentery, and other ailments common in the world prior to sanitation and antibiotics. Murderers from Roman times onward appreciated these advantages and made liberal use of them. This one element, more than any other, drove the fear that in turn drove the advances in chemistry, death investigation, and toxicology that would lead to the emergence of forensic science as a recognized scientific discipline.

Arsenic (As) is a metal with an atomic number of 33 (33 protons in the nucleus) and an atomic weight of 74.9 atomic mass units. Chemically, arsenic is a transition metal in the same family as phosphorus, antimony, and bismuth. Transition metals are valued for many reasons, one being their ability to form highly colored compounds. Other transition metals include cadmium, lead, and zinc. Anyone who has used watercolor paints will recognize their names. Zinc oxide is the white material used as a sunscreen, and most white paints contain titanium pigments. Lead, another transition metal, was formerly used in house paints until it was banned in the 1970s. Because arsenic has two oxidation states (arsenic III and arsenic V), it can exist in many solid and gaseous forms, as well as dissolved in water. Each of these forms, sometimes referred to as species, has different properties and toxicities. The organic arsenic compounds are those that contain carbon, while the inorganic compounds do not.

Arsenic was one of the earliest known elements, documented around 2000 B.C.E. In its elemental metallic form, arsenic is dull gray and brittle. The most common mineral form of arsenic is arsenopyrite (FeAsS) from which arsenic can be extracted using the alchemic tool of pyrolysis. Other natural varieties are realgar (ruby sulfur or ratsbane, As_2S_2); king's yellow, As_2S_3; and arsenolite (flowers of arsenic and later "inheritance powder," As_2O_3). The name *arsenic* may have originated from the Arabic term *az-zernick* or the Greek *arsenikon*, roughly translated as relating to the male or having potency. The Greeks associated gender with metals based on the use and properties. In the Bronze Age, arsenic was added to the alloy to make it harder, a property the Greeks linked to bravery and the male gender. The name *orpiment* for king's yellow probably derives from the Roman descriptor of the pigment, *auripigmentum*, referring to its yellow color. The Greeks assumed that mineral arsenics were the elemental form[1], a mistake unrecognized until the work of Boyle and others.

Is arsenic a drug or a poison? Both. The toxicity of arsenic depends on what form it is in and the size of the dose. Antimicrobials such as arsenic are poisonous to microbes that can cause disease and infection. Arsenic's antimicrobial and medicinal properties were recognized and exploited soon after its discovery. As early as 400 B.C.E., the Greek physician Hippocrates reported using it to treat ulcers. In the 1700s, Thomas Fowler created a solution of As_2O_3 and potassium bicarbonate to create a preparation known as *Fowler's solution* that was widely used to treat skin and other problems into the 1900s. *Salvarsan* (arsphenamine) was the first effective treatment for syphilis, a sexually transmitted disease caused by bacteria. German chemist Paul Erhlich (1854–1915) introduced this organic form of arsenic in 1901 as a replacement for toxic mercury-based treatments. He won the Nobel Prize in 1908 for this and many other achievements. In the 1930s, arsenic became one of the first chemotherapeutic agents, and physicians still use some forms of it in modern cancer therapy.

Along with medicinal uses, early metallurgists used arsenic to strengthen alloys much as the Greeks had. When firearms became common weapons in the fifteenth century, arsenic became an ingredient in projectiles. The metal is also essential to modern electronics and, until recently, was used as a wood preservative. Wood rots by bacterial degradation, so killing the microorganisms is an effective way to preserve wood. The use of arsenic as medicine was carried a bit far in the late 1800s and early 1900s, when some people took arsenic in dilute preparations as a general health tonic.

Arsenic was also widely used in cosmetic preparations and treatments from the late medieval period onward. The aristocracy of France exploited the bleaching properties of As_2O_3 to enhance a pale complexion. Fashion-conscious women swallowed arsenic to help gain weight and attain the favored plump figure of the time. Some thought that regular ingestion of small amounts of arsenic would lead to immunity from arsenic poisoning (a forlorn hope). Embalmers of the period used arsenic compounds to slow decomposition.

MECHANISM OF DEATH

As centuries of use attest, arsenic is not the most toxic substance, or even the most toxic heavy metal. Why did it become a preferred method of murder? First, arsenic was widely available given its use in medicines, industry, and cosmetics. Most households had arsenic in some form, and purchasing even large amounts rarely raised suspicion. It has a bitter taste, but one easily disguised. Coffee has been a favorite method of delivery because it is a bitter brew. The largest mass poisoning in modern American history took place in 2003 when a disgruntled church member dumped arsenic in a postservice coffee urn. Arctic explorer Charles Francis Hall (1821–1871) disappeared on an expedition. His crew made its way overland back to Canada and reported that Hall died of an illness. Hall's body was located in 1968, and when the tissues were tested, analysts found high arsenic levels. Historical and scientific analyses pointed to coffee as the likely delivery vehicle for the mutiny by arsenic.

As a powder, arsenic is easier and safer to handle than arsenic in liquid or gas form. Most importantly, the cumulative effects of repeated low doses mimic many diseases that were common before antibiotics and sulfa drugs were available. Until well into the twentieth century, people died principally of infectious diseases such as dysentery, typhoid fever, cholera, food poisoning, and other viral and bacterial diseases. Symptoms of these ailments include nausea, vomiting, diarrhea, weakness, headache, and muscle pain. Thus, symptoms alone were rarely sufficient to distinguish homicidal poisoning from illness. Until forensic science developed tests for poisons, symptoms and circumstances related by witnesses and accusers were all investigators had to work with.

A poison can cause harm and death in two ways. The first is the case of acute poisoning in which a single large dose is administered. Hydrogen cyanide (also called prussic acid, HCN) was used this way. Because of its high toxicity, a small amount can be immediately lethal. Accordingly, prussic acid has been used on occasion to commit murder. Using such a poison has a distinct disadvantage: death occurs rapidly after ingestion. The less time between the administration of the dose and death, the more suspicious the death becomes. From a killer's perspective, such a rapid and dramatic death draws far more suspicion than a gradual, illness-like one. Even so, arsenic has been used as an acute poison, with a dose of 60–300 mg typically being fatal. For comparison, a typical aspirin tablet contains 325 mg of aspirin. The second method of harm is through accumulation, or chronic exposure. For a substance to be an effective chronic poison, it must linger in the body. How long it remains depends on how the body reacts to it.

When a substance is introduced into the body by swallowing, a complex process begins. Toxicologists refer to this process as ADME, an acronynm for absorption, distribution, metabolism, and excretion. Some materials, such as aspirin, go through this cycle quickly, and all remnants are eliminated within a few hours. Other substances such as morphine, linger at detectable levels in the system for a few days. Persistence is often desirable for drugs, as it allows therapeutic effects to continue over longer periods, but the more persistent a drug, the longer the time that must pass between doses to avoid toxic effects.

One way to measure how long a substance stays in the system is by its half-life. The concept is the same as used to describe radioactive decay. One half-life is the time required to remove half the original substance from the body, and for arsenic, the half-life is about twelve days. A rule of thumb is that it takes ten half-lives to remove all detectable traces of a substance from the body, corresponding to about 120 days for arsenic. Assume a person is given a teaspoon of white arsenic (As_2O_3) every five days; this would lead to gradual build up of residual arsenic that would reach potentially fatal levels within twelve weeks. During these four months, symptoms would appear gradually and would not be obviously linked to any one meal or dose. Give the same size dose of cyanide to a victim, and he or she would be dead almost immediately with symptoms nearly impossible to confuse with any natural cause. For the patient perpetrator, arsenic is the perfect poison.

Arsenic does harm by several mechanisms. Arsenic is in the same chemical family as phosphorus. The common forms of arsenic are those bound to oxygen and sulfur, such as As_2O_3. The propensity of arsenic to combine with sulfur explains one of arsenic's mechanisms of toxicity; arsenic can disrupt bonds containing sulfur that occur in proteins, a generally bad outcome in a living organism. The body can mistake arsenic for phosphorus since it is in the same chemical family, wreaking further havoc in critical metabolic cycles. As if this were not enough, excess arsenic can impede the formation of hemoglobin, the red pigment in the blood that carries oxygen.

Another interesting aspect of the arsenic family is that all of these elements (phosphorus, antimony, arsenic, and bismuth) are often found together in nature such as in ores and deposits. Of this group, antimony and phosphorus were also used as poisons, with arsenic being more available and therefore the more common. Arsenic metal is rarely found in nature; rather it is usually found as mineral forms in soil in which arsenic is commonly bound with oxygen or sulfur. It was not until after 1000 C.E. that the difference between arsenic the metal and arsenic in minerals was understood, to say nothing of the existence of chemical families and the presence of antimony, phosphorus, and bismuth in arsenic-containing raw materials.

For medicinal use, this familial relationship is problematic. Since families of elements often coexist in nature, the same is true of the raw materials used to make medicines. Early pharmacists and physicians were unaware of this, and as a result, crude preparations of bismuth or antimony compounds could contain lethal doses of arsenic. Similarly, preparations containing low levels of arsenic could contain lethal levels of antimony. By the age of iatrochemistry, this problem was recognized and understood. Alchemists of the day worked to perfect the difficult separations required, building the foundations of modern analytical chemistry.

ELEMENTAL OR NOT?

Even after the Greeks formalized the practice of science, it took hundreds of years to elucidate a minimal understanding of arsenic chemistry. The first person to separate arsenic-containing minerals from each other was probably Jabir, around the year 800 C.E. The chemical relatives of arsenic, bismuth and antimony, were chemically isolated in the medieval period, but their relationship to arsenic was not yet understood or even suspected. The first milestone in chemistry that had direct forensic implications occurred in 1250. In that year or close to it, a true chemical separation of elemental (metallic) arsenic from minerals containing arsenic occurred. Albertus Magnus (1193–1280), a German scholar, alchemist, and theologian, managed the feat. While there was still no clear understanding of the differences between compounds and elements, the isolation of metallic arsenic proved that the minerals that the Greeks thought were arsenic were in fact combinations of materials. In forensic terms, Magnus was the first to use heat to drive arsenic metal off the chemical matrix of a mineral. Five hundred years later, the first forensic tests for arsenic would be based on the same principle.

Magnus noted that if sufficient heat were applied to minerals containing arsenic, the arsenic metal would sublime. Magnus trapped this vapor and allowed the metal to condense. The same trick had been used for gold, but Magnus was the first to realize that there was such a thing as metallic arsenic and that a fire assay could be used to isolate it just as fire could be used to isolate and purify gold. For the time, this was a significant insight. Gold exists as metallic gold in nature—it is not usually locked up in ores or rocks that don't look like gold. Arsenic is found mostly in mineral form as white, red, or yellow rocks or veins that look nothing like the dull gray metallic form that condensed in Magnus' experiments.

Magnus' breakthrough had enormous, if delayed, consequences in forensic science. That poisoning was rampant was an open secret, but there was no way to prove that a death was caused by a poison. The proof would lie in a definitive chemical test for arsenic found in the body. To find arsenic in the body required separation of arsenic from tissues, stomach contents, hair, and blood. This had to be done even if the arsenic had been chemically altered by biological processes and was no longer in the same form as when ingested. If arsenic powder just sat in the stomach, it would not be toxic; it had to be processed by the body in some way before the toxic effects were seen. Magnus' work was the first small step in that direction.

Magnus, also known as Albert the Great, is also notable for other contributions. He became a professor at Paris University and counted among his students Thomas Aquinas. He also rose to the rank of bishop in a time when early science and religion were uneasy bedfellows at best. He was quoted as saying, "The aim of natural science is not simply to accept the statements of others, but to investigate the causes that are at work in nature," a sentiment remarkable for its time. As an alchemist, he was adept at using nitric acid as a means of separating gold from silver. A similar technique would be central in separating arsenic from forensic samples a few centuries later.

Progress inched forward during the age of iatrochemistry. Paracelsus described a method for isolating arsenic metal from arsenic sulfide compounds, building on the work of Arab alchemists as well as that of Magnus. He also wrote a treatise on the effect of gaseous metals as poisons in the mining industry, focusing on arsenic and mercury. Medicines he prepared and prescribed included low levels of bismuth, arsenic, antimony, and mercury salts, and he is credited with formulating the first viable treatment for syphilis. For this, he concocted an ointment based on mercury. Robert Boyle was also in the hunt for an arsenic test suitable for death investigations. He tried bubbling gases through solutions containing dissolved arsenic but never achieved a reliable and reproducible method.

POUDRE DE SUCCESSION (INHERITANCE POWDER)

While chemical science sputtered along, the poisoners plied their art with relative impunity. The most famous form of arsenic poison is arsenic trioxide (As_2O_3), referred to as white arsenic or colloquially as arsenic. The French later dubbed it *inheritance powder*. The marriage of poison and politics has proven a long and stable one. The first known law specifically addressing it was passed by Rome in 82 B.C.E., although as early as 400 B.C.E., the Romans had declared poisoning to be an epidemic. The phrase "live by the poison, die by the poison" probably traces to a mass execution of women convicted by Roman authorities of poisoning several men including their fathers, brothers, husbands, and various others. The execution was carried out by forcing the condemned to drink the same mixture that they used in their crime.

Later in the empire's run, the infamous emperor Nero sought poison to kill his rival Britannicus. He turned to condemned poisoner named Locusta to obtain the material. She supplied it and offered to administer the concoction herself for a modest increase in price. Nero refused and did the deed himself. Britannicus survived, and Nero had Locusta flogged. She protested that the weak dose was designed to make the death seem natural. The second time, she supplied a stronger dose that Nero tested until it was of sufficient strength to instantly kill a pig. He then administered it to Britannicus and obtained the desired result. He pardoned Locusta and sent apprentices her way.

Nero's penchant for poison ran in the family. His mother was Agrippina, known to use poison as a tool for career advancement. Her poison of choice was likely white arsenic. She killed her husband with it, allowing her to marry the emperor Claudius and therefore put her son Nero in line for the throne. Of course, that required that Agrippina also poison Claudius' first wife since she would have undoubtedly protested her husband's second marriage.

To combat the epidemic of arsenic poisoning, the ancients took advantage of arsenic chemistry to create what they called a "poison cup." Such cups were made of bezoar stones which come from the gut of ruminant animals such as goats. Bezoar stones are high in sulfur and could effectively filter out some arsenic by allowing it to bond with the sulfur in the cup itself. The use of poison cups was based on experience, not scientific knowledge. Knowing a method to prevent arsenic poisoning was a long way from having the tools to reliably detect and thus deter it. Well into the 1700s, it was commonly believed that powdered emeralds were a universal antidote for poisoning and that a unicorn horn was a reliable detector of poisons.

During the early years of the Renaissance, city councils of Florence and Venice sanctioned poisonings, going so far as to post names, issue contracts, and record payments issued on delivery of service. The Borgia family, particularly the infamous brother-sister pair of Cesare (1476–1507) and Lucrezia (1480–1519), made liberal use of arsenic as a financial planning tool, increasing their family's power and wealth. Lady Toffana was known for an arsenic-containing concoction called *aqua toffana* used in cosmetics as well for nefarious purposes. It likely contained a potent arsenite compound, a few drops of which were fatal. Toffana was executed by strangulation in 1709 after more than 500 deaths were attributed to her deadly water.

Catherine di Medici (1519–1589) left Italy and ventured into France, taking her collection of potions, known as the poison cabinet, with her. In a practice pioneered by Cleopatra, she tested mixtures on people she treated as "patients," observing symptoms and the speed of onset. Not to be outdone, the French contributed such famous arsenic users as Madame de Brinvilliers and Catherine Deshayes, also known as LaVoison. Among LaVoison's victims were some 2,000 infants. The scourge of poisoning in the court of King Louis XIV (1638–1715) led to a special tribunal called the Chambre Ardente (1679–1680) that used interrogation, torture, and executions to investigate and stop the crimes. Autopsies were conducted on many of the victims. A key finding was blackening of the throat and stomach that was consistent with what was known at the time about the effects of arsenic poisoning. However, that was the extent of the scientific evidence available to the Chambre.

The celebrated proceedings emphasized the need for better testing, but the infant science of chemistry wasn't ready to provide it. What it could provide was a greater understanding of the characteristics of arsenic. The garlicky smell and physical appearance of various arsenic preparations was well known. Medical and police investigators knew the typical symptoms of arsenic poisoning and what to look for if a person had died under questionable circumstances. One of the first documented arsenic cases that utilized the scientific and the medical occurred in 1752, notable for the detailed investigation of the death scene and subsequent expert testimony. The tests used were not chemical tests, but scientific nonetheless.

FOR THE SAKE OF DECENCY, GENTLEMEN, DON'T HANG ME HIGH

Mary Blandy (1721–1752) was a woman in a difficult situation. Her father had advertised a large dowry for her hand in marriage, with the predictable barrage of unappealing replies. The one acceptable suitor was Captain William Henry Cranstoun, who joined the household headed by Mary's father. Things went well until it was discovered that the honorable captain was already married and had been since 1744. Mary remained devoted to him. Her father did not and threw Cranstoun out of the house. He returned to Scotland but continued to correspond with Mary. The following events allegedly occurred, leading to Mary's arrest and execution.

To counter his prospective father-in-law's hostility, Cranstoun instructed Mary to slip her father some powders that would lessen his ire. The powder contained arsenic. Mary placed small amounts of the powder in her father's gruel. Over several weeks, he became ill, as did household servants who ate the leftovers. Mary called for a doctor who must also have known something of the law; he advised Mary that she could be held responsible for the poisoning. She burned incriminating letters from Cranstoun and tried to get rid of the remaining powder, but some was saved by a household servant. Her father died after he granted her forgiveness; Cranstoun ran to France, and she was arrested.

A medical examiner named Dr. Anthony Addington compared the white powder recovered from the scene with known arsenic and testified that arsenic had been used. Addington was a medical scientist, skilled in investigation and testing, but not a medical examiner in the modern sense as described in Chapter 8. Other doctors testified of detecting a garlicky odor on heating the powder and on the remarkably well-preserved state of the father's organs. The implication was that they had been preserved by arsenic. Mary testified in her own defense, admitting using the powders but maintaining that she thought they would soften her father's attitude toward Cranstoun. Whether she believed it or used it as an excuse will never be known for certain. The jury dismissed her version, convicted her of murder, and sentenced her to death by hanging. The sentence was carried out on April 6, 1752, and her last words are cited above. She was concerned that unruly men and boys in the crowd would try to peek up her skirts if given the chance. She died with her toes dangling inches off the ground.

THE MARSH TEST

Addington's tests relied on human senses for detection, an inadvisable practice when the test material may contain a deadly poison. In 1827, William Brande gave a lecture to a scientific society in England describing the state of the art in arsenic detection. When heated, he noted, arsenic gives off a distinctive odor, adding, "[Its taste] is singularly nauseous; it creates a peculiar astringent sensation about the mouth and fauces, a great flow of saliva, and a painful feeling in the mouth which can never be forgotten by those who have made the experiment."[2] Not all agreed on the taste. Some noted sweetness; others claimed it was tasteless. The problem of subjectivity of test results that relied on human senses, such as sight and color judgment, would ultimately drive the development of instrumentation. Meanwhile, with the variety of sensations possible, a taste test for arsenic was as useless as it was foolhardy. Chemists around Europe were working to find a better way.

Shortly after Blandy's execution, Swedish chemist Carl Wilhelm Scheele (1742–1786) developed a postmortem test for arsenic. Scheele was an apothecary's assistant and an excellent technician who discovered the element chlorine. His arsenic test involved heating arsenic powder (As_2O_3) placed in a solution containing metallic zinc and nitric acid. The arsenic formed the arsine gas AsH_3 that smelled of garlic. Johann Metzger took a different approach, adding charcoal to a solution of arsenic trioxide, resulting in formation of metallic arsenic. Another qualitative test for arsenic developed during this period involved bubbling hydrogen sulfide gas (H_2S, which has the odor of rotten eggs) through the solution containing dissolved arsenic and hydrochloric acid. Any arsenic present would form solid King's yellow, As_2S_3.

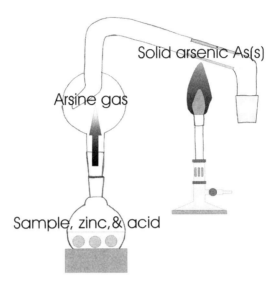

Figure 7.1 A schematic of the Marsh test apparatus. The sample is placed in a flask with zinc metal and acid. If there is arsenic present in the sample, heating it will produce arsine gas (AsH_3) which will travel up the glass tube. It will be heated again to break down the arsine to arsenic metal which will plate the glass tube that will turn into a gray mirror.

By the early 1800s, the first attempts to use these and related tests were reported. In 1806, chemist Valentine Rose attempted to detect arsenic in stomach contents by converting it to white arsenic and then using Metzger's technique. These early attempts were difficult, required great skill, and could not detect relatively low levels of arsenic. A famous case brought this limitation to light.

In 1832, John Bodle had been accused of poisoning his grandfather with arsenic placed in coffee. English chemist James Marsh was asked by the prosecution to check the stomach contents of the victim. Marsh used the hydrogen sulfide method and was able to produce a yellow solid consistent with the presence of arsenic. Unfortunately, the solid degraded between the time it was prepared and when it was presented to a jury. To Marsh's dismay, Bodle was acquitted. To add insult to injury, Bodle later bragged about his acquittal. Marsh took his anger and frustration and disappeared into his lab.

Marsh's goal was simple: develop a reliable and visually convincing method to detect arsenic in messy and complex samples like tissue and stomach contents. First, he turned to Scheele's procedure in which arsenic was converted to arsine gas. Marsh also knew that under the proper conditions, compounds containing arsenic, such as arsine, could be ma-nipulated to form arsenic metal. Magnus had demonstrated that conver-sion centuries earlier. Marsh realized that metallic arsenic is stable, and if he could capture the arsine gas, he could then obtain the metallic arsenic from it. Great idea on paper, but it took him four years to perfect what came to be known as the *Marsh test*. This famous procedure was the first reliable analytical test for arsenic. For his efforts, Marsh received wide ac-claim and a gold medal from the Royal Society of Arts.

The test incorporated all the advances in analytical chemistry made un-til that time. The method starts by converting the sample, be it a powder, stomach contents, or body tissue, into solution by adding hydrochloric acid. Shavings of metallic zinc are included in the mixture which is then heated. Under these conditions, arsenic forms arsine gas that rises away from solution. The innovation Marsh added was to trap this gas and direct it through a tube. The gas is heated again, causing the arsine gas (H_3As) to decompose to metallic arsenic which forms a gray coating on glass or a piece of porcelain. Unlike the arsenic compound formed with hydrogen sulfide gas, the metallic "mirror" is stable and makes ideal visual evidence for display before a jury.

The full impact of the Marsh test was not felt for decades. Several factors contributed to the delay. First, not everyone, including scientists, knew of the test. Second, the test was difficult to perform, even for Marsh. The test was a hybrid of an industrial-type test meant to identify arsenic in zinc and a toxicological test. At the time, much of the zinc and acids available had traces of arsenic in them. A positive result did not necessarily mean that the arsenic came from the tissue sample. These issues would be raised in years ahead as the Marsh test and modifications spread. Finally, scien-tific evidence and testimony was the exception and not the rule in legal proceedings.

Despite these issues, by the mid 1800s, all the pieces were in place to bring the marsh test to the public's attention. All it would take was a sensational and sensationalized trial to finally bring forensic science into being.

FORENSIC SCIENCE ARRIVES

The place was Brive, France, and the year was 1840. Marie LaFarge, an attractive young woman, was married to Charles LaFarge, a foundry owner. By most accounts, Charles was a scoundrel who lied to Marie and represented himself as far wealthier than he was. He had debts and saw Marie's dowry as the solution. Predictably, there was no love lost between the two since there was none to start with. They married in 1839, and Charles was dead by early 1840.

While on travel in December of 1839, Charles complained of stomach distress after eating a cake sent from his wife. He returned home, and she attended to him, notably preparing food and drinks for his convalescence. Despite or because of her attention, his condition deteriorated, and he died in early January. Suspicion focused on Marie given her behavior during the illness, her request for arsenic to "kill rats that were bothering the patient," and her handling of the food as witnessed by a servant. The evidence against her was significant, but not conclusive. She was arrested and charged with murder. Subsequent chemical tests on the food showed the presence of arsenic.

The investigation and trial was, much like the Blandy case, a national obsession. People waited hours in hopes of getting a seat in the courtroom. Marie was defended by a man named Maitre Palliet, a coincidence that raised the trial of Marie LaFarge from a tawdry repeat of the Blandy case to a milestone in forensic science. Palliet was also the personal lawyer to a man named Mathieu Joseph Bonaventure Orfila (1787–1853), a toxicologist working in Italy at the time. Had Palliet not known of Orfila and his work, it could have been another fifty years before a breakthrough case was heard.

Orfila has been christened the father of modern forensic toxicology. He was born in Minorca, a Spanish colony. He was a prodigy and quickly outgrew his first academic home in Valencia. The chemistry of oxygen, recently studied and revealed by Lavoisier's work in Paris, drew him to France as much as his disdain for his Spanish teachers who still taught from Greek and Roman texts. Orfila worked and wrote prodigiously, graduating with an M.D. in 1811.

Due to the Napoleonic wars, he was unable to leave Paris, so he continued his work there and eventually became Professor of Forensic Chemistry and Dean of the Medical Faculty at the University of Paris. He began publishing early, with his first paper on poisons in 1814 when he was twenty-six years old. During 1814–1818, he published his most famous and important work, a textbook on poisons and toxicology, as well as books on medicinal chemistry and other papers. He spent a good deal of time studying poisons, particularly arsenic. As a toxicologist, he concentrated on methods of analysis of poisons in blood and other body fluids and tissues. Thousands of dogs died during the course of his work.

One of Orfila's other passions was demolishing false ideas and traditional practices much in the vein of Paracelsus four centuries earlier. In the early 1800s, many remedies and medicines were concocted based as much on anecdotal evidence and folklore as on science. As an example, many preparations contained a substance called *nux vomica*, which is known to contain high amounts of strychnine. Orfila demonstrated clearly and experimentally the dangers of this material. His growing fame and expertise led to his appointment as the Dean of University of Paris Medical Faculty in 1831, a post he held until 1848. During that time, he added significantly to the work done by Marsh early in the decade.

One of the first problems noted with the Marsh test was a result of its sensitivity. Chemists found that samples that should not have contained arsenic, such as soil and bones, gave a positive result with the Marsh test. The latter occurred even when a person had died of natural causes and when special test solutions were prepared meticulously such that no arsenic should have been present. The test solutions revealed the importance of insuring that any reagents used in the Marsh test, such as the acids, were arsenic-free. Even when these precautions were taken, bones tested positive. Laborious experiments of Orfila and others were needed to prove that the human body naturally contains arsenic, albeit at levels far below what would be expected in poisoning cases. Orfila also pointed out that arsenic concentrates in bones and that most arsenic delivered as a poison would be found in the stomach and other tissues at concentrations well above background. Orfila conducted many experiments to determine background levels of arsenic in soil. An important finding was that most of this arsenic was in a form that was insoluble and thus unlikely to infiltrate a grave in any significant quantity. These soil studies would play a major role in the LaFarge case, as would Orfila himself.

Marie LaFarge's lawyer, Palliet, had an excellent defense strategy for her case. He knew that the evidence against her was strong. He knew that the prosecution was vulnerable because it lacked a credible finding of arsenic in the body. He reasoned that if he could cast doubt on the scientific tests already performed, he could raise further doubts and mitigate any positive results that might later be obtained from the body. Hoping to discredit the prosecution's scientific analysis, Palliet took the test results to Orfila for review. His effort was rewarded when Orfila delivered a withering criticism of the techniques and results used during the initial tests. Palliet put the report to good use during questioning of the doctor who had performed the tests. The *"Perry Mason moment"* came when Palliet forced the doctor to admit he had not heard of James Marsh, and, by implication, the Marsh test. Palliet asked that Orfila be called to perform further testing, but the prosecution argued against it, citing the cost and delay of having Orfila travel so far.

Instead, the court turned samples, including stomach contents, over to two analysts based in Paris. The two had heard of Marsh and the Marsh test, but failed to mention that they had never done the test themselves. Undaunted, they set about performing the tests and reported back to the court that they were unable to detect any arsenic in the stomach contents or tissue of the deceased. Palliet and his client were overjoyed, but they had a hard lesson to learn about courtroom strategy.

The prosecution had been taken by surprise by Palliet's initial attack on the scientific results. During the recess taken for the second analyses, the prosecutor learned what he could about toxicology. His research revealed that a negative result for stomach contents did not rule out poisoning but rather indicated that testing of other organs such as the liver should follow. The prosecution made exactly that argument before the court. Now it was the defense's turn to scramble and object, but it was too late. Another round of testing was ordered, necessitating the exhumation of Charles LaFarge. The liver and spleen were tested, again with negative results. In a final challenge, the prosecution asked that the food evidence be retested using the same techniques. This time, the results appeared conclusive. One sample, eggnog, was reported to "have been enough to poison at least ten persons."[3]

The prosecutor moved in for the kill. So certain was he of the damning results that he now agreed with the defense's original request to have Orfila review all of the test results. Palliet could hardly disagree since he had been the one to bring Orfila to the court's attention in the first place. Rather than just review the results this time, Orfila came himself and set to work repeating all of the tests. He insisted that all of the chemists who had done the previous work be there to witness what he did.

Three long days later, Orfila rose and read his results to the court. One can only imagine how Palliet felt when he heard his friend and acknowledged expert state, "I shall prove, first, that there is arsenic in the body of LaFarge; second, that this arsenic comes neither from the reagents with which we worked nor from the earth surrounding the coffin; also, that the arsenic we found is not the arsenic component which is naturally found in every human body."[4]

Maria was found guilty and sentenced to life with hard labor, which the King commuted to exclude the hard labor. This step was probably in deference to the "LaFargists" who apparently had little else to do but follow the trial and agitate for mercy for the attractive young woman who had put on a dramatic and emotional show for the court. She spent ten years under confinement and was released shortly before she died of tuberculosis.

The début of the Marsh test was not exactly a triumph. The contradictory results obtained by different chemists did not instill confidence in the method, particularly since it appeared to be so difficult to perform. It would soon be revealed that although far better than any tests before it, the Marsh test was not specific to arsenic. Antimony, the close chemical relative of arsenic, would also form a solid under its conditions, but it was a whitish solid rather than a mirror. Marsh worked to make the test more specific, as did other investigators. Because antimony was also used as a poison, this cross-reactivity was actually useful for detection and was not entirely detrimental.

Finally, it must be emphasized that the Marsh test, state of the art in 1840, would not be accepted in a modern court as definitive proof of arsenic. This is not the fault of the test but simply an acknowledgement that science is a process that is designed to improve over time. An article in the *London Medical Gazette* (1840–1841) summed it up: "The certain test of

1820 is no longer the certain test of 1840; and who can answer what this will be in 1860? Until chemistry becomes a fixed science, and the action of every possible combination of substances has been tried, how can we be sure of our facts, and confidently prove a negative? Every story, says the vulgar proverb, is good, till another is told; and every test is valid, till a fallacy is discovered in it."[5]

The LaFarge trial was a landmark. The sensational nature of the trial, the central role of science, and Orfila's dramatic and now famous testimony as a recognized expert in forensic toxicology marked the beginning of modern forensic science. In a trend repeated today, students studying chemistry vied for the chance to study with Orfila and to become forensic toxicologists themselves. Prosecution and defense counsel alike now realized that scientific analysis of evidence could be the crux of a case or the undoing of it rather than an afterthought. Orfila's testimony and the acceptance of the Marsh test did not end poisoning, nor did they do anything to prevent accidental exposures to arsenic. Eventually that would come, but as is often the case, the scientific advance aided law enforcement and also forced murderers to alter their tactics.

Forensic science was born.

8

A Visit from God

More than any other circumstance, forensic science is concerned with the circumstance of death, particularly when the death is suspicious. Once science provided the first simple tools to separate the extraordinary from the ordinary death, the investigation of questioned death became the nucleus of what would become forensic science. Organized forensic laboratories took shape out of public health and sanitation bureaus with rudimentary forms of autopsy and toxicology. The Marsh test was instrumental in deterring the use of arsenic, but there were plenty of other poisons. The difference was that now science was capable of mustering a counterattack. As forensic medicine became an accepted and established medical specialty, its successes were instrumental in driving the expansion of forensic science in new directions.

NASH

A person can die by his or her own hands, or death may be caused by another person, either purposefully, negligently, or by accident. If death is caused by someone else, the killing may be premeditated or spur of the moment, aggravated or unprovoked. How society views the circumstance of a killing dictates the severity of the punishment. Suppose a body is found in a well in a rural area. The victim is clearly dead, and a homicide has occurred, but under what circumstance?

Consider the instructions given to a trained investigator facing such a situation:

> The similarities between those who jump into wells, those who are thrown in, and those who lose their footing and fall are very great. The differences are slight.... If the victim was thrown in or fell in accidentally, the hands will be open and the eyes slightly open, and about the person he may have money or other valuables. But, if he was committing suicide, then his eyes will be shut and the hands clenched. There will be no valuables on the body. Generally, when someone deliberately jumps into a well, they enter feet first. If a body is found to have gone in head first, it is probable that the victim was being chased or was thrown in by others. If he lost his footing and fell in, you must check the point where his feet slipped to see if the ground has been disturbed.[1]

There is nothing surprising about this passage, except that it was written in 1247 C.E. The concern with manner of death is as old as civilization; circumstance defines murder.

Death investigation took on importance as society and governments advanced for many reasons, aside from the obvious one of detecting a murder. The manner of death, natural, accidental, suicide, or homicide (abbreviated as NASH), determined where the money (taxes and inheritance) went. Modern humans are hardly the first to escape the dual certainties of death and taxes. As soon the concept of personal property was established, so were the concepts of theft and inheritance. Depending on the manner of death, a person's property would be passed on to the family or surrendered to the government. Once inheritance became an issue, the manner of death took on a broader social consequence beyond the familial unit in which it occurred. The investigation of death and its circumstance (medicolegal investigation of death) is the earliest identifiable ancestor of forensic science. *Medical* because someone trained in medical arts is the best qualified to investigate death; *legal* because of the social consequences.

POSTMORTEM

The Sumerians possessed significant medical knowledge and practiced surgery. They referred to the opium poppy as "joy plant" indicating more than a passing familiarity with the effect of opium and the morphine that could be extracted from its milk. The Egyptians also had extensive knowledge of natural medicines and by 300 B.C.E. were teaching classes in anatomy and performing occasional autopsies. Like the Greeks, the Egyptians observed and documented the cooling (algor mortis) and stiffening of a body (rigor mortis) after death. By the second century A.D., they were performing medicolegal work and investigations.

Early medical testimony usually involved a postmortem examination of the body. This examination could be external, internal, or both, but was rarely a systematic dissection. The Greeks contributed the concept of autopsy (from *autopsia*, the act of seeing for oneself). The autopsy was used as a teaching tool as well as an investigative and legal one. The physician Hippocrates, after whom the famous oath has been named, was writing extensively around 400 B.C.E. on topics of forensic and medicolegal importance including what type of wounds were likely to be fatal. He also discussed topics ranging from epilepsy to medical fraud. Hippocrates' work formed the foundation for the important body of medicolegal knowledge that was exploited by Greeks, Romans, and those who followed. In 130 A.D., a doctor testified in a court concerning wound characteristics, the first such record to come out of Greece. Rome recorded one of the first recorded testimonies of a scientific expert in a legal matter, when Antistius testified about the death of Caesar.

Similar progress was being made in India in this later period, where dissections were being advocated for training surgeons. By the third century A.D., they had produced documents relating to the investigation of questioned deaths. The Chinese were equally progressive, having addressed topics such as herbal medicines (including marijuana) and poisons as early as 2800 B.C.E. Records of caesarean sections existed by 300 A.D., and expert testimony by a physician named Wu P'u in medicolegal matters had been recorded. There are also indications that a text devoted to medicolegal matters was written by Hsu Chich-Ts'si in the sixth century, but the actual text apparently is lost. It was not until 1247 that a surviving text on legal medicine was written, this one by Sung Tz'u and entitled *Hsi Yüan Lu*, translated as *The Writing of Wrongs* or *The Washing Away of Wrongs*, which was quoted above. Incredibly, this book was used into the twentieth century and included information on strangulation, drowning, wound characteristics, poisons, and even a dash of forensic dentistry. Characteristic changes in the postmortem interval (PMI) were discussed to provide a means of estimating how long a person had been dead.

Sung Tz'u's work was notable because it was a manual expressly for death investigators. The death investigator was charged with providing information that would be used during an inquest. An inquest is an investigation of a questioned death held at the behest of government officials. In English law, the procedure became known as a coroner's inquest. Such investigations were common throughout recorded history. Sung Tz'u was the earliest known record of death investigation in the forensic tradition. Death investigators during his time were typically not physicians. This was true in the West as well. The role of a physician during the age of testimony by ordeal was to examine his patients to certify that they were strong enough to undergo torture. It would be several hundred years before physicians took the lead in medicolegal investigation. Even in modern medical examiner's offices, physicians typically are not called to the death scene. Rather, initial investigation is undertaken by trained death investigators trained using manuals not all that different from those used in China.

One of the first uses of an autopsy in the Middle Ages was reported in Bologna, Italy, in 1302, but the practice was not mentioned with any significance until the 1500s. It was during this century that studies of human anatomy began in earnest. Dissection was one of the primary tools of this renewed exploration. Governments in Italy and France began to call on medical practitioners in legal matters. In 1579, an official report was filed in Bologna regarding the examination of a body found hanging near the outhouse of the dead person's home. The report noted no signs of external injury other than those due to the noose. No specific mention is made of the manner of death, but the clear implication was that it was a suicide. In Italy, the physicians Fortunato Fidelis and Paolo Zacchia undertook systematic dissections to understand the signs of drowning, strangulation, sexual assault, gunshot wounds, and infanticide.

VISITS FROM GOD

The British Isles adopted a coroner system near the turn of the first millennium to investigate deaths. The protocols they developed and followed formalized the relationship of the two inevitabilities—death and taxes. The term "coroner," loosely traced to the term "crowner," originated in England. The English coroner system began some time in the eighth or ninth centuries. The coroner's responsibilities included collection of revenue due to the government, oversight of inquests into questioned deaths, and record keeping. Formal elections of coroners to serve specific counties began in 1194, and the system was designed to insure that money due to the crown as a result of death was delivered to the government and not to corrupt local sheriffs. Corruption is a contagious disease, and many of the coroners became as shady as their predecessors. One of the job requirements for a coroner was that he own land in his district. The logic behind this requirement was simple: if the coroner was caught embezzling, the crown seized his property. Not to be outwitted, many coroners owned a small piece of land in their jurisdiction—a burial plot, which they were happy to surrender in exchange for their ill-gotten gains. The land ownership requirement was abolished in 1926.

The early English coroner system had other design flaws. Because the coroner was elected, medical training was not required. When medicine itself was primitive, this was not a particular problem, but by 1800, medicine had evolved sufficiently that laypeople typically lacked the background necessary to investigate the medical aspects of a questioned death. There were also fines and penalties aplenty, some of which worked against the system. When a body was found and the death questionable, the person who found the body was supposed to notify the coroner and accompany him when he came to examine the body. The *first finder* was also obligated to accompany the coroner to an appearance before a court, which could involve several days' travel. For the medieval farmer, this could be a significant hardship, and as a result, many first finders were probably better classified as designated finders; that is, the persons who drew the shortest straw. Other first finders accepted the fine rather than leave for a court appearance.

In some cases, a homicide or other type of sudden unexpected death could bring a fine on the local parish. If a murder occurred during the day and the killer escaped, it was assumed that the community was at fault for not capturing the killer. The government was more forgiving if the crime occurred at night since it was presumably easier for the perpetrator to escape. Predictably, many bodies found their way to other parishes before being discovered. Any time a body is moved, vital information about the context of the death is lost, making a difficult job even harder.

As for cause of death, the coroner relied primarily on external examination of the body. One of the earliest autopsies recorded in Britain took place in 1635. The subject was a man named Thomas Parr, and he was reputed to have died at the ripe old age of 152. The King commissioned the well-known physician William Harvey to perform the procedure in hopes of uncovering the secret of such longevity. Apparently, the King (Charles I) failed to pick up any pointers for increasing the length of his reign, which began in 1625 and ended with his execution in 1649.

With autopsy rare and medical knowledge still primitive, most deaths investigated by coroners were attributed to *ex visitatione divina*, or a visit from God. Barring obvious wounds or other visible symptoms, most deaths, including sudden or unexpected ones, were usually ascribed to a visit by the deity. As noted in the previous chapter, this bias made it easy to get away with a well-executed poisoning. Acts of God were still the most commonly assigned cause of death in Britain well into the 1800s. Other interesting causes of death recorded over the centuries included evil, lice, lethargy, and French pox (syphilis).

Physicians and surgeons were frequently called on to determine if a dead baby had been stillborn or had been killed after a live birth. A clever Danish physician named Bartholi devised a simple test in the late 1600s in which he placed the body in water. If the corpse floated, he reasoned, then there was some air in the lungs and the child had been alive long enough to breathe on its own. By the middle of that century, students in many medical colleges were given some training in death investigation.

By the late 1700s, textbooks devoted to the medicolegal investigation of death had been published in French and German. This coincided with a growing enthusiasm for microscopic studies of tissues made possible by the invention and perfection (in a limited sense) of the microscope. These new skills and knowledge evolved at a time when cities were growing more centralized and populous, bringing on new problems in health and sanitation. The era of plagues and epidemics added to the pressing need.

The plague ravaged Europe for decades and killed untold thousands. It was blamed for many other deaths, including that of a man named Ansovino, who died in Rome during the early 1600s. He was involved in a fight with a man he knew named Silvio, who struck Ansovino on the head. Ansovino was seen by a surgeon who noted that there was a cut but no bone fractures and that the wound was not particularly serious. A few days later, Ansovino developed a fever that accompanied the formation of black spots around the wound. He died shortly thereafter and Silvio was charged with capital murder. His defense was that his dead companion had died as a result of the plague, not from the blow. How the court saw the cause, and thus the circumstance, of the death would determine Silvio's fate.

Postmortem examination of the body revealed extensive black spotting and other symptoms consistent with the plague. The prosecutor's argument that a blow to the head was dangerous was rebuffed by the surgeon's report indicating laceration but no fractures. Finally, testimonies of others revealed that one of the men who had tended Ansovino after his brawl also contracted plague. In this case, scientific testimony was crucial in proving that the plague was the more probable cause of death than the wound.

In response to the need for public health and sanitation controls, local governments around Europe began forming government offices responsible for public health, sanitation, and death investigation. Although it may not be as obvious as it once was, these topics are inseparable. Often death investigation was conducted as a public health service to identify outbreaks of disease and order quarantines or other measures to limit the spread. This trend continued across Europe and was well established by the late 1700s. Across the Atlantic, the Massachusetts Bay Colony had a ship quarantined in 1647 as a public health measure, the first such act recorded in the American colonies. New York City noted one of the earliest postmortem examinations of a case in which poisoning was suspected, that of Henry Slaughter who had just been elected governor of the state in 1691. The autopsy pointed instead to natural causes.

By the end of the eighteenth century, governmental institutions and offices staffed by medical experts were in place and were routinely conducting public service and medicolegal activities. Death investigation via coroners and other systems was an accepted aspect of governmental responsibility. Scientific advances, particularly in chemistry and microscopy, had opened the door to much greater understanding of anatomy and physiology on a chemical and cellular level. This newly acquired knowledge and experience was being employed to develop diagnostic and investigative tests such as the Marsh test. By the end of the century, books had been published relating to forensic medicine, notably *A Treatise on Forensic Medicine and Public Health* by Fodere and *The Complete System of Police Medicine* by the German Johann Peter Franck. As was the case with arsenic, by the turn of the nineteenth century, all the pieces were in place to allow for a breakthrough in forensic death investigation. Britain and the rest of Europe were to take center stage.

THE CRITICAL CENTURY, 1800–1880

The nineteenth century introduced the pioneers and practices of modern forensic death investigation several factors contributed to this timing. First was the increasing skill of physicians and chemist/toxicologists such as Orfila. By 1791, medical colleges in Britain were presenting their students with information related to medicolegal topics and scientific investigation of death. The first institute of legal medicine was formed in Vienna in 1804. By 1833, such courses became mandatory in British medical schools. Paris was home to the first institute dedicated to forensic medicine, founded in 1794. At the same time, books on forensic death investigation, even if they did not carry those exact words in their titles, were being widely disseminated. A textbook entitled *The Epitome of Judicial or Forensic Medicine; for the Use of Medical Men, Coroners, and Barristers* appeared in London in 1816, nearly 600 years after Sung Tz'u's handbook covering the same topic appeared in China. The coroners continued to play a role in death investigation as the nineteenth century unfolded, but as time went on, coroners increasingly called on the expertise of the "medical police" to fill in the scientific and medical blanks that arose during the investigation and in criminal and civil proceedings.

In the field of forensic medicine, Alexandre Lacassagne joined the faculty at the University of Lyon as the first to hold the chair in the newly created department of forensic medicine. He took this place in 1880, and this university in France became the incubator for many prominent forensic scientists, including Edmond Locard. A similar position had been created at the University of Edinburgh in 1807, and this somewhat smallish and isolated school became the cradle of forensic medicine in the United Kingdom and other English-speaking countries. It also marked the first strong entry of Britain into the progressive march of forensic science, which had previously been dominated by the continental powers of Germany and France.

Some of the famous alumni of Edinburgh fanned outward, carrying with them knowledge and appreciation of matters and procedures forensic. Robert Christison (1797–1882) was appointed chair of medical jurisprudence in 1822. He had studied in France under Orfila and began a long and storied career in forensic toxicology and chemistry. He was recognized for applying many advances in analytical techniques to toxicology and in 1829 became the medical advisor to the Scottish Crown, a position he held for nearly forty years. Doctors James Stringham and William Dunlop (1792–1848) set up shop in the United States and Canada respectively. Stringham became a professor in New York in 1813, while Dunlop set out for what was to become a colorful career in Canada. At the age of twenty-one, he was an assistant surgeon treating soldiers wounded during battles in the War of 1812. A tough man, his nickname was Tiger, and he performed many forensic autopsies. In Canada especially, he is well known for blunt honesty, which included such statements as "I leave Parson Chavasse a small token of my gratitude for the service he has done my family in taking a sister no man of taste would have taken."[2]

The first known scientific testimony in Canada came in 1859 by Professor Henry Holmes Croft in the case of the murder of Sarah King. Croft, English by birth, trained in Berlin and at the tender age of twenty-three, was a rising star in chemistry. Upon the recommendation of Michael Faraday, Croft returned to Canada to assume the post of Professor of Experimental Philosophy and Chemistry at Kings College in Toronto. His lab was built away from the main building to prevent his odorous samples from entering the building. In the King case, Dr. William Henry King was accused of killing Sarah King using poison. Croft found arsenic in the stomach, but little in the liver, and he testified that the amount found there would not have been enough to kill Sarah. Moments before his execution, Dr. King admitted his guilt, claiming to have used morphine rather than arsenic.

TIME, CAUSE, AND MANNER

Along with the cause and manner of a death, investigators in the nineteenth century were becoming concerned with the time of death. The easiest phenomena to exploit are the cooling rate of the body (algor mortis), stiffening of muscles and then softening (rigor mortis), and settling of blood that is no longer circulating (*lividity* or *livor mortis*). While undoubtedly all three were known from ancient times, how or if they were used in death investigation is not known until the 1800s.

Rigor mortis was first studied in detail and described by a Belgian physician named Pierre Nysten in 1811. He noted that the process begins with stiffening in small muscles such as the jaw and proceeds to the larger muscles followed by relaxation in the reverse order. Onset varies but typically begins within three hours of death. Fiction writers frequently use "stiff" as a synonym for a dead body, but that is only true for the freshly dead; rigor is usually completely released within three to four days. Lacassagne studied rigor as well, determining that the process actually appeared to begin with the heart. One of the first textbook mentions of rigor came in the 1882 edition of *Legal Medicine* by C.M. Tidy.

More attention has been paid to body temperature and how it changes after death. The first research into the topic appeared in 1839 in a book by Englishman Dr. John Davey based on work done in the tropics and in Britain. In several cases, he noted an increase in temperature. Since some of his subjects had died of infectious disease accompanied by high fever, he wisely put little weight into these findings. An American, Dr. Benjamin Hensley, followed up with a similar report in 1846, but neither author attempted to derive a mathematical relationship or formula to relate body temperature to a specific time of death.

Time of death remains notoriously difficult to determine. Dr. Davey had identified a factor in its determination, the condition a person was in just before death. Diseases that cause high fever throw any calculations into doubt, as does intense activity just before death such as running for one's life. The environmental conditions are equally critical, as is the surface area of the body and how much skin is exposed. Other key factors recognized by early forensic practitioners was where in the body the temperature was taken and how often. Core temperature of a body will differ from skin temperature just as rectal temperature will differ from liver temperature. The first truly comprehensive study considering many variables appeared in England in 1863 and was derived from studies on a hundred bodies. The authors showed that skin temperature was not as reliable an indicator of cooling as an internal temperature such as one taken in the rectum. A simple mathematical approach to estimating the time of death based on rectal temperature appeared in 1868. Graphical methods were added to the arsenal in the 1880s, but it was recognized that even complex mathematical approaches were generally inadequate to deal with the variety of environmental conditions in which bodies were found.

Only in the 1950s did forensic pathologists revisit the relationship of body temperature to the estimated time of death. One of the first reports to tackle the problem of environmental conditions appeared in 1955 and was based on carefully controlled studies conducted on the bodies of executed criminals. The report, published by Dr. G. de Saram, noted among other findings that cooling rates varied significantly from body to body even under similar environmental conditions. A study published in 1957 recommended the use of multiple sites of measurement as well as continuous measurement rather than readings taken at intervals. The authors also emphasized the temperature difference between the body and the environment rather than just the body's temperature in their work and concluded that the most reliable temperature measurements for estimating the time of death were taken in the brain. The findings confirmed what research from the 1800s and anecdotal information from Sung Tz'u forward had shown: a body cools approximately 1.5°F per hour at room temperature.

THE RISE OF MEDICAL EXAMINERS:
SIR BERNARD SPILSBURY

The nineteenth century saw enormous progress in the forensic investigation of death, but the discipline was still in its infancy. Within the medical community, it lacked the respect and prestige of many other specialties. Progress was slow and uneven. Forensic science was still not a recognized science, and it was often considered as more of a sideline, avocation, or hobby. Physicians working in forensic medicine often did other types of analysis and were sometimes called to testify concerning the results of tests they did not themselves perform. Death investigators of this age were true generalists, and the best of them recognized the limitations of this approach and pushed other specialists such as microscopists, chemists, and biologists to bring their skills to bear on death investigation. These men were the forerunners and founders of the medical examiner system (or the equivalent). The nature of the challenge and the work drew an interesting lot of characters who echoed in some ways the likes of Paracelsus, Newton, Hooke, and Boyle. As a result, the late nineteenth and early twentieth centuries mark the beginning of forensic celebrity. Through their work, extensive public exposure, and involvement in high profile cases, these men jumped into the public and scientific limelight.

One of the first was Sir Bernard Spilsbury in England. His colorful career was the subject of several books, including *The Scalpel of Scotland Yard: The Life of Sir Bernard Spilsbury*. His life and, ironic given his profession, his death had just the right touch of theater for the age. Spilsbury was born in 1877, and he died near his office in 1947, committing suicide using carbon monoxide gas. His public life was one of fame, his private later life one of tragedy. Two of his sons, also doctors, died during the war period. The first to die was Peter, who was killed in an air raid in 1940. This was also the year of Spilsbury's first stroke. The next year, his sister died, and in 1945, his son Alan died of consumption. Before the 1940s signaled the beginning of the end, Spilsbury made an indelible mark as a forensic pathologist and death investigator. He performed thousands of autopsies, many of them on criminals he had helped send to the gallows. He used what he learned to study death by sudden blow and to recommend more humane methods of hanging.

Spilsbury began training in medicine in 1899 at St. Mary's Hospital in London, one of the key facilities associated with legal medicine. St. Mary's became famous in 1928 because of the work of Alexander Fleming, who discovered penicillin while working there. Spilsbury didn't discover a new substance while there but rather his own incredible aptitude for meticulous investigation and analysis required for death investigation. He was able to study under some of the most famous forensic pathologists and toxicologists of the day, men who were themselves representative of the first and second generations of true forensic scientists who emerged after Orfila. By 1809, he was senior pathologist and the Home Office pathologist at St. Mary's.

His celebrity was launched with a murder case in 1910. The accused was a fellow physician named Crippen whose wife had been reported missing in early January. The badly decomposed body was found in July, buried in their cellar. His work was hampered because the killer had removed the head, bones, limbs, and sexual organs from the body. All Spilsbury had to work with was a decomposed torso. Analysis of the tissue revealed the presence of a compound called *hyoscine*, better known as scopolamine in the United States. This drug is a naturally occurring alkaloid that is readily absorbed through the skin, but it is not as toxic as other poisons common in the day. Spilsbury's testimony centered on the difficult task of identification which he was able to do using a scar found on the abdomen. Crippen was convicted.

The second case that established Spilsbury's reputation was the Seddon case in 1912. Frederick Seddon and his wife operated a rooming house that was home to Eliza Barrow, whose life ended soon after she changed her will and left all her property to the Seddons. She was buried but later exhumed and tested for arsenic by Spilsbury. The Marsh test was used and the arsenic mirror was shown to the jury. Frederick Seddon was convicted and hung for murder.

The most famous case Spilsbury worked came three years later and was known as the "Brides of Bath." George Smith stood accused of murdering three young women. In sequence, he courted, married, and insured each, with their deaths following shortly after the last step. All three had died in the bathtub, but the deaths occurred in different places across England. Once suspicion was raised, all three bodies were exhumed. Spilsbury determined that all had died by drowning. Through experimentation, Spilsbury showed that Smith had managed to yank the women by the feet while they lay reclined in the tubs. A strong violent jerk, he demonstrated, could cause the victim to become immediately unconscious. They drowned without struggle. While doing the experiments, Spilsbury's willing subject, a nurse, passed out and had to be revived. The story added to Spilsbury's notoriety. In 1923, after several more high profile cases and convictions, he became Sir Bernard Spilsbury.

One of the most ironic and interesting cases Spilsbury worked on occurred in 1924. A woman named Emily Kaye was killed inside a small house on the southeastern coast of England. Her body was dismembered by a saw, the parts further chopped and then boiled, and parts including the head were never located. The bloody saw was found in a suitcase belonging to Patrick Mahon. Spilsbury arrived on the scene and managed to find a few bone fragments in the room that he concluded were from a large woman who was pregnant at the time of her death. The remains also showed evidence of violent blows inflicted at the time of death. Spilsbury's testimony was crucial in convicting Mahon, who was subsequently executed by hanging. Spilsbury performed the autopsy on Mahon. Based on his findings in this and subsequent autopsies of executed criminals, Spilsbury made several recommendations to make death by hanging as quick and painless as possible.

Spilsbury's prime as a medical detective spanned the 1920s and 1930s, although stress was beginning to take a toll. In 1940, at the age of sixty-three, he suffered the first of what would be several strokes and the death of one son, the first of several deaths of loved ones. His final case came in 1947, and shortly after it, he committed suicide. There has been speculation that his suicide was driven also in part by mistakes he had made in earlier cases, amplified in the harsh light of his fame. Whatever the reason, none since in the United Kingdom have been able to claim the same degree of public recognition as Spilsbury did in the early part of the twentieth century.

AMERICA AND MEDICAL EXAMINERS

The United States relied on the coroner system that it inherited from Great Britain. The first coroner system was set up in New York in 1664 when the Dutch surrendered control to the English. The city has always been a gateway with a huge population of immigrants, and the link between forensic death investigation and public health naturally played out there. Little changed until the late 1800s, when post-Civil War advances in forensic science paralleled those in Europe and the United Kingdom. Medical experts were playing an increasingly important role in death investigation, and as their European counterparts, they faced their greatest challenges in cases where poisoning was suspected. Autopsies were rare, and as was the case in the mother country, death was frequently attributed to a visitation by God.

As was occurring in England and Europe, the increasing awareness and use of scientific methods of analysis began to presage change. A landmark American case was heard in 1871 in Annapolis. In many respects it was the American replay of the LaFarge case from thirty years earlier. The victim was General W. Scott Ketchum, who died three days after eating a meal at the home of Elizabeth Wharton. At the time, Ketchum was attempting to collect on a large loan to Wharton that had come due.

Elizabeth was a wealthy woman active in the Episcopal Church. Ketchum was her financial advisor and a friend of her family. After dining with Wharton at her home, the General was taken ill and lingered for three days before dying. Later, Wharton invited Eugene Van Ness to her home, as he was the financial clerk who handled her accounts and records at the Baltimore firm of Alexander Brown and Sons. Van Ness had been keeping two sets of records for her, the official one and a second duplicate set of secret ones. After visiting Wharton, he developed symptoms similar to Ketchum's but survived. The doctors who treated him were now suspicious. Their misgiving deepened when it was learned that Wharton's son had died suddenly a year earlier, leaving her a substantial fortune from a conveniently and unusually large life insurance policy. She was arrested as she was preparing to leave for Europe.

Ketchum's personal physician conducted the autopsy and requested that colleagues at the University of Maryland test the stomach contents. Professor E.A. Aiken performed the analysis and found large quantities of antimony in the sample, as well as in a glass that had been used to serve punch to Ness. Witnesses at the trial noted that Wharton had purchased a substance called tartar emetic, a substance that contains antimony and that was used in small amounts to induce vomiting. The tonic was used as the syrup of ipecac is used today.

Being a woman of means, Mrs. Wharton hired a crack team of defense lawyers. They focused their attacks on the chemist (Aiken) and on Ketchum's physician. They hired other chemists and toxicologists that testified the expertise and techniques used were inadequate and unreliable. In what was to become a frequent occurrence, the case became a highly publicized *battle of the experts* at a time when experts were still learning. Because of doubt cast on the prosecution's work, the judge had the body exhumed and samples delivered to another chemist, William Tonry, who worked out of the U.S. Surgeon General's Office. His results confirmed the earlier testing that indicated poisoning. Undeterred, the defense produced more expert witnesses, principally physicians, who raised meningitis as an alternative mechanism as the cause of death. In the end, Wharton was acquitted. Public reaction was immediate and unflattering to those involved.

"The case, we suppose, has scarcely a parallel as a doctors' war, chemical experts having been arrayed for weeks in hostile squadrons, through after all nothing seems certain about their conflicting tests unless it is their uncertainty,"[3] said *The New York Evening Post*. Many commentators stated that money rather than science dictated testimony and noted with dismay that it appeared that testimony was auctioned off to the highest bidder. The trial and the aftermath generated many legislative attempts at reform during the 1870s and 1880s, none successful. The controversy highlighted the need for reliable and unbiased scientific examination and testimony. Only a government entity had any hope of fulfilling that charge, but it would take another forty years for that to occur.

NEW YORK CITY

The state of Massachusetts created the first medical examiner system in 1877, not long after the Wharton case hit the presses. A medical examiner (ME) is a physician whose charge it is to investigate deaths, determine cause and manner, and, if a crime is involved, pursue the investigation. This sounds like a coroner, but there are two fundamental differences. An ME is a physician with a specialty in pathology, whereas a coroner may have no medical training. Second, the ME is an appointed or hired position rather than an elected one, which goes a long way toward shielding him or her from the political controversy that always accompanies the job and high profile cases. The Massachusetts system was the first to attempt this, although it was not centralized in the sense that one ME handled all death cases in the state. It was an important step though and was used as an example when New York City instituted the first true medical examiner system in 1914.

In 1900, the murder of William Marsh Rice in New York City marked a turning point. Rice, a wealthy elderly man died under suspicious circumstances. Rice's attorney, Albert Patrick, was charged with hiring Rice's butler to kill him using chloroform. Chloroform is an organic solvent that was used as an anesthetic. In fiction, it is often used to incapacitate a victim after a few frantic breaths into a saturated rag. In reality, chloroform not meted out in carefully controlled doses causes convulsions and death. This was apparently Rice's fate. The coroner conducted the inquest and commissioned postmortem examination. The physician testified that death was caused by chloroform. A second doctor, hired by the district attorney at first disputed this finding but later changed his mind and concurred with the chloroform theory. For his work, this doctor was paid $18,000, which was about three times his yearly salary and roughly the equivalent of $350,000 today. Patrick was convicted despite the lack of concrete scientific evidence and findings to support the chloroform findings.

Fortunately for Patrick, this was not the end of the case. While he was in prison serving a life sentence, a second chloroform case occurred. This time, there was a thorough autopsy including an examination of the lungs and a definitive identification of chloroform within them. The description of the lungs was nothing like what had been reported in the Rice case. A group of 500 medicolegal practitioners (toxicologists, doctors, and pathologists) signed a letter urging that Patrick be granted a new trial. The request was not honored and Patrick had to wait until 1912 for his release.

Because of this and other problems, the press, including *The New York Times*, began to openly and frequently point out problems surrounding the coroner system. Revelations of corruption and mishandling of bodies increased. An example was moving a body from Brooklyn to Manhattan or vice versa so that two coroners could collect fees rather than one. The final nail in the coffin occurred when one of the mishandled bodies happened to be that of a friend of the Mayor. The Mayor established a commission to study the system in 1914, and in 1915 its report supported abolishing the coroner system and replacing it with a medical examiner system. The Office of the Chief Medical Examiner of New York City came into existence in 1918.

The skills required of the ME were far different from those required (if any were required) of coroners. The ME had to be listed as a civil service job applicant, had to be a physician, and had to be skilled in the use of a microscope. The ME was charged with investigating and documenting cause and manner of death and authorizing autopsies when deemed necessary. These autopsies were to be performed only by qualified medical examiners working for the Chief.

The first man selected for the job was a bit of an ironic choice, Dr. Patrick J. Riordan. He had been the coroner during the time when the system had come under the scrutiny that ultimately led to its demise. Outcry ensued and Riordan's tenure lasted a month during which he interviewed other candidates. The man selected for the job was Dr. Charles Norris, who had trained extensively in Europe (including at Vienna and Edinburgh) and was considered an expert in forensic medicine. He was also a New York native and grasped the problems faced by the enormous city and the surrounding areas. As it turned out, Norris was the right man in the right place at the right time, and he served with distinction until his death in 1935. Colleagues described him as firm yet dignified, favoring frock coats and firm decisions.

His tenure spanned a horrific explosion on Wall Street and the implosion of the stock market in 1927, resulting in many suicides. Gang warfare was rampant, and prohibition came and went, but the seemingly routine deaths dominated the workload. Gone were the days where insurance companies and families could negotiate and bribe the coroner into a ruling favorable to them, and many cases that would have never been investigated got the attention they desperately needed. In an example, a policeman saw a longshoreman throw a bag into the water and further investigation revealed body parts strewn along the river. The man was arrested and he confessed to killing his girlfriend at her apartment, where the head and torso of the woman was found. The man told police that he had awoken after a night of intoxication and found his girlfriend dead on the floor next to him. He assumed that he had killed her while drunk and to hide the crime had dismembered the body and attempted to dump it. Investigation by the ME told a different tale, one of death by carbon monoxide poisoning, and the man was released.

Norris's tenure was not without problems and conflicts. He resigned twice and twice returned after the Mayor pleaded with him to do so. Both incidents were precipitated by budgetary issues. In the first, the city refused to cover the cost of an office car and driver and expensive items that Norris paid for out of his personal money. The second incident began when city officials had the clocks removed from the morgue, no doubt to encourage longer workdays. Norris was quick to make his displeasure known in both cases.

Norris was succeeded by Dr. Thomas Gonzales, another veteran of the 1918 birth of the office. One of his key contributions was hiring of Dr. Alexander Wiener, a scientist who had worked with Karl Landsteiner, the Nobel Prize winner who discovered the ABO and Rh blood groups. Wiener took charge of serological evidence such as blood and body fluid stains. One of the assistant MEs under Gonzales was Dr. Milton Helpern (1902–1977). Helpern later became Chief and one of the first of the celebrity forensic scientists of the twentieth century.

Gonzales was a key figure in the foundation of the American Academy of Forensic Sciences in 1947, the first forensic professional society to encompass many forensic specialties. One of the most noteworthy cases during his time was the 1945 crash of an Army B25 bomber into the Empire State Building. Gonzales retired with distinction in 1953 and was succeeded by Helpern, who had been with the ME's office since 1931.

Helpern shared much in common with Spilsbury in that he became one of the first medical examiners known by name to many in the public outside his local jurisdiction. He participated in many high profile and controversial cases, and founded a museum associated with the ME's office. Like Spilsbury, his death was tinged with irony; his last illness came on during the annual meeting of the American Academy of Forensic Sciences being held in San Diego in 1977. A famous quote came from the trial related to the murder of Malcolm X. The defense attorney stated that Helpern didn't know who killed Malcom X to which Helpern replied, "I don't know and I don't care; I'm interested in what did it, not who done [sic] it."[4]

Helpern was a prodigious writer, authoring articles in scientific journals and coauthoring a text with Gonzales and Dr. Benjamin Vance entitled *Legal Medicine and Toxicology*. His public recognition came in part from books he wrote for general audiences, the most famous of which was modestly called *Autopsy: The Memoirs of Milton Helpern, the World's Greatest Medical Detective*. Although Helpern was not the first to author a popular book, his started a trend joined by other MEs such as Michael Baden, who later held the same position as Helpern. Baden took this a step further by overseeing a television series on HBO called *Autopsy* and by frequently appearing on cable television networks.

Forensic medicine evolved elsewhere besides the United States and the United Kingdom. In Russia, forensic medicine was recognized as early as 1716. The Tsar, Peter the Great, recognized the value of postmortem examinations in case of violent death and included regulations to that effect in military codes. A system of district medical examination grew out of this structure, which remained in effect until the turbulence of 1917 and the end of the monarchy. A formal medical examiner system was put in place by the communist government that built on the previous bureaucracy, and it remained in place throughout the Soviet era. Unlike the U.S. system (or patchwork of systems), the Russian system was a national one with district offices working under the national structure. The Research Institute of Forensic Medicine was created in 1932 in Moscow as a national center for examination and research. In Austria, the Viennese Institute of Forensic Medicine appeared in 1805 and from the outset placed emphasis on forensic chemistry and forensic toxicology.

Death Investigation and Forensic Toxicology

THE CHAIN OF PRESUMPTIONS

Forensic toxicology exists at the nexus of three forensic disciplines—medicine, biology, and chemistry. It was also the first discipline to emerge from medicine as a distinctly forensic practice with the descriptor *forensic* preceding it. Poisoning, and fear of it, spawned the study of poisons that later bloomed into postmortem toxicology. As medical diagnostic skills and techniques improved, forensic toxicology extrapolated backwards to the living. Toxicologists applied their skills to identify causes of intoxication to help direct treatments.

The next leap in forensic toxicology came in the early 1900s with the advent of automobiles and accidents caused by intoxicated drivers. Indeed, it is only relatively recently that the term *intoxication* has become synonymous with the results of excessive alcohol ingestion. As poisoning became easier to detect, killers adopted different weapons and means. Now, postmortem and human performance toxicology make up the bulk of the forensic toxicology casework.

As an author of the time noted, "Poisoning trials presented a uniquely instructive illustration of proof by circumstantial evidence. Such proofs riled on arriving at the truth of an unknown by agreed-upon indicative means—'presumptions.'"[1] These presumptions arise from circumstance revealed through circumstantial evidence. The difference by 1840 was that presumptions founded on scientific evidence joined the legal mix. Scientific analysis such as Orfila's in the LaFarge case produced circumstantial evidence. The presumptions are the results of analytical tests such as the

Marsh test. The trier of fact presumed, based on Orfila's results and presentation, that arsenic was present in Charles LaFarge's remains. From the totality of the other evidence, the court presumed Marie put it there. The case highlighted more than forensic toxicology; it thrust circumstantial evidence supplied by science into the public and legal spotlight.

The much-heralded Marsh test was no panacea. Any metal that could combine with hydrogen can produce a *false positive* test. Antimony, another common poison over history, is one such metal. Recognition of false positives led to push from the scientific community for adoption of more specific tests and utilization of a layered series of tests, the results of which could be chained together to increase confidence in a scientific finding. A prominent toxicologist of the period wrote of scientific and circumstantial evidence in arsenic cases: "[W]here several tests, based on principle totally distinct, are applied to different portion of a suspected substance, and give each the characteristic results of a know [*sic*] poison, the chances of error are indefinitely removed, and the proof of the existence of that poison in that substances comes short only of positive demonstration."[2] The concept of combining results of increasingly specific tests is a distinctive element of forensic science. There is legal parallel referred to as the *preponderance of evidence*.

Scientists and legal scholars in the 1800s noted the parallels between the legal concept of the preponderance of evidence and chemical testing. In the courtroom, the prosecution presents witnesses and testimony countered by those offered by the defense. Alone, no one piece of information makes the case. It is the combination of evidence and elucidation of the most probable explanation that leads to the verdict and resolution. A forensic chemist or toxicologist such as Orfila, when handed evidence, started with simple tests such as heating the sample and noting the odor or other simple observations. Next, the sample would be tested with other reagents, leading up to the most specific and selective test for arsenic available. For Orfila, this was the Marsh test. The combined results of the tests taken as a whole would lead to the most probable conclusion and resolve the question, "Is there arsenic present or not?" The chemist relied on collective experience and personal knowledge to make the call.

Although chemical and toxicological tests have evolved over the years, the underlying philosophy is entrenched as a pillar of modern forensic science. Forensic analysis begins with simple general testing and moves toward the more specific and selective. Modern analyses rely less on subjective observation (color changes, heat evolved, smell, bubbling, etc.) and more on instrumental data and comparison to known and reliable standards. Test results are still interpreted based on the collective knowledge of scientists working in that area, just as testimony and evidence are judged based on collected human experience (i.e., common sense). In the mid 1800s, science was sufficiently advanced to be applied to the legal and social world in an expansive and systematic way. The manifestation of forensic toxicology is a good example of this process.

POISONS AGAIN

Although the Marsh test had already been accepted and used, it took years for the technique and practice to spread. An improved version of the Marsh test, called the Reinsch test in honor of its inventor, Egar Hugo Reinsch (1809–1884), appeared in 1841. The procedure was easier to perform than the Marsh test and comparably sensitive but not foolproof. Variations of the test were widely used well into the twentieth century and still are in some cases. Alternatives to these tests, more improvements than innovations, evolved throughout the 1800s.

One of the most famous post-Marsh test arsenic poisonings were those attributed to Mary Ann Cotton (1832–1873). Her victims, at least twenty, included most of her close relatives including her mother, several children and stepchildren, three spouses, and one lover. Her motive was insurance money and her downfall was excess. She killed her children (whose deaths were initially attributed to gastric distress) when their existence interfered with impending relationships and marriages to obtain the money. The last child she killed was her son Charles. The attending doctor was suspicious and obtained samples from the boy's body. Using the Reinsch test, he found arsenic, leading to Mary's arrest. The trial itself had to await the birth of yet another child who owed his life to fortunate timing, a timely conviction, and the gallows. The jury rejected Mary's suggestion that arsenic vapors given off from wallpaper killed her son.

Despite improvements such as the Reinsch test, poisoning reached its zenith in the late 1800s. Plant-based toxins such as morphine, nicotine, strychnine, atropine, belladonna, and hemlock joined arsenic and its cousins, as well as substances such as chloroform and cyanide. As it became clear that medical science and chemistry could develop tests for other poisons, a self-sustaining pressure built for them to do so. The Coroner's Act of 1887 passed in England was driven in large part by fear of poisoning and the continuing difficulty encountered in detecting it. At the same time, the courts were leery of expert witnesses, in part because of problems in such cases as the Smethurst (described shortly) and LaFarge cases. As one judge remarked in 1889, "[O]ne has to take a great deal of the scum from the testimony of skilled witnesses."[3]

As toxicologists became more adept at detecting heavy metal poisons, poisoners turned increasingly to plant-based poisons. Within this family, alkaloids are infamous and familiar. Caffeine is one of many alkaloids present in coffee, and nicotine is one of many alkaloids found in cigarettes. Chemically, alkaloids are alkaline (basic), the property from which their name arises. One of the earliest (and foolhardy) methods of detecting an alkaline substance was to taste it; basic substances are bitter to hot while acidic substances such as citric acid or vinegar (acetic acid) are sour. Originally, alkaloids were classified as vegetable bases because of their characteristic chemistry and origin. That is the extent of the simplicity. Alkaloids are further subdivided into families. The milky exudates of the dried seed-pod of the opium plant, called latex, are the source of opiate alkaloids. Morphine, thebaine, codeine are found naturally in this extract and can be used to make other opiate alkaloids such as heroin, oxycodone, and hydrocodone. The killing compound in hemlock is the alkaloid coniine. Caffeine belongs to the xanthine alkaloids that also include theophylline found in tea and chocolate. The tropane family includes cocaine.

Unlike the metallic poisons such as arsenic, alkaloids encompass thousands of compounds, making isolation and detection of any single one a difficult challenge even today and a monumental one during the 1800s. Given the size and variety of alkaloids, it is all the more remarkable that reliable tests for many of the alkaloid poisons appeared not long after the Marsh test. Chemists used the tests years or decades before the chemical structures of the substances they were testing for were even known.

The man who would make the crucial breakthrough for isolation and detection of alkaloid poisons was Belgian Jean Servais Stas (1813–1891). Like many of his day, he had gone to Paris to study toxicology under the famous Orfila. By 1850, he was back in Brussels serving as a professor of chemistry. The murder of a man named Gustav Fougnies was to alkaloid poisoning what the LaFarge case had been to those perpetrated by arsenic. Gustav had the misfortune of being the brother of Lydie Fougnies. She married a man named Bocarme who had married her for the money she supposedly had, but in fact did not. Undeterred by the lack of love and money, they enjoyed the wild life and generally lived beyond their means.

By 1849, the hard-partying couple realized that their only hope of financial salvation was the death of Gustav and the inheritance that would provide. Gustav's bad luck continued; in 1849, he was recovering from an amputation and had not yet married. If he died as a bachelor, all his money would go to Lydie since his fortune originated from the death of their father. Lydie and her husband might have been willing to wait for a little while to see if the post-amputation trauma would kill her dear brother, but Gustav sealed his fate. His final mistake was finding a suitable bride. The rumors of impending marriage surfaced in 1850, prompting a swift response. He died on the eve of announcing the wedding, his sister attributing his death to a stroke.

The initial postmortem immediately ruled out a stroke. The investigators noted Gustav's blackened throat and stomach and wondered if acid, another common poison, was involved. The examiners had the foresight to remove critical organs and place them in alcohol, arrest Lydie and Bocarme, and request Stas' help.

Stas worked patiently from late 1850 into early 1851. He employed alcoholic extractions of the tissues and evaporated off the alcohol, which left a thick syrup. During one of these evaporations, Stas detected the odor of vinegar and during another, the odor of coniine. This compound was one of two that had been identified by that time, the other being nicotine that killed in doses of as little as 100 milligrams. By way of comparison, a typical "baby" aspirin contains about 80 milligrams of aspirin.

Stas now believed that Gustav had alkaloid poison in his tissue, but he was not yet confident of which one. Meticulously, he refined his extractions, one of which yielded large quantities of nicotine, a fatal dose of which could easily be concealed in food. One of the confirmatory tests Stas used was the taste test; he noted that the typical burning of the nicotine lingered in his mouth for hours. While foolhardy in retrospect, early chemists relied on their senses for detection because it was often the only procedure available.

Much as Dr. Addington had done a century earlier during the Blandy case, Stas compared the brownish material he extracted with known nicotine to confirm his identification. He also had an explanation for the vinegar odor he had detected. When an acid is mixed with a base, the result is neutralization of both. It was possible that Lydie and Bocarme had tried to neutralize the alkaloid poison using the vinegar to confound any chemical testing. Bocarme's cleverness betrayed him. By adding the acidic vinegar to the basic nicotine, the neutralized nicotine became water soluble and much easier to detect.

Stas reported the results to authorities who quickly determined that the suspects had extracted large amounts of tobacco in the days before the murder. Investigators located bodies of animals used in experiments on the property and on the strength of the scientific evidence and the investigative information it provided, a court convicted Bocarme of murder and sent him to the guillotine. Lydie escaped, likely because the jury was squeamish about sending a woman to the same fate.

Stas' work, much as Marsh's and Orfila's a decade earlier, led to a flurry of activity related to the detection and identification of alkaloid poisons. Many of the tests developed in the wake of Stas' breakthrough are still used in forensic labs, although their function has changed as the science also has. What were definitive tests in the nineteenth century are now classified as presumptive tests, meaning that a positive test indicates that the suspected material is probably present but not definitively present. The same holds for a negative result—the suspected material is probably, but not definitively, absent.

Stas' breakthrough had more to do with the chemistry of separation and extraction than with identification. With the separation methods available to him, the way opened for other chemists to devise chemical tests to identify alkaloids present in the extracts. Finding caffeine in stomach contents is far less sinister than finding coniine or strychnine, for example, even though all are alkaloids. Thus, it was important to be able to test extracts further to identify which alkaloids might be present. A series of tests appeared in the mid to late 1800s, most named after their German chemist inventors. The list includes the Marquis, Froedhe, Mecke, and Mandelin tests, all of which are still used. These tests are called color tests because when the reagents are added to the alkaloid or an extract containing it, a distinctive color change is noted. The Marquis reagent turns a deep purple in the presence of heroin, morphine, or related substances, but will turn orange in the presence of methamphetamine (a synthetic alkaloid). The colored substances created are dyes, a subject of surprising importance in forensic science.

Stas collaborated with German chemist Friedrich Otto who improved upon Stas' method, allowing a larger number of alkaloids to be extracted and in higher purity. The Otto-Stas method was announced in 1856, heralding a marked acceleration in progress in forensic chemistry and toxicology. European chemists, particularly the English and Germans, led the way. In contrast, progress across the Atlantic was slower, partially due to the time it took news to cross the ocean. The United States also lacked the medicolegal infrastructure that had taken root across the continent and in England.

One of the key players of the period was Irish chemist Richard Kirwin (1733–1812), who worked to identify minerals and ions from minerals in water. In Germany, Karl Remegius Fresenius (1818–1897) devised a series of tables used to systematize analytical chemistry and lent his name to the first journal dedicated solely to analytical chemistry. The journal, *Fresenius' Journal of Analytical Chemistry*, is still published. He authored the first textbook on qualitative chemical analysis, first published in 1841 and evolving through an astounding seventeen editions. Because qualitative chemistry (wet chemistry, color tests, and the like) was the heart and sole of early analytical chemistry, Fresenius had significant impact in forensic chemistry and toxicology. Stas and Otto had developed extraction methods and others had devised color tests to help identify materials in the extracts.

Poisoners did not stand still in the battle of technology. In addition to arsenic, other products and substances were entering the market that could do the job just as well. Among the nastiest were the strong acids, *lysol*, a caustic mix containing phenols (used as a disinfectant) and cresols, prussic acid (HCN), oxalic acid, laudanum (an opiate derivative used as a medicine and a chemical pacifier for children), mercuric chloride (also called "corrosive sublimate"), strychnine, brucine, and the complement of alkaloids that seemingly grew by the year. Death investigators (doctors, toxicologists, and chemists) had their work cut out for them.

TWO STEPS FORWARD, ONE STEP BACK

A notorious arsenic poisoning case in England in the 1850s did nearly as much to discredit scientific analysis of arsenic as Orfila had done to push it forward. The accused was Dr. Thomas Smethhurst, arrested on suspicion of killing his mistress. The doctor analyzing the evidence was Alfred Swaine Taylor (1806–1880). Taylor had established a reputation as one of the best of the early forensic toxicologists. As a young medical student, Taylor went to Paris to attend lectures by Orfila. Once on a memorable trip, he studied gunshot wound patterns, and these experiences solidified his interest in legal medicine. In 1831, he assumed the position of lecturer in medical jurisprudence at Guy's Hospital in London. He was twenty-five. He began to appear as an expert witness and studied the literature of the law with the same intensity he devoted to chemistry and medicine.

Taylor also recognized that chemical analysis of the time was not definitive but probabilistic. The role of chemical findings, whatever they were, was to support medical and clinical findings. In his view, finding traces of arsenic in tissues alone was not enough to prove poisoning. Many other factors, including the limitations of the testing method, played into the overall conclusion. Equally or more important were clinical observations made by the physician while the victim still lived. Taylor also recognized that quantity of a poison was critical, echoing Paracelsus but updating the information to the forensic application. Arsenic was common in the environment of Taylor's time; finding it in small amounts in tissue alone was unremarkable. If arsenic was found in a suspected poisoning victim, Taylor integrated and weighed the merits and limits of clinical data with chemical findings to unravel the circumstances that led to finding the arsenic.

Taylor was forward thinking in other ways. He noted the importance of the chain of custody and recommended that samples be stored in clean jars, tested immediately, and stored where there was no question of tampering or adulteration. This practice amounted to tacit admission of the need for peer-review, independent confirmation, and the inevitable development of better methods to come. Taylor's insight sprung from scientific training, legal knowledge, and acumen that he passed along in his lectures. He authored several books beginning in 1836, including the well-known *A Manual of Medical Jurisprudence* and *On Poisons.*

Taylor was an early adopter of the Marsh test and used it extensively in casework. He also favored the Reinsch test over the objections of his contemporary Fresenius, who argued that the test was too sensitive. Without the proper controls, Fresenius argued, such as testing reagents and apparatus to insure they were not contaminated, results of the Reinsch test were problematic. Potential interferences included lead, copper, bismuth, and mercury, some of which were nearly as common in the nineteenth century as arsenic. Testing for all of these in addition to arsenic would be a chore in a modern lab, let alone a nineteenth century one. Recognizing this, Taylor concluded that the complexity of eliminating every possible false positive was much more likely to lead to false conclusions than a careful application of the test alone. Taylor also believed it was unlikely that this particular group of elements would innocently coexist with arsenic in tissues or other evidence associated with a suspected poisoning. Taylor noted, "[A] court of law requires to know whether arsenic was present and was the cause of death, rather than whether it was mixed with traces of bismuth, or lead, a fact which however interesting in a chemical, is wholly unimportant in a medico-legal way."[4]

Taylor may have been right, but his reliance on the Reinsch test in spite of its limitations hurt him and his reputation during the Smethurst case. In his testimony, Taylor admitted that the arsenic he detected could conceivably have come from his own reagents and techniques. Taylor was further misled by the medical findings that he valued so much; the clinical evidence strongly suggested that some type of irritating poison was involved. Taylor applied the Reinsch test to one sample and obtained a positive result, a finding that led to Smethurst's arrest. When he obtained other samples (over twenty) from other tissues, he found no arsenic and only traces of antimony. There was some thought that Smethurst, being a physician himself and possibly knowing that Taylor would use the Reinsch test, had administered a chlorate substance to his victim to speed removal from the body. There was no evidence to support this conjecture. Even with the results of the chemical analyses thrown out, the court convicted Smethurst, although the conviction did not stand.

This was not Taylor's first baptism through controversy. In 1856, he had been involved in another murder case, another poisoning, and another conflict of chemistry and clinical findings. The suspect was William Palmer, the victim J.P. Cooke, and the method, suggested by pre-death symptoms, was strychnine. Analysis of the stomach and intestines failed to reveal any. With modern hindsight, the lack of strychnine means little; the substance rapidly enters the bloodstream. Taylor and his contemporaries did not know this, and predictably, Taylor fell back to the clinical observations. Despite his inability to find strychnine, he believed Cooke died by murder with strychnine.

The defense countered that Cooke had died of tetanus and that the chemical evidence to the contrary was laughably inadequate. Taylor never wavered, to no avail. He regretted the outcome of the trial and was disheartened that courts and the public now often viewed chemical analysis as the weak link of a weak profession. The later Smethhurst controversy added to the cloud that hovered over him and his profession in the later part of the 1800s. Not until the time of Sir Bernard Spilsbury did a sense of public trust came to forensic death investigation.

ANOTHER HOLMES

One of the United States' earliest practitioners of forensic medicine was Oliver Wendell Holmes (1809–1894), who was also renowned as a doctor, poet, activist, writer, and humorist. He obtained medical training in Paris and much as Taylor, strongly advocated the use of clinical as well as post-mortem findings to delineate the cause of death. In 1845, Holmes became the dean of the newly formed Harvard medical school, where one of his first acts was to emphasize microscopy in the curriculum. By 1849, he was embroiled in a sensational Boston murder trial in which the victim was a Harvard surgeon and the suspect a Harvard chemistry professor.

Dr. George Parkman, an eccentric physician and surgeon at Harvard, was famous for his pointy chin, extreme wealth, and ruthless financial management. Parkman had donated most of the land on which the Harvard medical school was located and Holmes held the Parkman Professorship of Anatomy and Physiology. Parkman also owned many of the most downtrodden tenements in the city and had a reputation as a heartless landlord.

Dr. John White Webster was a professor in chemistry of average skill and limited financial resources. To address the latter, he borrowed money from friends and acquaintances, including Parkman. As his situation degraded and his debt increased, Webster borrowed more and sometimes offered collateral he did not have. By 1849, Webster was thousands in debt, his mortgage in Parkman's hands. Once Parkman realized that Webster had falsified collateral, he began hounding him to repay his considerable debt. One afternoon in November 1849, Parkman strolled out of his home and never returned.

Suspicion immediately fell on Webster. Fearing the worst, investigators searched the grounds of the medical school, including the discard pile from the anatomy lab. A detective attempted to enter Webster's laboratory only to be warned that hazardous materials were stored there and might explode. The prudent detective replied, "Very well, then, I will not go in there and get blowed up."[5] The warning did little to allay suspicions, particularly of a custodian who recalled an altercation between Webster and Parkman the afternoon Parkman vanished. Webster subsequently locked the janitor out of the laboratory and gave him a Thanksgiving turkey, which was unprecedented and out of character. The janitor further noted smoke rising from a chimney the Saturday after Parkman's disappearance and the sound of continuously running water.

The custodian, a man named Littlefield, was nothing if not persistent. Littlefield testified that once Webster left, he entered the laboratory and searched it. Webster had built an indoor outhouse in the lab, the shaft of which led to a storage area in the subbasement. Because the building was located on the Charles River, the water would occasionally rise and flush out the area. Littlefield noted that the key to the toilet was gone and the door locked. Undeterred and only slightly delayed, Littlefield armed himself with a sledgehammer, ventured to the basement, and, working in bursts spread over several days, managed to tear an opening in the toilet shaft. He found bones, a pelvis, and dentures. Because Holmes had mandated that all dissected bodies receive a proper burial after study, there was little doubt what Littlefield had found. Once the news was out, several hundred Bostonians flocked to the scene.[6]

Webster's trial began in April of 1850 and turned into an American version of the LaFarge trial that had taken place ten years earlier in Paris. During courtroom sessions, people were shuttled in for ten-minute periods and hustled out, allowing nearly 60,000 to see at least some portion of the trial. This number represented nearly half the population of the city. Forensically, there was one question—whose bones and teeth were found in the toilet shaft? Holmes testified twice about the body parts, but the key testimony came from Dr. Nathan Cooley Keep (1800–1875), a physician and dentist who made Parkman's dentures. Both doctors, Keep and Holmes, knew and liked both Parkman and Webster, making their testimony more dramatic and difficult. The press relished it, lavishing prose on every gruesome nuance.

One of those was the condition of the dentures recovered from the shaft. All of the tissues had been exposed to extreme heat, making identification nearly impossible. However, Keep was able to show how the dentures fit the molds he had in his office of Parkman's mouth. He further explained that the artificial teeth were made of porcelain, which normally explodes when exposed to such high temperature. The only reason they had not was that they had been protected from the heat by the head itself. The defense offered their own experts, but none were able to discredit Keep's findings and testimony. The Parkman trial was the first in the United States to revolve around *forensic odontology* (dentistry). The jury needed only three hours to reach a guilty verdict. Prior to his execution in August, Webster admitted the killing but maintained it was unintentional.

THE UNITED STATES AND ELSEWHERE

By the early 1900s and the advent of routine trans-Atlantic travel and communication, the gap in forensic progress between America and Europe narrowed to insignificance. Arsenic poisoning waned as detection methods improved; killers increasingly turned to the alkaloids. An interesting and ironic case in Canada illustrates the changing of the guard. In

1859, Dr. William Henry King faced trial for murdering his wife by poison. The chemist charged with the analysis reported finding arsenic in the dead woman's stomach. The court convicted King and sentenced him to death. On the gallows, he confessed to the crime but claimed to have used morphine, not arsenic, to kill his wife.

In the United States, the close association with medicine and toxicology was evident in the New York City Medical Examiner's Office. One of the men hired by Dr. Norris in the early years was Dr. Alexander O. Gettler (1883–1968) who organized a chemical analysis laboratory within the ME's office. Gettler's lab became the nexus of toxicology in the United States under his direction and lasted until his retirement in 1959. He testified hundreds of times and contributed in many areas. One example was in cases of suspected drowning, where he noted, "Years ago, medical examiners and chemists only guessed when they gave 'drowning' as a cause of death. I wanted to find some positive way of telling and finally evolved a way precise and beyond contradiction." He did so via a comprehensive study of both sides of the hearts of drowning victims. Specifically, he measured the amount of chloride in the serum in the separate chambers.

Freshwater rivers and the sea surround New York City, so a determination of drowning as a cause of death tells half the tale. If a person drowns in salt water, he or she inhales it, along with the high concentration of sodium chloride it contains. Blood leaving the right side of the heart travels to the lungs where it picks up oxygen. This blood then travels to the left side of the heart and on out to the body where oxygen is consumed. If there is seawater in the lungs, the chloride ion moves into the blood that ends up in the left side of the heart. Since the heart stops beating relatively quickly after immersion, this high chloride ion concentration does not have time to disperse and even out. The concentration of chloride ion in the blood in the left side of the heart will be higher than that of blood in the right side of the heart.

Gettler's work provided a definitive and quantitative method of determining drowning and in what type of water. He also improved testing methods for detection of poisons and worked with testing of blood and body fluid stains. The many toxicologists he trained spread his practices and ideas to other cities and jurisdictions. Among them were graduate student Joe Umbarger, a tobacco-spitting toxicologist, and Sidney Kaye, who later gained fame and praise for his own toxicology skills.

ALCOHOL WAS INVOLVED

In modern forensic toxicology labs, many cases involve blood alcohol samples. Professor Erik Widmark (1889–1945) developed the first reliable methods for determining alcohol concentration in blood in 1922. Widmark, a Swede, worked in the University of Lund. His methods remained the standard worldwide into the 1970s. Widmark's studies extended to the metabolic pathways ethanol followed once ingested.

Widmark received an M.D. in 1917, but he gravitated toward research from early in his career. His thesis centered on measurement of acetone in blood and other tissues and fluids, a common occurrence in people with diseases like diabetes. This work set the stage for his research with alcohol, a compound that behaved similarly to acetone. Unlike most drugs, acetone and alcohol (specifically ethanol) are appreciably volatile. Consequently, ethanol is detectable in exhaled breath, and its concentration depends directly on the blood concentration responsible for intoxication. Widmark's research allowed work to move from concept to applications such as the modern Breathalyzer.

Upon graduation, Widmark accepted a position at the University of Lund in 1918, and he competed successfully for a full professorship there in 1921. His main competitor for the position was Dr. L. Michaelis, who later became famous for his work relating to role of enzymes in biochemical reactions. A fundamental equation related to enzyme reactions, the Michaelis-Menton equation bears his name in testament to his accomplishments. This equation remains central in describing how quickly enzymes in the body work to eliminate ethanol from the system.

Alcohol intoxication has been an issue throughout human history, but it became much more of a problem with the introduction of the automobile. Operating a horse while drunk is a nuisance; operating several tons of metal while drunk endangers the public. The same applied to other modern machinery such as airplanes and boats. Being able to detect and quantify the degree of intoxication became a medicolegal question. Law enforcement agencies and the courts needed reliable methods to gauge the severity of the intoxication, the degree of public threat, and ultimately the penalty or treatment.

By the late 1920s, several trends were clear. First, automobiles were soon to become the primary means of transport for most people. More cars meant more drivers, more drunk drivers, and more accidents. Given the poor roads and lack of even rudimentary safety engineering, even seemingly minor accidents could cause injury and death. The judicial system needed a quantitative chemical test of blood alcohol concentration that could prove intoxication. Widmark was ready to meet the need.

The first test he devised for blood alcohol was crude but effective. For each, he collected five small tubes of blood collected from the earlobe. He then transferred a carefully weighed portion to a small cup suspended over a solution containing an oxidizer of sulfuric acid and dichromate ion. As the ethanol evaporated, it diffused into the oxidizing liquid below. The resulting chemical reaction consumed the oxidizer in proportion to the amount of ethanol, and by calculating the concentration of the remaining oxidizer, the concentration of ethanol in the blood could be determined.

Testing five samples instead of one increased the reliability of the results. With a valid analytical method in place, Sweden was among the first countries to establish a DUI law, with the intoxication limit set at 0.80 milligram per gram (0.08 percent) in 1941. As methods improved, the limit fell to 0.05 percent in 1957 and 0.02 percent in 1990, which remains one of the lowest limits worldwide. By comparison, the US federal standard is 0.08 percent.

Another of Widmark's key contributions was in deciphering the process and speed of ethanol elimination from the body. Beginning in 1924, he published a series of papers describing mathematical equations relating blood alcohol concentration to the time and amount of ethanol ingested. Alcohol is rapidly absorbed into the bloodstream in the stomach and upper gastrointestinal tract, leading to a spike in blood concentration. Assuming an empty stomach and no further ingestion, metabolic processes remove alcohol at a steady and predictable rate. Variables include sex (women on average metabolize and remove ethanol faster than men) and genetic variations. Widmark's equation remains the standard for determining how much alcohol a person drank and when, starting from the blood alcohol concentration (BAC).

Widmark's blood test and metabolic understanding was critical to forensic toxicology, but the problem remained of how to determine intoxication in the field. A police officer cannot draw blood from each person he or she stops; nor will everyone stopped on suspicion of intoxication actually be so. Law enforcement needed a field test that could provide both probable cause of intoxication or reliable evidence of its absence. In the United States, the National Safety Council became involved in issues of alcohol intoxication, and it appointed a commission to study the issue. This work led to the first discussions of using breath as a means of estimating intoxication.

Ethanol, with two carbons, is a small molecule by biological standards. It is soluble in water and water-like systems such as blood, but it is also appreciably volatile. The warmer the liquid, the greater the tendency of ethanol to evaporate out of it. In the human body, blood comes in direct contact with the atmosphere deep in the lungs. There, some ethanol will evaporate out of the blood and into the exhaled air. Because body temperature is nearly constant for all people, the concentration of ethanol in exhaled breath is directly proportional to the concentration of ethanol in the blood, and that proportion can be calculated using simple equations.

Technology caught up the science in the late 1930s. The first significant breakthrough came in 1937 when Dr. Rolla Harger of the University of Indiana introduced what he called the *Drunkometer*. The device was a great help to patrol officers and, as such, a tangible deterrent to driving while intoxicated. Robert Borkenstein developed its widely used sibling, the Breathalyzer, in 1954. Variants of this instrument are standard equipment in most patrol cars today. Many still rely on color changes in dichromate solutions, the same substances used by Widmark.

The most recent advances in toxicology, those following World War II, involved movement away from tedious wet chemical methods to instrumentation. The first instrument to appear in most toxicology labs was a spectrophotometer capable of scanning in the ultraviolet range. Arnold Beckman developed one of the earliest designs, called the DU spectrometer. A car battery powered it. The unglamorous DU proved to be workhorse, replacing the old Stas method for detecting many organic compounds such as alkaloid poisons. Next to appear in labs were spectrometers capable of scanning in the infrared region and gas chromatographs, both described in the next chapter. Sidney Kaye, the toxicologist who had worked with Gettler in New York, described the period spanning roughly 1945–1960 as truly revolutionary.[7] By this time, he had left New York, worked in St. Louis, and set up three new toxicology laboratories. These labs are direct descendants of the early New York ME system that catalyzed medicolegal science (death investigation and forensic toxicology) in the United States.

Forensic Chemistry: The Color of Evidence

By the mid to late 1800s, chemistry was undergoing significant changes, particularly in Europe. These changes spilled over into forensic chemistry as it coalesced as a specialty within forensic science. There difference between forensic chemistry and forensic toxicology was (and remains) malleable, based more on the type of sample than the science used to analyze it. Both practitioners are chemists, but toxicologists moved to confine their efforts to biological samples while forensic chemists began to focus on physical evidence such as powders, plants, fabrics, fibers, soil, dust, and glass. The division between forensic chemistry and forensic toxicology was emblematic of the changes taking place within chemistry itself during the nineteenth century.

Orfila's career straddled the old and the new orders in chemistry. When he assumed his position at the Faculty of Medicine of the University of Paris, it was that of chair of medicinal chemistry while the other chair oversaw organic chemistry and pharmacology. During Orfila's tenure from 1823 to 1853, his specialty grew to encompass forensic medicine and toxicology. After Orfila died in 1853, committees reshuffled and divided the areas of emphasis into pharmacy/organic and mineral chemistry. The bureaucratic shift reflected growing specialization and interest in organic chemistry.

Organic chemistry, the study of carbon compounds, required exacting analytical skills to isolate compounds from their biological matrices such as plants. By the end of the nineteenth century, organic chemists were learning to modify these extracted compounds and eventually to synthesize them from distant precursor compounds. Two classes of synthetic and semisynthetic compounds—drugs and dyes—played critical roles in the progression of forensic chemistry as it diverged from toxicology. The measurement of color would lead to the first chemical instruments (colorimeters), which would prove indispensable for chemistry in the decades to come.

COLOR AND CHEMISTRY

From the late 1700s until the early 1900s, chemists had little in their analytical arsenal save wet chemical methods. Wet chemistry involves sample manipulation and extraction coupled with simple tests. Detection of compounds relied on one of the human senses. Chemists and toxicologists debated the true taste of arsenic and argued the merits of smell but acknowledged the eye as the most exquisite of detectors. The Marsh test is a classic example of the eye as detector. The only proof of arsenic's presence was the chemists seeing a grayish metallic mirror.

The first significant advances in color-based identification and analysis trace back to Robert Boyle. His work contains the first reference to a chemical color test or "spot test." In his case, he used extract of a gallnut as a test for iron. He was apparently not the first to use this test; reportedly, Pliny used a similar extract around 60 C.E. to test for iron in vinegar. However, Boyle was first to develop a systematic analytical scheme for mineral water and was among the first to note that arsenic was acidic. His analytical approach was meticulous, detailed, and thorough, taking advantage of selective precipitations and color-based reactions. This protocol was the foundation for qualitative and quantitative analysis used by forensic chemists until the 1950s.

BUNSEN AND BEER

Primitive instrumentation appeared in the late 1800s. These devices were designed to detect elements such as arsenic based on interactions with visible light; that is, based on color. Generically, instruments that respond to visible radiation are called *colorimeters*. Newton was the first to record the breaking of sunlight into the component colors, red, orange, yellow, green, blue, indigo, and violet, using a prism. Two centuries later, the first colorimeters relied on prisms. Colorimeters belong to a class of instruments called *spectrophotometers* or *spectrometers*. The first forays into spectrometry reflect two of humankind's earliest fascinations—fire and color.

The color of a flame, even a simple wood flame, changes depending on what is burning. German chemist Andreas Sigismund Marggraf (1709–1782) studied the colors of flames salted with different materials, and his work was crucial to early spectroscopy. The compounds he used were sodium nitrate (NaNO$_3$) and potassium nitrate (KNO$_3$). He observed that the sodium salt produced vivid yellow flames and potassium, a lavender color. The use of flame color to reveal the presence of elements such as potassium or sodium is called atomic or elemental spectroscopy. The role of the flame is to decompose compounds to free atoms capable of generating color by emission.

For inorganic compounds and salts, flame emission spectroscopy is ideal. Unfortunately, the same technique is not useful for organic such as aspirin or morphine. Organic compounds typically contain carbon, hydrogen, oxygen, and nitrogen. Therefore, it is not the elements but how they are arranged in the molecule that matters. Flames destroy molecules while providing no useful information. The development of *molecular spectroscopy* methods capable of detecting these compounds would take another century.

Marggraf also was the first to produce phosphoric acid (H$_3$PO$_4$) and an analytical test for iron based on cattle blood and potassium. The process is not as wild as it seems; his procedure of heating potassium salts in the presence of cattle blood produced potassium ferrocyanate (from the iron in hemoglobin) with a blue substance referred to as Prussian blue. Microscopy was also one of his skills, and he pioneered early microscopic identification of materials based on crystal structure and microchemical reactions.

The first true spectrometer, dated to the 1850s, was the culmination of much foundational work and two familiar names: chemist Robert Wilhelm Bunsen (1811–1899) of the Bunsen burner fame and physicist Gustav Kirchhoff (1824–1887) known for Kirchhoff's law. In 1860, Bunsen and Kirchhoff published a paper describing the first instrument designed specifically to study the light emitted from different samples. The device consisted of a flame created by a burner, optics (a telescope) that directed the light into a small box and prism, and another telescope to project the lines for evaluation. The burner was critical to the design since it provided a steady (not flickering) hot flame free of smoke. The impact on the scientific community was immediate and spectacular. Qualitative analysis of elements changed as close to overnight as possible in the time, as did the definition of a pure substance. With newer and more sensitive instruments, constituents that escaped detection with crude wet chemical methods were now revealed. In short order, many new elements such as cesium and gallium were identified using flame emission spectrometry.

Bunsen did not consider himself to be a forensic chemist, but he had a forensic mindset. Practical to the bone, he once said, "A single determination of one fact is more valuable than the most beautifully constructed theory." Like Orfila, Bunsen drew crowds of students and admirers to his labs, where he believed in hands-on learning by example. Among his pupils were many soon-to-be-famous chemists including Adolph Baeyer

(1835–1917). Upon receiving one of many awards, Bunsen once remarked, "Oh my God! The only good thing about these honors was that they made my mother happy, but she, poor soul, is dead."[1]

At the same time Bunsen and Kirchhoff were working on flame spectroscopy, Frenchman Jules Dubosq (1817–1886) designed and demonstrated the first viable colorimeter in 1854. The instrument produced qualitative and quantitative information based on color and the absorbance and transmittance of visible light. His first application was a measurement of the amount of caramel in syrup. The technique found widespread acceptance throughout the remainder of the century, although technical issue related to the detector (still the human eye) hobbled it. Early detection schemes relied on sets of colored materials such as glass discs that the observed matched to the color of the solution. One instrument that utilized colored standards was called the Lovibond comparator, which was introduced in 1890 as a method for measuring the color of beers. The comparison standards were again colored glass disks. Because color perception ability varies among people, the eye can never be an objective method of detection.

Speaking of beer (or Beer), the ability to use a colorimeter for quantitative work depends on a mathematical method of linking the instrumental output to a concentration. Intuitively, the concentration of an analyte will determine the depth of the color, but intuitive must be translatable into mathematical to devise a quantitative method. The first steps in that direction predate Bunsen and Kirchhoff by several decades. A French physicist and sailor who worked extensively with optics presented Bouguer's law in 1729. Using studies of glass and of the atmosphere, Bouguer stated that the thicker the media, the greater the absorption of light and thus the lower the intensity of emitted light.

Furthermore, Bouguer noted that this was an orderly and predictable change and that "if a certain thickness" intercepted "half the light, the following equal thickness" would "intercept not the entire second half but only half of this half, reducing it accordingly to one-quarter of its original brilliance."[2] It was the first recognition that absorbance of light was a logarithmic phenomenon. In 1760, J.H. Lambert (1727–1777) published a paper entitled "Photometry, or the Measures and Levels of Light, Color, and Shade" that derived a mathematical expression for the degree of absorbance as a function of the distance traveled. Chemists were using these crude but effective equations for quantitative colorimetry by the 1820s.

Beer (not the beverage but the man, August Beer, 1825–1863) published a paper in 1852 and a book in 1854 that further refined the formula for relating concentration and absorbance to the length of the path traveled by light. From this time until the late 1880s, quantitative colorimetry became an important analytical tool based on the relationship that Beer and many of his contemporaries, Lambert, and Bouguer had elucidated. How the name for the most-used version of the equation[3] became known as Beer's law is not clear. Perhaps one word was easier than three, and if one has to choose, it would seem appropriate to select the most colorful. The first articles to use the term "Beer's law" appeared much later, in the late 1880s. Regardless of how the name came to be, the equation made possible quantitative spectroscopy across the electromagnetic spectrum, most of which have been used in forensic chemistry.

COLORS, DRUGS AND DYES: ENTER THE GERMANS

If blood and death belonged to the English and the Americans, forensic chemistry belonged to the Germans and the Austrians. Much of this heritage is unappreciated outside Europe, given language barriers and the lack of English translations of many pioneering papers.[4] Once Otto Stas had provided the means to extract poisons from tissues, the issue of which poison was present remained. This led to color-based tests that were used to tease out likely identities. The color produced in most tests is the result of dye formation. Many of the earliest tests developed to screen for certain drugs and toxins carry the name of the men who developed them, including Marquis (a student of the German chemist Kobert), Dragendorff, Mecke, Ehrlich, Frohde, Liebermann, and Zwikker. Most of these tests were described in publications from 1870 to 1905. Forensic chemists and law enforcement officers still use these tests today. In the 1960s and the 1970s, German chemists published articles describing how the color tests worked on a molecular level.

This litany of names shows how German chemists excelled in two areas intimately related to forensic science—dyes and drugs. There is a neat symmetry here; the color tests mentioned earlier work, in many cases, by forming a dye; many drugs were made accidentally while the chemists were busy trying to make dyes, and vice versa. Explosives manufacturing closely connected to both. It might seem that drugs and dyes have little in common with each other, but chemically, these families share common roots. Drugs are of obvious forensic importance, but the role of dyes is less so.

Dyes, along with pigments, are colorants that impart color to the substrate to which they are applied. Solubility dictates the distinction between them; dyes dissolve in solution like food coloring in water while pigments form a suspension in solution and dry as a coating on a surface. The chemical structure alone does not automatically dictate which is which since a change in solvent can change solubility. The forensic importance of dyes and pigments, particularly from a chemical point of view, is a recent development that traces back to the introduction of materials that use them.

Pigments are widely used in paints and inks and as colorants for fabrics and fibers. It is this last application that spurred the chemical developments that would have the greatest impact on forensic science.

The first mention of dyes appeared during 2000–3000 B.C.E. The dye compounds came from extracts of plants, leaves, and other colored materials. The ancients derived pigments for paints by grinding up colored minerals and suspending them in water or other slurry materials. The Chinese and the Egyptians made inks and paints using charcoal suspended in oils or animal fats. Along with medicines and metallurgy, interest in colorants was a primary driver of early chemistry. Once beyond simple extracts and slurries, progress in colorant chemistry had to wait for techniques of chemical synthesis to evolve, a process that picked up dramatic speed in the late 1800s.

Many naturally derived drugs share chemical similarities with naturally derived dyes. The alkaloids for example, a class of drugs that include heroin, morphine, and cocaine as well as thousands of others, are based on a structure called a tertiary amine. Indigo, the dye used to make blue jeans blue, also contains tertiary amine groups. The first synthetic dye created, mauve, was an accidental by-product of an attempt to make quinine to treat malaria. It is not surprising then that the chemical histories of drugs and dyes run parallel. Before the advent of synthetic organic chemistry, drugs and dyes could only be obtained from natural sources such as extracts, teas, and mineral preparations. Chemists lacked that knowledge and tools to create new molecules and thus new drugs from precursors.

Drug chemistry diverges from that of dyes in an important and obvious way: people can abuse drugs. Pinning down the definition of abused drugs begs a definition of abuse. This is a social rather than a scientific question, the answer to which depends on the circumstance and the place in history. The Sumerians and Egyptians were excellent brewers, with the former showing a penchant for brewing beer, while the Egyptians were particularly adept at winemaking. Hair analysis from ancient samples from Peru revealed the presence of metabolites of cocaine, which supports the notion that chewing coca leaves began in South America around 2000 B.C.E., if not earlier. Marijuana was mentioned in Chinese texts from the third century B.C.E., and because the marijuana (hemp) plant is hardy (i.e., a weed), it grows almost anywhere. It is not surprising that use of its products was widespread in the ancient world. The pursuit of medicines and treatments remained separate from chemistry until Paracelsus and his followers began to bring chemistry into the search for medicines, a search that predictably led to the discovery of drugs of abuse. What was not predictable was that dye chemists would be the ones leading the way.

Of all the colors, the most sought after in ancient times were the blues and the purples. Indigo, one of the earliest blue dyes, comes from the *Indigofera tinctoria* plant. The leaves and their extracts are not blue and require chemical processing for the blue color to emerge. The extract is first soaked in a basic solution and then oxidized by exposure to air. Likely, this was an accidental discovery, but the realization that colors could be coaxed from colorless materials was a chemically important step, even if ancient dye makers did not understand the fundamental chemistry they were practicing.

Chemists exploited indigo for analytical purposes in the 1800s using a reagent consisting of indigo dissolved in sulfuric acid. If a sample contained nitric acid, the indigo was bleached from the characteristic blue to a clear solution. The test was used forensically in the early 1800s until William Brooke O'Shaughnessy (1809–1889) published his first paper in the medical journal *The Lancet* in 1830, describing the shortcomings of the test. This was important because some poisoners used nitric acid. O'Shaughnessy, who was twenty-one when he wrote the report, pointed out that other compounds besides nitric acid reacted with indigo. In noting this, he was contradicting some of the early English forensic scientists of note including Robert Christison, who had a medical degree from the University of Edinburgh. It was a courageous action for such a young chemist.

Not satisfied with debunking the existing method, O'Shaughnessy described three tests that were specific for nitric acid: first, nitric acid would turn orange in the presence of morphine (forming another dye); second, it would form a solid when added to urea nitrate; and third, it would facilitate formation of silver fulminate. Detection of the latter was simple, obvious, and hazardous given that silver fulminate is an explosive. In publishing the paper, O'Shaughnessy was following Christison's advice to forensic chemists that it was the job of the analyst to provide more than some evidence but to provide the best evidence possible given the limits of scientific knowledge of the time. For a short period, indigo dye and other tests represented those limits.

Another famous ancient dye was royal purple, also called Tyrian purple for the coastal city where its manufacturing was centralized. Tyre, once part of the ancient Phoenician Empire, is on the coast of Lebanon, a city build on mounds of mollusk shells used in the production of the dye. The process of making Tyrian purple started by gathering mollusks and extracting their glands. Next, the extracted material oxidized to form the final color, much like with indigo. The process required thousands of purple snails to make any appreciable amount of dye, and it is not surprising the species nearly became extinct. The dye was one of the most valuable commodities in the ancient world. Alizarin was another ancient dye, red in color.

The dye industry was central to manufacturing and trade from the ancient times until well into the nineteenth century. The nature of the manufacturing process was labor and material intensive, making dyes too expensive for most people to afford. In the 1700s, interest turned to find-ing ways to synthesize dyes from cheaper and more abundant resources. One of the first to try was Peter Woulfe who began with indigo in 1771. He treated it with nitric acid to make picric acid, a lovely yellow compound. Its dye applications were short-lived. When dry, picric acid is unstable and detonates easily, a generally undesirable feature for clothing. Regardless, the recognition that dyes could be converted to other dyes with chemical treatments was an important step forward even if picric acid (thankfully) never made a significant impact on the dye industry.

In 1858, Johann Peter Griess (1829–1888), a German chemist, described a type of reaction called diazotization in which an amine compound (one containing an -NH$_2$ group) reacts with nitrite ion (NO$_2^-$) under acidic conditions to yield diazonium salts that are often highly colored. The re-action can continue on to coupling reactions that produce highly colored products. Uncovering the reaction led to production of azo dyes by 1861. The coupling reactions, often considered a nuisance in salt production, have been utilized extensively in forensic chemistry as color-based pre-sumptive tests for drugs and in other forensic applications.

For much of the last century, the Griess test was one of the principle screening tests used for detection of gunshot residue (GSR). In this test, the analyte of interest is not the amine but the nitrite, which is a by-product of combustion of gunpowder. An acidic solution of the starting amine (naphthylamine) is added to the sample suspected of containing gunshot residue. If nitrite is present, the dye formation proceeds to yield a red dye. A modified version detects nitrates (NO$_3^-$) in water. The source of this material is usually runoff water containing fertilizers, which are high in nitrates. Ammonium nitrate (NH$_4$NO$_3$) is one of the main culprits and is used as an ingredient in explosives. The bomb used in Oklahoma City in 1995 was made of ANFO, a combination of ammonium nitrate and fuel oil.

Griess did not actually make the first synthetic dye. That honor goes to William Henry Perkin (1838–1907), mentioned briefly above. He was an eighteen-year-old chemist who was working to improve treatments for malaria. He was interested in making quinine, which at the time (1856) was the only known effective treatment for the disease. Quinine was made from extracts of coal tar in a complex process that Perkins hoped to sidestep by starting from simpler ingredients. He did not succeed in that quest, but he did manage to create an intense purple-blue solution that not only dyed cloth but also did not weather, fade, or wash out. He quickly abandoned the quest for quinine, patented the dye called mau-veine (*mauve*), and started a company in London called Perkin & Son. The name was a gesture of gratitude to his father, who helped fund his work. Perkin's contribution to dye chemistry was to show that it was possible to start from compounds found in coal tar. This and other related materials

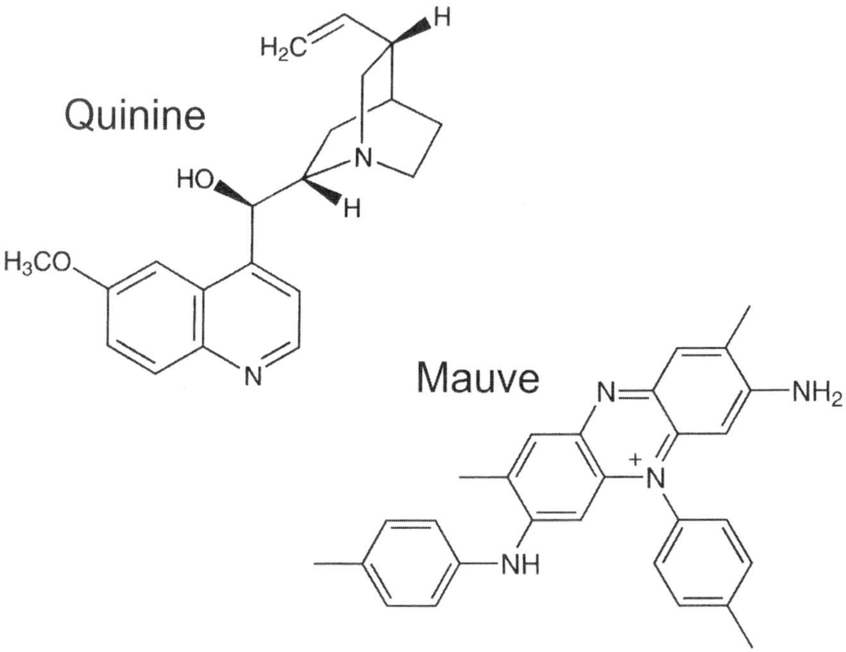

Figure 10.1 Perkin was attempting to make the antimalarial drug quinine (top left). Instead, he created the first synthetic dye, mauve.

were and remain relatively cheap and abundant. This freed the dye chemists from scarce and costly natural materials such as plants, mollusks, and other living precursors.

By 1868, Carl Liebermann and others had created colorants consisting of metals and dyes. They understood that the key structural feature of dyes responsible for color was a series of alternating double bonds, such as those found in mauve. Knowing this, Liebermann was able to focus his efforts. During the 1870s and 1880s, he developed color tests based on dye formation and remained a central figure in early colorant and dye chemistry. The Liebermann test is still used occasionally to detect the presence of phenol groups (benzene rings with −OH attached as in aspirin). A positive reaction produces a colored dye product. The Ehrlich reagent (1901) consists of p-dimethylaminobenzaldehyde, which reacts with indoles such as LSD and mescaline to form colored dyes, purple in the case of LSD.

Paul Ehrlich (1854–1815) was one of the more productive and colorful of the color chemists. He often carried a box of cigars under one arm, of which he smoked around twenty-five a day. He was also reported to eat little and to frequent beer halls where he got into spirited discussions and debates. Despite—or because of—this eccentricity, he won a Nobel

Prize in medicine in 1908 for work related to both medicine and dyes. He worked with stains used to color tissues and microorganisms. His work in the late 1880s was the foundation of the Gram staining procedure still used today to differentiate bacterial types. In the 1890s, Ehrlich turned his attention to immunological work and later to medicine and pharmacology. He screened hundreds of compounds to treat the spirochete that was known to cause syphilis. Prior to his work, mercury was the only viable treatment for the disease, resulting in many fatalities. After screening more than 600 compounds, Ehrlich identified one that contained arsenic and became known as salvarsan, discussed previously. Another German dye making company, Hoechst Dye Works, marketed the drug starting in 1910. In a replay of the Baeyer aspirin story, the success of the drug allowed the company to move more aggressively into pharmaceuticals.

Perhaps the most versatile color test used in forensic drug analysis is the Marquis test published in 1896. The ingredients are simple—formaldehyde and sulfuric acid. The Marquis reagent reacts with many alkaloid drugs to form a variety of colors. Amphetamine and methamphetamine create orange dyes, while the opiates react with the reagent to form purple ones. Ninhydrin, a common reagent used for visualizing fingerprints, was introduced in the early 1900s and reacts with the amino acids to form a purple colored dye. As a result of the rapid advances in the late 1800s, forensic chemists entered the 1900s with a rich toolbox of extraction and detection methods, all based on classical wet chemistry.

O'SHAUGHNESSY

The emergence of a reliable set of classification and identification tests for drugs typified forensic chemistry in the decades to come. A notable forensic chemist to champion such a methodical approach was Sir William Brooke O'Shaughnessy, introduced earlier for his role in debunking the specificity of the indigo test for nitric acid. In a classic example of the interplay of public health and legal matters in the early history of forensic science, O'Shaughnessy took on a project in 1830 at the request of the editor of the prestigious medical journal *The Lancet*. He developed a systematic method of testing candy for the presence of organic and inorganic poisons that found their way there by accident or design. Mindful of the tendency of children to suck on the candy wrappers, he considered those as a possible mode of ingestion. He eventually identified a number of contaminants and adulterants including oxides of lead and antimony, mercuric sulfide, copper carbonate, calcium sulfate, and Prussian blue. To confirm the presence of the metals, he isolated the elemental form, presaging the work of Marsh to come. The work spurred public concern and further investigation of adulterated products, with offenders having their names published in *The Lancet*.

O'Shaughnessy, like many of his contemporaries, had an abundance of self-confidence and the will to use it. He would challenge any authority, and he was right more often than he was wrong. He once wrote of Orfila's work related to lead detection in poison, "Nothing can be more practically absurd than Orfila's directions in this instance."[5] In contrast, he embraced the Marsh test and was among the first to recognize its value in forensic toxicology, writing in 1842, "The moment I read Mr. Marsh's notice I saw at once its extra-ordinary value.... That week I applied it in the investigation of two cases of arsenic poisoning received into Police Hospital, and I was subsequently the first to publish the practical results of its application to legal analysis."[6] He was not in fact the first to do so; Orfila had beaten him by two years with the LaFarge case. O'Shaughnessy had a good excuse for the lapse. Frustrated by not being named to a post in medical jurisprudence at the University of London, he joined the East India Company as an assistant surgeon and went to Calcutta in 1833. He had wanted to return to his practice of medicine, but his forensic chemical skills kept interfering with this plan. In India, he was given the post of chemical examiner at Calcutta Medical College. This assignment was in addition to his medical duties. It was there that he demonstrated the Marsh test and began to use it. True to form, he was the first to point out one of its shortcomings.

When the Marsh test was first introduced, chemists assumed that any form of arsenic would respond. In Europe and England, white arsenic (As_2O_3) was the commonest form of arsenic used as a poison. In India, yellow arsenic (As_2S_3, kings yellow) was easily available in bazaars and thus accessible to would-be murderers. It was this form of arsenic that Marsh had obtained in the Bodle case in 1832 and that had motivated him to devise the better test. O'Shaughnessy enters the story in 1838, two years after the publication of the Marsh test. Using it, O'Shaughnessy examined the stomach contents and lining of a victim of suspected arsenic poisoning. He could clearly see the yellow solid clinging to the stomach lining, but the Marsh test yielded negative results. To prove his suspicions, he dissolved the yellow solid in nitric acid and then performed the Marsh test, obtaining the positive result. He would also later point out, as did others, that antimony yielded a positive result with the Marsh test. More importantly, he noted the forensic implications of this finding. At the time, a treatment used in the case of suspected poisoning was to administer an emetic to induce vomiting. A common emetic was potassium antimonyl tartrate. The problems were obvious to O'Shaughnessy.

O'Shaughnessy's contributions to forensic chemistry were among many other accomplishments. His role as physician led him to pioneer the use of cannabis (marijuana) to English medical practice as a treatment for tetanus, cholera, and convulsive problems. Having worked with many cholera victims early in his career, he became adept at looking at stomach contents and judging if a death was due to a disease or arsenic poisoning. In India, he became an assayer at the Calcutta Mint and was instrumental in bringing telegraphic service to the country. He wrote a book on forensic chemistry in the form of a medical manual for students in Calcutta and was knighted in 1856.

The Eye of the Beholder

In no other area is the overlap of society and science more glaringly apparent than in the area of abused drugs. Although drug analysis is perhaps not as glamorous as toxicology or death investigation, drug cases often constitute around half of all cases submitted to modern forensic science laboratories. Forensic drug chemistry combines elements of analytical chemistry and forensic investigation in a way unique to forensic investigation. The cat and mouse game between forensic drug chemists and their clandestine counterparts is one of the interesting untold stories in forensic science. The history of drug development is intimately tied with the development of dyes, which have their own unique place in forensic science, as related in the last chapter.

The definition of a drug is straightforward: a substance that when ingested results in a therapeutic effect. The definition of abuse is forever nebulous and controversial. What one culture values, another fears; what was once accepted has become the scourge of youth. However, drug abuse was not a notable social problem until drugs became easily available and inexpensive and nearly as accessible as alcohol. For the most part, this occurred in the 1800s as chemists (many dye chemists) learned to convert simple precursors into potent drugs.

BAEYER AND BARBITURATES

What mauve and Perkin are to the story of dyes, Hoffman, Baeyer, and aspirin are to drug chemistry. Aspirin is the trade name of the compound acetylsalicylic acid. Hippocrates recommended that his patients chew on

willow bark leaves to relieve pain, not knowing that the related compound salicylic acid was the active ingredient. Paracelsus used the bark
to treat fever. By the mid-1800s, salicylic acid had been prepared from
plant extracts, and the fever-reducing properties of the substance were
recognized. Frederic Gerhardt reported the first synthesis of acetylsalicylic
acid in 1853, and from that time until about 1880, various improvements
and alternatives surfaced. Merck & Co. marketed acetylsalicylic acid in
the 1880s, although there was little medical or commercial excitement.

During the latter part of the nineteenth century, there were few reliable medicines and preparations to treat fever and pain. Of the ones that
were useful, opium was frequently used for pain and quinine to treat fever
(and malaria). Both are plant-derived materials, and as their use increased,
so did the price. Quinine was extracted from the Cinchona tree native to
Peru, and the powerful addictive qualities of opium were quickly realized,
providing incentive for chemists to look elsewhere for substitutes. This
interest was an important driver because it created a market for viable alternatives, preferably less addictive and found locally. Although willow
was still a natural product, it was plentiful in Europe, and attention returned to this material. As early as 1830, the active ingredient in willow
bark had been extracted by a German chemist (Johann Buchner) and went
by the name salicin. Another German treated salicin further and oxidized
it to salicylic acid. The first useable product related to this was salicylic
acid made from phenol (also called carbolic acid) that was marketed as an
alternative to phenol, a common antiseptic of the time.

In 1863, German chemists Friedrich Baeyer (1825–1880) and Johann
Weskott, both dye makers, founded the company that would become
Baeyer (Bayer in the United States). The pharmaceutical group was not
formed until 1881 when there was already a significant body of understanding about salicylates. The first Baeyer pharmaceuticals were
phenacetin (still used as an analgesic and fever reducer) and heroin. At the
time, heroin was heralded as a great improvement because it appeared to
be less addictive than morphine found in opium. That drug would have
a significant impact on forensic chemistry, but not until well into the next
century. Phenacetin was first made as a by-product of reactions used to
make dyes.

At Baeyer during these early years, Felix Hoffman was working to find
an alternative to salicylic acid to aid his father, who suffered from rheuma-
tism and disliked the drug. Hoffman revisited and repeated the synthesis
of acetylsalicylic acid in 1897. Testing on the substance began in earnest.
As was typical of the time, Baeyer's pharmacists undertook animal tests
as well as self-testing. They found the substance to be safe.

The step that would bring Baeyer fame and wealth was the mundane
one of patenting the drug and assigning it the name aspirin. Baeyer, a
dye company, began to market aspirin in 1899 as a pain reliever and fever

reducer. If it had not been for all the money made in dyes, it is unlikely that Baeyer would have ventured into the pharmaceutical market at all. Interestingly, dyes later served as precursors for initial work leading to sulfa drugs, the first family of effective antibiotic drugs.

Baeyer was just getting started. As it had with aspirin, it took previous work by others and moved forward, this time into the family that would become a forensic mainstay, the barbiturates. Swedish chemist Scheele, introduced earlier for his early arsenic work, isolated a compound now called uric acid from urine in 1776. From then until the middle of the 1800s, chemists toyed with the compound and were able to make derivative materials. It was Baeyer himself who in 1863 combined these findings and made barbituric acid. The name is the subject of much debate, speculation, and wishful romanticism. It may have been named for a woman Baeyer may have had his eye on. Barbituric acid proved to be a versatile chemical scaffold on which to build related drugs that came to include secobarbital, phenobarbital, and pentobarbital. One of the first derivates, barbital, was made in 1882 and was found to have hypnotic (sleep-inducing) properties. Barbital was marketed under the trade name *Veronal* starting in 1903.

Barbiturates were quickly successful. The success spawned further work and advances in barbiturate chemistry. The year 1911 saw introduction of phenobarbital and in 1928, amobarbital, which found use as an anesthetic. During the century, over 2500 compounds were produced, of which about fifty were used for sleep-inducing and sedative effects. The greatest dangers of barbiturates were that they were addictive and could cause death with relatively small overdoses. Abuse patterns became apparent in the 1930s when young people started to use the drugs recreationally.

At first, public reaction focused on the role of barbiturate intoxication in causing traffic accidents. This was a repeat of the pattern seen with alcohol earlier in the century. By 1940, several states had placed some controls on the sale and availability of barbiturates. It was not until the 1960s, when viable alternatives appeared, that the trend seemed to improve briefly. It was short-lived. The advent of the drug culture and widespread drug abuse, including barbiturates, took hold in the late 1960s. The abuse of barbiturates receded only in the 1980s when substitutes became available and legitimate use declined. With less legal use, the supply diminished and since the drugs were not easy to make, abuse declined in parallel.

Barbiturates were used to treat sleep disorders and anxiety as well as high blood pressure. One of the first and most successful synthetic sedatives was Valium (diazepam), first synthesized in 1958. Valium went on to be the most prescribed drug in history for the time. It is still widely used because the dose is small compared to barbiturates with far less side effects. The smaller dosage is a result of targeting; pharmaceutical chemists employ their knowledge of metabolism and response to synthesize the drug to do one thing only. In practice, there are always some side effects, but targeted design drastically reduces them. Targeting to a specific symptom or ailment avoids many of the side effects associated with drugs with more generalized action. This trend is now firmly entrenched in pharmaceutical research and development.

As an example, barbiturates were often used to treat anxiety but caused general sedation, sleepiness, tolerance, and dependence as side effects. Valium and other benzodiazepines had far fewer side effects but could still cause drowsiness. As such, these drugs were still subject to abuse by those seeking out the side effects, but the extent of abuse is much less compared to barbiturate abuse. The next generation of synthetic drugs for depression were the selective serotonin reuptake inhibitors (SSRIs) such as Prozac and Paxil that came on the market in the 1980s. As the name indicates, the SSRIs target one biochemical process. As a result, they do not cause sedation or significant sleepiness and have little potential for abuse.

THE ANTI-BARBITURATE

Barbiturates, in drug culture parlance, are *downers*. Their opposites were *uppers*. Generically, these drugs are based on a skeleton consisting of a benzene ring, an ethyl group, and an amine group called *phenylethylamines*. The most familiar members of the family to the forensic chemist are methamphetamine and amphetamine. Methamphetamine was first synthesized in the late 1880s by German chemists, but it was not until the 1930s that the compound was thoroughly studied. Amphetamine appeared on the market in 1932 and was an ingredient in a nasal inhaler used to relieve congestion. Most of the drugs in the family such as pseudoephedrine, phenylpropanolamine, and ephedrine are effective decongestants. Their side effects brought them to the attention of forensic chemists. Users quickly noted the stimulant effects of amphetamine, and soon doctors prescribed it for conditions such as narcolepsy, depression, and appetite and weight control.

College students were among the first to use amphetamine to ward off sleep in the 1930s. Their sources were campus research labs. Athletes and long-haul truck drivers were soon among those using the drug, but the issue did not attract as much attention as the barbiturate problem. This was probably because accidental overdoses leading to death were more of a concern with barbiturates. By the mid 1940s, most states had laws that limited access to amphetamines, barbiturates, or both. The federal government, through the Food and Drug Administration (FDA) entered the picture in 1938 through the Food, Drug, and Cosmetic Act. This act took the first steps toward uniform federal regulation of drugs subject to abuse. It also mandated the first significant use and precaution labels for prescription drugs.

As the use of amphetamine became more restricted, abusers began to turn to illicit sources, starting with the inhaler form that was still available. Since the inhaler was not covered by FDA regulations during the 1940s, abusers would purchase it, tear open the canister, and retrieve the folded paper on which the drug was impregnated. Users dipped it in drinks or simply swallowed it as it was. The FDA responded by requesting manufacturers to make an impregnable canister. No feat of affordable engineering could make such a canister. Efforts moved to spiking the paper with agents that cause nausea when swallowed. Abusers confounded this by accepting an upset stomach as a side effect. By 1949, the inhaler was off the market.

World War II contributed to the use and abuse of amphetamine and methamphetamine, both of which were supplied to armed forces personnel from many countries. The number of pills issued may have numbered in the millions. Americans used the drugs to help bomber crews stay awake, as an example. German and Japanese soldiers used methamphetamine, and Japanese civilians working in war-related industries were also supplied with the drug. After the war, ample supply of methamphetamine plus general acceptance led to widespread abuse. The problem was so severe that it was estimated that in 1948, about 5 percent of the Japanese population had a methamphetamine abuse problem. To put that number in context, the same percentage of the American population would number nearly 15 million people. By 1951, Japan had controlled methamphetamine and had developed aggressive treatment and intervention laws designed to curb abuse and accompanying crime. In the United States, methamphetamine was widely prescribed in the 1950s and 1960s as a treatment for depression and obesity. Doctors even occasionally prescribed methamphetamine to treat heroin addiction.

The war saw copious use of barbiturates to treat the wounded and for other applications. Wartime needs led to high production that flooded the market with both families of drugs, increasing accessibility and thus abuse. Although the drugs were legal if prescribed, diversion, particularly with the available surplus, was not challenging for determined abusers. A black market for barbiturates, especially those used as sleeping pills quickly developed, as did one for amphetamine. Estimates in the 1950s and early 1960s put the amount of diverted drugs at about half of the available supply. Sources were often pharmacists or drugstores with access to quantities of the drugs coupled with lax or nonexistent enforcement of regulations and laws. As with antibiotics today, doctors of the time tended to overprescribe amphetamines and barbiturates, fueling the abuse in the middle class. Abusers often took both, one as a counter to the effects of the other in a vicious cycle called *bolt and jolt*.

Once again, drug abuse, intoxication, and driving were the catalysts for public outcry. By the late 1950s, significant enforcement attention was focused on amphetamine abuse among truck drivers. This well-publicized problem, coupled with press attention, led to research into substitute drugs with less potential for abuse. The efforts for barbiturates were more successful than for the amphetamines because amphetamines are among the most effective decongestants ever discovered. During the 1960s, the diversion problems with both drugs began to subside as alternatives came on the market. The worst of the amphetamine problem was yet to come, in the form of methamphetamine.

OTHER DRUGS

Many abused drugs belong to the alkaloids (*vegetable bases*), which also include many of the first plant-based poisons such as nicotine described earlier. In the late 1700s, Scheele had isolated acidic ingredients from plant matter, and by the early 1800s, neutral species had also been derived. As the nineteenth century dawned, two plant-derived extracts were widely used as medicines: quinine from cinchona bark for malaria and morphine from opium extracts. Opium has a particularly long history, although a first use is impossible to identify. Robert Boyle worked with opium, treating extracts with substances such as potassium carbonate. In 1670, laudanum was introduced, a product of an alcohol extract of opium and thus high in active ingredients of morphine and codeine. By 1800, many scientists were attempting to isolate the active ingredient in opium, not realizing that there were several. This and the confusion about the inherent acidity or basicity of the compounds presented a significant problem to these early chemists.

Work proceeded in earnest in the nineteenth century with several reports of partial success. In 1815, F.W. Serturner (1783–1841) used acetic acid to extract opium. The acid turned the basic alkaloids into water-soluble forms that he was able to extract and convert to salts. He called the extracted substance *morphium* in homage to the god of dreams. By self-administration, he was able to confirm the analgesic and sleep-inducing (hypnotic) effects of the salts. Apparently, Serturner did not appreciate the broader significance of the work, and he still dismissed the possibility that what he had isolated had to be a base and thus an alkaloid. It took a few years and a much bigger scientific name to publicize the work. Guy-Lussac (1778–1850), the French chemist, read Serturner's work, verified his results in the lab, and published a translation of the original paper in the widely read *Annales de Chimie* in 1817. The republication included an editorial in which Guy-Lussac pointed out the importance of the discovery. Now chemists had a method, crude as it was, to isolate alkaloids, convert them to powdery salts, and make much more effective medicines. Guy-Lussac also suggested the name morphine for the substance Serturner isolated. This set the precedent that is still followed. All alkaloids are given a name (informal rather than chemical) ending with *ine*.

Significant research went into isolating and studying the alkaloids. In 1817, an extract of root of *Ipecacuanha* plant was found to contain a substance that induced vomiting, later to become known as ipecac. In 1819, strychnine was isolated from *nux vomica* and went on to infamy as poison. Many alkaloids, including morphine, were widely used as murder weapons, particularly as chemical methods for detecting arsenic and metal poisons improved.

In 1820, quinine was first isolated by French chemists Joseph B. Caventou (1795–1877) and Pierre J. Pelletier (1788–1842). They built a factory that was producing over 3 tons of quinine as a sulfate salt in 1826 to satisfy the demand for quinine as a malaria treatment. Chemical advances and commercial success kept the chain going. By 1930, about 300 alkaloids had been extracted and isolated; about a thousand by 1950; the current total exceeds 10,000.

Cocaine is a tropane alkaloid and is unique in forensic history for both its real and fictional roles. Sherlock Holmes was an addict, preferring a dilute 7 percent solution of the drug. Freud loved the stuff, and his widely publicized enthusiasm (*Uber Coca*, 1884) was likely the model for Holmes' use. The Coca-Cola Company used it in their product until the 1920s, but it was the ancient peoples of South America who probably were the first to use cocaine. They obtained it from chewing the leaves of the *Erythroxylon coca* plant native to mountain valleys in Bolivia and Peru. The cocaine content of the leaves is typically around 1 percent. According to a legend, the plant was first noted growing from the ground above a grave of a beautiful woman who had been executed by being cut in half for committing adultery.

Cocaine is abused as a stimulant but is also an effective local anesthetic along with related compounds of lidocaine, novocaine, and benzocaine. The ancient Peruvians probably used it in this role, applying saliva obtained from chewing the leaves to the scalp to numb areas before boring into the skull. The Spaniards, who invaded the region, adopted the use of coca leaves and their extracts to treat a variety of conditions. The Spanish brought coca back to Europe where it received little attention until the search for medicinal alkaloids was in full swing. Even so, cocaine was one of the last of the major alkaloids isolated (1855). In 1859, it was being touted as a stimulant and antidepressant. Use and acceptance soared.

The medical community recognized the value of cocaine as a local anesthetic. A physician in Vienna and friend of Sigmund Freud first used cocaine to numb a frog's eye as well as those of other animals and himself. He presented his results in 1884. In the same year, an American doctor named W.S. Halstead (1852–1922) used an injection of cocaine into a nerve to create what is now called a nerve block anesthetic in which all sensation below the point of injection is lost. The pharmaceutical company Parke-Davis manufactured several cocaine-containing medicines in the 1880s, including cocaine-laced wine and coca cigarettes. One advertisement suggested that "[it was] not too much to suppose that coca and its derivatives [were] the universal panacea for all human ills."[1]

Cocaine enjoyed a brief period of mass consumption as an ingredient in beverages. In 1896, Angelo Mariana concocted a cocaine wine called *Vin Mariani* that quickly became famous in the United States. His was not the first to enter the lucrative American market. A chemist working in Atlanta named John Pemberton (1831–1888) made a wine containing coca extracts. Portions of the public reacted negatively to the wine part, not the cocaine part. The nonalcoholic version was released a year later. This drink contained syrupy extracts of the African kola nut (high in caffeine) and coca leaves with sugar added to offset the bitter taste of the two alkaloids. Permberton's company marketed Coca-Cola as a drink to instill "vim and vigor" and to treat headaches. For a short while, it was extremely popular. It was so popular that the dangerous addictive side of cocaine became more obvious. By 1906, it was no longer an ingredient in the soft drink. The change was due to the Food and Drug Act of 1906 that required a label that included all ingredients. Cocaine remained legal, but it had fallen from public grace so quickly that having it on the label poisoned sales. By 1912, most states had relegated cocaine to the status of prescription-only.

The last drug category of significant forensic interest is the hallucinogens. Many drugs are stimulants and hallucinogens, the dose making the difference. Large doses of methamphetamine can produce psychoses, as can large doses of cocaine. The drugs abused for the hallucinogenic effect include mescaline (from peyote cactus), LSD (lysergic acid diethylamide, derived from a fungus that grows on grains such as rye), and marijuana. Marijuana has the longest documented known use with references dating back to ancient Chinese texts of the third century B.C.E. Hashish is a concentrated form of the marijuana plant, obtained from oils from the flowering tops. The resin is more potent than the leaves and the stems of the plant due to higher concentration of the active ingredient, THC (Δ^9-tetrahydracannibinol). THC is a complex molecule and, unlike the majority of other plant-derived drugs, is acidic and oily rather than basic. Because marijuana is a weed, it is hardy and easy to grow. As a result, in forensic labs that have drug analysis sections, marijuana usually dominates the caseload.

Chemist Albert Hoffman in 1938 who was working for Sandoz in Germany discovered LSD. Hoffman was attempting to isolate and adapt the active ingredients from ergot fungi that grow on rye. These fungi had been used by midwifes to induce labor, but their poisonous properties were well known. Chemists working in the United States had already identified an active ingredient, lysergic acid. Hoffman was interested in modifying its molecular skeleton to make other useful pharmaceuticals. LSD was the twenty-fifth compound he made during these studies. At first, he noted nothing of interest about the compound and set it aside.

Hoffman returned his attention to LSD in 1943. He synthesized the compound again and noted mild hallucinogenic properties, which he at first attributed to the solvent he was using. Ever the experimentalist, he then inhaled solvent fumes to see if it recreated the effect. It did not. He knew immediately what had happened: "LSD spoke to me....He told me, 'Don't give me to a pharmacologist, he won't find anything.'"[2] Hoffman experimented with the drug for a short time but soon realized that it was so potent that it was best taken under tightly controlled circumstances. He stopped taking it after a bad experience resulting from a combination of amphetamines and LSD.

For about ten years, psychotherapists used LSD, but the side effects proved undesirable. Although not as popular as in the 1960s and 1970s, the drug is still encountered, sold most often on tiny blotter papers with patterns on them, or soaked into sugar cubes or tiny tablets that come in many different colors. These tablets are often named "haze" based on the color of the tablet; the term "purple haze" made famous by rock musician Jimmi Hendrix in the 1960s may well refer to a purple LSD tablet and the effects it produced.

LSD is an ergot alkaloid derived from lysergic acid. Lysergic acid is a compound produced by a fungus that attacks grasses such as rye. Another precursor, lysergic acid amide is found in the seeds of the morning glory flower. There has been speculation that historical incidents of mass hysteria or otherwise unexplained behavior, such as the Salem witch trials, can partially be attributed to infected grains that were used in foods such as bread. Baking the fungus would have produced LSD. The chemical synthesis of LSD is difficult, but determined clandestine chemists have managed the feat.

LSD and THC are examples of drugs that are difficult and costly to extract or synthesize. This has important forensic consequences. Pelletier and Caventou set up a factory to extract and process tons of cinchona bark to make quinine sulfate. This relatively pure powder proved much more effective for patients than chewing on the bark itself. The powder also produced fewer side effects like nausea. Similarly, patients treated for pain get morphine sulfate, not an opium poppy. The same is true of abused drugs, and the same economics apply.

Skilled chemists can synthesize cocaine, but it is extraordinarily difficult and expensive compared to harvesting and extracting coca leaves. The same is true of opiates and their derivatives such as heroin. Synthetics such as barbiturates, benzodiazepines, and others sold as prescription medications are diverted to clandestine use far more often than they are made in clandestine labs. There are two glaring exceptions. One, methamphetamine, has become a primary concern of forensic chemists in the past few years and will be discussed shortly.

SOCIETY STEPS IN

The definition of drugs of abuse highlights the most obvious interaction of society and the law in the forensic context. It is a simple matter to identify cocaine and heroin chemically, but society identifies them as illegal and thus of forensic interest. Many abused drugs were first introduced to combat abuse of others. Heroin was touted as a less addictive drug than morphine, and cocaine was seen as an antidote to morphine abuse. The same pattern was seen with amphetamine and barbiturate abuse. Which drugs are defined as abused dictates which types of drug evidence will appear in the forensic laboratory. To the forensic chemist, the legal categorization of a drug is nearly as important as the chemical and the physiological ones.

The term "drugs of abuse" applies to drugs and related compounds that are subject to regulations and laws because of their potential to be abused and cause harm. Abused drugs are usually addictive, causing physiological dependence, psychological dependence, or both. Physical addiction is traceable to a biochemical or physiological change caused by repeated use of the substance. In the case of morphine discussed above, repeated regular use can lead to a decrease in the number of active opioid receptors in the brain and central nervous system. Since there are reduced receptors, the user cannot simply stop taking the drug without feeling symptoms of withdrawal. Ever-increasing doses are needed to elicit the desired effect, a phenomenon referred to as *tolerance* which accompanies physical addiction. Psychological dependence does not have a direct physiological cause but is rather rooted in emotional needs and responses.

In the United States, the first recreational drugs were the opiates such as morphine and opium, introduced by Chinese immigrants in the mid 1800s. San Francisco was the first city to pass a law regulating drugs in 1875. The first federal law regarding drugs was the Pure Food and Drug Act of 1906 which required labeling of patent medicines. This was the law that led to the removal of cocaine from Coca-Cola. The first federal agency with a responsibility for drug control, the Bureau of Revenue, was formed in 1915. This organization was a precursor to the Drug Enforcement Administration (DEA).

The history of the DEA began in the early 1900s when predecessor agencies formed within the Department of the Treasury. From 1927 to 1930, the Bureau of Probation handled federal drug enforcement when it was renamed the Bureau of Narcotics. It remained such until 1968. In that year, the Bureau merged with the Bureau of Drug Abuse Control (under the

Food and Drug Administration) to form the Bureau of Narcotics and Dangerous Drugs within the Department of Justice. Further consolidations resulted in the creation of the Drug Enforcement Agency in 1973. Among other functions, the DEA develops and tests methods for forensic chemistry and drug analysis and conducts research on newly discovered drugs, designer drugs, analogs, and new methods of drug synthesis.

In the United States, the federal government regulates drugs under the Controlled Substances Act (CSA) passed in 1970. The CSA divides drugs into categories called *schedules* based on their medical uses and potential for abuse. The Act specifies criminal penalties for violations ranging up to twenty years in prison and $1,000,000 in fines for the first offense involving a schedule I substance, down to a maximum of one year/$100,000 for a first offense involving a schedule V substance. The federal Anti-Drug Abuse Act of 1986 expanded the list to include "designer drugs," synthetically produced analogs to controlled substances.

While substances such as cocaine and heroin require extensive extraction and chemical processing before they are fit for ingestion, drugs such as PCP (phencyclidine or angel dust), GHB (a date rape drug), and methamphetamine are relatively simple to make. An effective tool to minimize illicit production of such drugs is to limit access to the precursors from which they are made. Accordingly, the Controlled Substances Act has been modified to include many of the key precursor chemicals needed for making methamphetamine and other clandestinely made drugs. Rather than list all precursors as controlled substances in 1988, the Congress passed the Chemical Diversion and Trafficking Act (CDTA) in 1993. This legislation created two lists of regulated chemicals designed to deter diversions of these compounds for clandestine synthesis.

THE CURRENT SCOURGE AND CLANDESTINE LABS

Drug use and abuse is cyclic. Cocaine ruled the late 1980s and 1990s, and by the early 2000s, methamphetamine surged ahead. A decade from now, it will be something else. The actors change, but the script does not. The pattern of introduction, use, availability, widespread abuse, demand, and then decline repeats for each new fad. Methamphetamine appears to be leveling out and starting to decline, thanks to legislative actions that mirror those taken to combat barbiturates and amphetamines. The only question is what will take its place.

Methamphetamine is available by prescription but produced in small quantities. However, it is easy to synthesize using minimal equipment and chemical skill from easily available precursors. Pseudoephedrine is an active ingredient in many over-the-counter cold medicines. With a little practice and recipes available over the Internet, a clandestine cook can whip up a batch of methamphetamine in a lab no bigger than the trunk of a car. PCP falls in the same category, but clan labs producing this substance are less common. Given the right precursors, amphetamines are also easily prepared.

Pseudoephedrine and ephedrine have been around for decades, as has the chemical knowledge of how to convert them to methamphetamine. As the drug culture took hold in the late 1960s and moved through the 1980s, there were few sources of information easily available and understandable to the typical drug abuser. With increased controls on access to commercial sources of methamphetamine, the turn toward clandestine manufacturing was inevitable. In 1962, clandestine methamphetamine labs appeared in San Francisco, which would become the spawning ground for many illegal drugs and the resultant culture of use and abuse.

The starting material (precursor) seen in that era was phenyl-2-propanone (P2P or phenylacetone), a common solvent. The synthesis of methamphetamine from P2P is relatively easy but yields a mixture of optical isomers of methamphetamine. As is common with many drugs that have such isomers, one form is more potent and biologically active. The product made by this process was not as strong as commercial methamphetamine, which contained principally the most active isomer. The first mentions of methamphetamine in the forensic literature came in the late 1960s, in the context of poisoning. The first forensic analytical procedures to identify methamphetamine were published in the early 1970s. This does not indicate a lack of forensic attention but rather reflects that the analytical methods that worked for most alkaloids were also easily adaptable to methamphetamine.

Regardless of purity issues, clandestine methamphetamine grew. Large-scale trade became dominated by motorcycle gangs that spread the drug along the California coast and then nationally. In the 1980s, other chemical methods entered the fray, using ephedrine as a starting material. Large labs sprang up in Mexico and much of the methamphetamine on the market originated from those sources. In the 1990s, the percentage of methamphetamine coming from small clandestine labs skyrocketed. This led to a series of laws in the United States, starting with the Comprehensive Methamphetamine Control Act in 1996 that attempted to limit access to precursors. This and related measures made the synthetic route starting with P2P prohibitively difficult. Unfortunately, the ephedrine methods had become so widespread that these quickly became favored. Recently, some clandestine cooks have turned to products related to *ephedra*, a grass that contains ephedrine.

A key and often unappreciated factor in the evolution of clandestine methamphetamine labs from nuisance to crisis was the advent of the Internet in the 1990s. Within a few years, easy and consequence-free access to recipes and instructions was available to anyone who could get access to the Internet. By the year 2000, that list included everyone, and meth labs proliferated. In response, legislatures and law enforcement agencies are turning toward control of precursors as a means of controlling the problem. In 2001, Oklahoma led the way by legislating controlled access to pseudoephedrine. Other states quickly followed. As of late 2005, federal legislation was pending to extend some measure of control across all states and major retailers were taking actions on their own to limit access.

These actions will undoubtedly have an impact, but in the larger forensic picture, the effect is like squeezing the balloon. Popularity and abuse of any one drug follows some form of a bell-shaped curve. When first introduced, abuse is limited, but if word-of-mouth is enthusiastic, abuse grows dramatically. Society and law enforcement responds, popularity wanes, and the abuse rolls back to some level of equilibrium that ebbs and flows with popular culture. Cocaine was fashionable in the 1990s. From the days of Baeyer through the 1950s, amphetamines and barbiturates were the rage. Everything seemed popular in the 1960s through the 1980s when marijuana rose to the top. LSD came and went, although seems to be undergoing a small revival. The train never stops; it only jumps tracks.

12

Gunpowder and DuPont; Dyes and Polymers

Dyes were nearly as important to the development of explosives as they were to the development of drugs. When wet, picric acid is a yellow dye; when dry, it is a dangerous contact explosive. Guncotton, an ingredient in smokeless powder, begins with the natural polymer cellulose that constitutes cotton. As chemists in the late 1800s became more adept at manufacturing materials, explosives, propellants, and polymers joined the list of synthetic compounds. Some form of all has found their way into forensic laboratories.

GUNPOWDER

The invention of the first gunpowder (black powder) has been attributed to many cultures including the Chinese, Arabs, Greeks, and Indians. Black powder contains charcoal (carbon) at about 15 percent by weight, potassium nitrate (KNO_3 or saltpeter) at 75 percent, and sulfur at 10 percent. The first written formula dates to around 1000 C.E. A story describes an accidental discovery in the third century B.C.E.: Chinese alchemists, working to purify gold and silver by separating them from an ore sample, added sulfur and saltpeter to it before placing it in the furnace. The procedure also called for the addition of charcoal, but apparently, an absent-minded alchemist forgot this step. Realizing the mistake, he added it but at the end of the procedure rather than at the beginning. The mistake did not go unrewarded. The result was not the separation of gold and silver but the production of black powder, resulting in a large explosion in the Chinese lab.

The hardest of the three ingredients to obtain was KNO_3. It seeped out of damp basement and cellar walls, forming a white crust. The Sumerians and the Egyptians noted it, although how it was used by them is not known. Around 400 B.C.E., it may have been used as part of a simple refrigeration method, since dissolving the solid in water significantly cools the solution. Soils containing nitrate became precious resources. Governments in England and France authorized the seizure of such soils for use in national defense. Stables with animal manure were prized for this purpose. By 1835, Swedish landowners were required to turn over a set quantity of saltpeter to the government.

The first uses of black powder were for fireworks, but the potential as a weapon was recognized by around 1000 C.E. Later in that century, the Chinese were using arrows loaded with black powder as incendiary devices. These early powders were not effective as propellants. As formulas improved, mostly by increasing the amount of KNO_3, the powder burned faster and became viable for that purpose. The idea behind burning a chemical to propel something is to harness the hot expanding gas produced by rapid burning of the powder to move a projectile forward at rapid speed. This requires a powder that burns quickly but not too fast (i.e., not resulting in an explosion) and a device that can contain the reaction long enough for pressure to build up behind the projectile. Initial efforts in China produced devices that launched arrows or bundles of small pellets in the manner of a crude shotgun.

By the late 1200s, the first gun-like devices appeared. They were made of bronze and fired rocks or iron balls. It was about this time that knowledge of black powder made its way to Europe. How it got there is not known, but by the middle of the thirteenth century, there were records and writings referring to it. German monk Berthold Schwartz began making and studying black powder in earnest early in the 1300s, speeding the adoption of the technology. The first European gun was produced in this century, a simple iron tube that was filled with powder and ignited by the insertion of a hot wire. It worked, but not well.

The problem was the formulation of the powder. To make an effective propellant, the burn rate had to be just right. The chemical formula was one aspect of that, but equally important is the physical form of the powder and the shape and size of the granules. Air has to be able to reach the particles, but the particles also have to be in contact to initiate the successive burning that generates the most effective pressure wave. In 1425, a process was perfected that allowed for optimized grain size. This spurred the development of small arms, grenades, and improved cannons and artillery. Black powder also was used in mining and construction starting in the sixteenth century.

In the United States, the Du Pont family dominated the early production of black powder. They built a factory in Delaware that began production in 1804 and produced several tons a year. Unfortunately, a huge explosion leveled the site in 1818, killing thirty-six and injuring many more. Other accidents followed, but the factory continued to produce powder under the leadership of Henry du Pont (1838–1926). In the middle and later parts of the century, the family dominated powder production in the New World. Chemist Lammot du Pont (1831–1884) produced one of the first powders specifically designed for industrial use in the late 1850s. Pennsylvania coalmines quickly put it to work. Eventually, DuPont, working through dubious business practices, absorbed most American powder production. Only in 1971 would DuPont finally end production of black powder.

With the increased production, the United States began to take the lead in firearms technology, led by men such as Samuel Colt (1814–1862) who designed the famous Colt revolver was first produced in the late 1840s during the Mexican-American war. Colt also mastered factory production methods for guns, using technology adapted from Whitney's cotton gin. Using this method, firearms production soared, and guns were soon widely available.

Black powder had several shortcomings. For military use, black powder weapons produced copious smoke that either quickly obscured the view or gave away the position of those firing. In construction, the powder lacked the explosive power needed to carve out tunnels in rock and other large jobs. The father-son team of Emmanuel (1801–1872) and Alfred Nobel (1833–1896) harnessed nitroglycerine (NG, discovered in 1846) for construction in 1859. The family had returned from Russia to their native Sweden, which had become a prominent center of explosives manufacturing. Alfred obtained patents, and in 1862, he built a plant for manufacturing NG outside of Stockholm. An explosion there in 1864 killed Alfred's younger brother. Unfortunately, NG exploded with extraordinary force, which was too easy to initiate.

In response, Nobel developed a method of using diatomaceous earth as an absorbent for the nitroglycerine that was much more stable. To ignite it, he used blasting caps that he had also invented. The cap consisted of mercury fulminate, a contact explosive first prepared in the 1600s and used as an igniting material for black powder. The cap was ignited by a flame that propagated down a fuse, allowing for a safe time difference between lighting and detonation. Nobel named the combined invention "dynamite," and it quickly replaced black powder for use in construction.

In the United States, Lammot du Pont was quick to see the advantages and opened a dynamite factory in 1880. The factory in New Jersey would prove to be his grave; he was killed in an accident in 1884. The DuPont family and company continued to grow despite the setback and expanded into the production of other chemicals. A chemist working for DuPont made a synthetic silk known as nylon in 1938 that opened the door to a world of synthetic fibers that have become a common part of trace evidence. The DuPont Company also invented Dacron, Orlon, Tyvek, Nomex, Kevlar, and neoprene. Back in Sweden, Alfred Nobel went on to become a rich man. Much of that fortune would eventually support the Nobel Prizes.

Parallel developments occurred in the area of propellants for firearms. Nitroglycerine is made by nitrated the -OH groups in glycerin. Chemists realized that cotton and cellulose, being rich in the same type of chemical functionality, were prime candidates for the same treatments. Among others, Friedrich Schonbein (1799–1868) of Switzerland, working in the 1840s with cotton, nitric acid, and sulfuric acid, created the highly flammable substance now called guncotton. When cotton is processed this way, the -OH groups in the cellulose are replaced with the $-NO_2$ group. Guncotton is rated according to its nitrogen content. Early guncottons, like nitroglycerine, proved to be unstable. It was not until the 1860s that manufacturing methods improved sufficiently to afford large-scale manufacturing. Field hospitals used the thick liquid form of nitrocellulose to bind and protect wounds suffered by soldiers in the Civil War.

POLYMERS AND EXPLODING BILLIARD BALLS

The tenuous mastery of guncotton (nitrocellulose) production set the stage for the next evolution in gunpowder. It is here that polymers enter the story. In the 1860s, billiards was a popular game. The balls used at the time were made of ivory, an expensive and difficult material to find. The company that made the most billiard balls in the United States offered a $10,000 prize to anyone who could offer a suitable replacement for ivory. A printer named John Wesley Hyatt (1837–1920) took nitrated cellulose, dissolved it in camphor, and poured the hot solution into a mold. It hardened (polymerized) and assumed the shape of the mold, including the spherical shape of a billiard ball. This material, called celluloid, proved hard as billiard balls. The drawbacks? Celluloid has a tendency to burn (as does celluloid film).

The ability to pour and mold the mixture appealed to those working on propellants because it made it easier to control the shape of the propellant granules. Work began in earnest in the late 1800s with the French army playing a central role. By the 1880s, plasticized guncotton was available, and when burned as a propellant, it produced far less smoke than black powder. Alfred Nobel added nitroglycerine to the nitrated cellulose, which remain the principle ingredient in modern propellant powders. An advantage of these materials is that they can be forced through molds to make prescribed shapes such as extruded cylinders. The materials are then hardened and cut into a variety of shapes including disks, balls, and flakes. Shaping the propellant grains affords careful control of burn rate and allows the chemists to optimize the grain size and shape depending on the application, be it propelling projectiles from 0.22 bullets to artillery shells. Almost overnight, black powder became an anachronism. Throughout the century, incremental improvements in formulation and shaping occurred, but the propellants and propellant residues seen in forensic laboratories today are not much different than those seen a century ago.

Propellants burn too slowly to be used as explosives, the job of which is to shatter and push by way of sudden enormous pressure waves. Dynamite, a combination of nitroglycerine and later nitrocellulose and ammonium nitrate, was one of the first true explosives. To simplify, explosives burn much faster than propellants and other combustibles and release their energy much faster. Explosives detonate, meaning that the reaction is initiated by compression rather than by flame or heat. Confinement of the reaction is also an important factor. The reaction rate of explosive detonation is so fast, often exceeding the speed of sound, that oxygen has to be supplied from the explosive molecules or formulation itself rather than from the atmosphere. Explosives can be classified as high explosives, which are relatively stable, and low explosives, which are less stable. Black powder is a low explosive that burns too slow to detonate. Secondary high explosives will not detonate without significant input of energy, necessitating devices such as Nobel's blasting cap. The German chemist and dye maker Griess, mentioned earlier, worked briefly with the material diazodinitrophenol before realizing its explosive potential. This substance is a primary high explosive. Substances that are quite sensitive are frequently used to initiate detonation of secondary high explosives. These initiation devices are usually made of shock, electrical, or heat-sensitive compounds that are set off remotely to initiate the detonation of the high explosives. In practice, an explosive device may incorporate several charges into the initiation chain. The power of an explosive expresses how fast it produces hot expanding gases. Most explosives are characterized by high amounts of nitrogen (which produces the highly stable N_2 molecule) and oxygen such as in the -NO_3 or the -NO_2 chemical groups.

An explosive of forensic interest is ammonium nitrate (NH_4NO_3), produced in large quantities as a fertilizer since the late 1800s. Nobel included it as a booster in later formulations of dynamite. Its value as an explosive was recognized, but dangers in handling it coupled with the difficulty in making it limited its use. This changed when the German chemist Fritz Haber (1868–1934) perfected the Haber process of making ammonium nitrate, starting from atmospheric nitrogen and using high pressure, temperature, and catalysts. Haber, an ardent German patriot, studied under Bunsen and Liebermann at German universities. He won the 1918 Nobel Prize in chemistry for his contribution to food production, but his work significantly aided the German cause in World War I. In 1914, the army

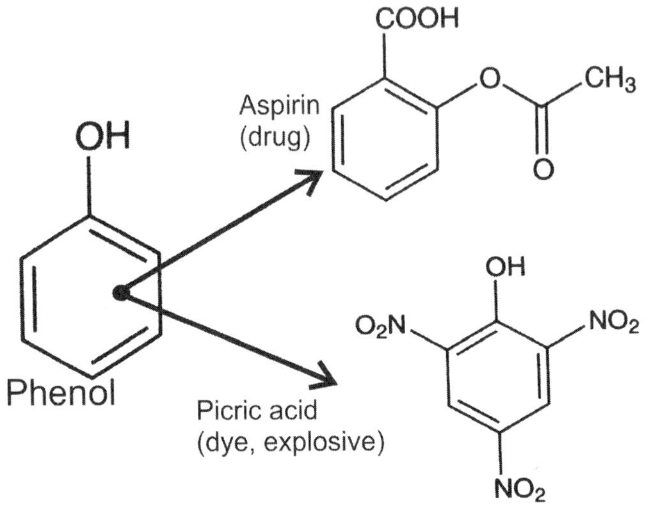

Figure 12.1 Phenol, isolated in the late 1800s, provided the
raw material to make drugs, dyes, and explosives.

was nearly out of nitrates for ammunition, and Haber was instrumental in
filling that need and thus prolonging the war. Haber is also remembered
for his role in early chemical warfare, helping to launch chlorine gas (Cl_2)
into allied trenches in 1915. For that reason, his receipt of the Nobel Prize
was controversial.

Ammonium nitrate is most effective as an explosive when combined
with hydrocarbons such as fuel oil. The explosive ANFO is a mixture of
95 percent ammonium nitrate and 5 percent fuel oil. Timothy McVeigh
used ANFO in the 1995 bombing in Oklahoma City. Previously, a massive
explosion of fertilizer in the hold of a ship docked in Texas City, Texas,
killed more than 500 people in 1947. The first bombing attack on the World
Trade Center in 1993 also used ANFO formulations.

As effective as ANFO is for blasting and for improvised explosives, it
lacks the focused, shattering powder desired for military explosives. The
starting place for the modern family of such explosives is the molecule
phenol, which was derived from coal tar and used as an early antiseptic
in the 1860s by Joseph Lister (1827–1912). The crude extract was called
carbolic acid, from which Lister eventually was able to isolate phenol as a
white crystalline material. Like cotton and glycerin, the molecular skeleton of phenol is a good platform on which to make explosives, principally
by adding oxygen and nitrogen in the form of nitro groups.

As noted in the last chapter, trinitrophenol (picric acid) had an explo-
sively short career as a dye. For a short time in the late 1800s, it found use
as a propellant and explosive, but it was touchy and corrosive to metals

used in munitions. Much of that problem vanished if the -OH group did. In 1902, Europeans began working extensively with trinitrotoluene (TNT) which had first been made in the 1860s. The experiments were successful, and picric acid went the way of black powder and just about as fast. By the onset of World War I, TNT was the standard military explosive. From the turn of the century through World War II, many additional explosive compounds and formulations were introduced, including tetryl, nitroguanidine, PETN, HMX, and RDX. Combining explosives with plasticizing agents allowed for molding and shape changes and their conversion into *plastic explosives*. A bomb made of PETN brought down Pan Am Flight 103 over Scotland in 1988, and PETN was part of the bomb in the shoe of Richard Reid in 2001.

FORENSICALLY SPEAKING

The underlying theme of drugs, dyes, propellants, and polymers is the advent of synthetic organic chemistry coupled to the industrial revolution. These two factors enabled mass production of items like guns, synthetic polymers, plastic, fabrics, and fibers—all the stuff of physical evidence. A goal of mass production is to insure that the widget coming off the line now is the same as the one before it and the one after it. Mechanization facilitates interchangeability. If the barrel of a gun is damaged, the owner can order a new barrel that will drop right in where the old one was. Everything is the same.

By 1900, it was clear that the lifeblood of forensic science was classification and comparison. Does this extracted material react the same way an extract containing arsenic does? Is this fragment of cloth the same or different from one recovered from the body? Is this powder residue consistent with gunpowder or not? All are comparisons in some sense, the goal of which is to say something is the same as or different from something else. Enter mass production, and the problem becomes far more complicated.

Consider a gun: If the barrel is made by hand, each barrel is unique. If it is made by a machine, the uniqueness vanishes to nearly indistinguishable. If the fabric that makes up a blouse is woven by hand, each garment has its own unique characteristics. Woven on a mechanical loom, yards and yards of that fabric are made to the same specifications hour after hour. As machinery improves, the forensic problem worsens.

Forensic chemistry is unique in that the comparative aspect is less obvious and easily overcome. Chemical analysis, beginning with the systematic use of wet chemistry and color tests, employs a series of increasingly specific tests that produces a conclusive result. It did not start that way; the Marsh test was not specific to arsenic although it represented the state of the art in 1840. However, with the advent of modern instrumentation and redundant testing, the identification of a drug or poison, be it in blood or a plastic baggie, is reliable because it can be compared to how a known sample of the same drug responds to the same test.

Chemists now understand why compounds react the way they do. Comparison is still part of the process but a much diminished and subtle one. This is not the case for most other types of forensic evidence from DNA to firearms. Nowhere are the comparative aspects of forensic science and the difficulties that are present in the modern area more apparent than in the microscopic world of trace evidence. Trace evidence can literally be anything. The best definition is that of *transfer evidence*. Anything that passes between a person and another or a person and a place can become transfer or trace evidence. The myriad of hairs, fibers, and dust particles clinging to someone's jeans is transfer evidence that tells the story of where they have been recently. To examine trace or transfer evidence, the oldest of instruments—the microscope—has reigned indispensable since its unveiling in the 1600s.

13

Microscopy and Trace Evidence

MICROCHEMISTRY AND FORENSIC MICROSCOPY

Microscopy was well on its way in the 1700s. The most important modification came with the introduction of polarized light microscope (PLM) in the early 1800s. PLM became and remains invaluable for the analysis of fibers, explosives, drugs, and many other materials. From the forensic perspective, it is a story of ascendancy, near death, and revitalization made possible by computers, hyphenation, and improved instrumental design. Reinsch, the developer of the toxicological test for metal poisons, said in 1881, "The use of the microscope in analytical tests becomes more and more important, and approaches the spectroscope in the filed [sic] of analysis of small samples. It gives even more information about the substance, because the approximate amount of the latter can also be determined."[1]

The statement summed up the path of forensic analytical chemistry for the next hundred years. The two pieces of equipment that defined early forensic science were the microscope and the colorimeter (spectrometer). Eventually, these two instrumental methods merged into microspectrometry (or microspectrophotometry), creating a new family of hyphenated instruments that are rapidly eclipsing their larger macro counterparts in forensic labs. One of the advantages of these techniques is that they are minimally destructive, always a desirable feature when irreplaceable evidence is involved. From the mid 1800s to the mid 1900s, microchemistry was an essential tool of forensic science and in particular, forensic chemistry. Later, microscopy, microchemistry, and microspectroscopy moved into trace evidence examination as well.

Microchemistry is a tool for identification rather than for quantitation. Many substances can be identified based on the morphology (form, features, and shape) of their crystals or crystals formed with chemical reagents. Reinsch's technique was typical—he would place a sample on a slide, add some reagents, mix, and allow the solution to dry slowly, allowing crystals to form. Beginning in the late 1880s, several books were published in Europe cataloging microcrystal tests for various substances. Overall, these works did not impress the larger scientific community since many of the tests used were adaptations of qualitative tests already practiced on a larger scale such as in test tubes. Forensic chemists, often working with tiny fragments of evidence and sample, were more appreciative of microcrystal tests.

Microchemistry is useful for inorganic as well as organic analysis, and work in the latter began in earnest in the twentieth century. Among the notable pioneers was Austrian Fritz Pregl (1869–1930), who received the 1923 Nobel Prize in chemistry for his work. If a reaction could be done in glassware and on a bench, Pregl could perform it on a slide. More importantly, he developed microscopic methods for quantitative analysis. Although these methods were never transferred to widespread forensic applications, it garnered enough attention to keep microscopy on the forefront of chemical science. Pregl's publications were also important in spreading the techniques, particularly to the United States.

Arguably, the first forensic chemical microscopy book was also a toxicology text, *The Microchemistry of Poisons,* written in 1867 by Theodore G. Wormley. Wormley was a physician and professor with a deep appreciation and understanding of chemistry and microscopy. Microscopists hailed the book for its detail and meticulous illustrations, made from steel engravings. Wormley had been unable to find someone willing to do the engraving, so his wife taught herself how and worked with him to complete the work. This was no small feat considering the intricate details needed for the drawings. The book is considered not only a milestone of chemical microscopy but also the first comprehensive American toxicology text. Wormley noted in the preface, "Heretofore the microscopy has received but little attention as an aid to chemical investigations, yet it is destined to very greatly expand our knowledge in this department of study."[2]

Back in Europe, Fritz Feigle (1891–1970) assembled a collection of microchemical tests that provided a systematic method of identifying many organic compounds. Feigel's methods were useful even with a microgram (a millionth of a gram) of sample. His tests used color changes and crystal structure, and many of these methods are still used as screening tests in forensic chemistry.

In the United States, Cornell University in New York became the nexus of chemical microscopy led by Emile Chamot (1868–1950), Clyde W. Mason, and their more famous student, Walter McCrone (1916–2002).

Chamot had already published two books entitled *Elementary Chemical Microscopy* and *Handbook of Chemical Microscopy* before 1920, and the books were used in forensic applications. McCrone was the first chemical microscopist who could be fairly described as a forensic chemist. Much of his work spilled over into historical artifacts. The latter led to his public fame, particularly because of work he did on the Shroud of Turin and the Vinland map. He embraced the simplicity of microscopy in the age of instrumentation and was responsible for training thousands of forensic scientists in that art. He founded the McCrone Research Institute in 1960 to conduct research and training courses.

McCrone obtained his Ph.D. from Cornell in 1941, already highly skilled in microscopy. He went to Chicago and began teaching microscopy. In 1956, he started a consulting company, McCrone Research Associates. Thousands of forensic chemists trekked (and continue to trek) to Chicago to take McCrone training courses covering all aspects of microscopy. McCrone was the first forensic scientist to have such reach and influence. No one person did as much to help resurrect polarized light microscopy as a forensic tool when other chemists were abandoning it for instrumentation.

One of McCrone's earliest and most important forensic work began during the World War II years when he was exploring the use of microchemistry to identify explosives. The work began while he was still at Cornell and culminated with a publication in 1944 entitled *The Microscopic Examination of High Explosives and Boosters*. He developed specialized methods of microchemistry that are still taught through McCrone's courses. He also published 600 plus articles and a collection of microscopic data called *The Particle Atlas* widely used in forensic laboratories.

McCrone became a big fish in the forensic pond soon after his training courses hit their stride in the late 1960s and 1970s. He came to the attention of the general public through his work with the Vinland map and later on the Shroud of Turin. The Vinland map case began quietly in the early 1970s but erupted later in his career. The case centered on the question of authenticity of the Vinland map, which contains what appears to be the outline of the part of the coast of North America. This was intriguing because the map was purported to have been drawn before Columbus sailed. If genuine, it would lend support to the idea (now proven) that others such as the Vikings had been the first Europeans to reach the New World. More importantly, it would make an otherwise unremarkable parchment priceless.

At the behest of Yale University, McCrone and others at the McCrone Research Institute studied the map and concluded that it was a forgery likely dating to the 1920s. They based their opinion on the type of pigment found in the ink, a type not widely available until after 1916. However, this was not to be the last word, and what followed was linked to another famous historical and forensically mysterious artifact—the Shroud of Turin.

Like the map, the Shroud was not another forensic or art case. It was both, wrapped up in passion and emotion on both sides. As a result, the work and his subsequent defense of it were emotionally difficult and draining. The Catholic Church has preserved the Shroud as a relic, and many believe that the ghostly image clearly visible on it is the image of Jesus. The less romantic alternative is that the Shroud is a clever medieval fraud. In 1978, McCrone was allowed to take several tape lift samples from the Shroud, and he analyzed them, publishing the results in a book and several articles. McCrone concluded in his typical definitive style that a diluted type of water-based paint created the image and that the purported bloodstains were paint augmented by red pigments. In other words, the Shroud was a forgery. His results were supported when subsequent carbon-14 dating placed the origin of the Shroud to the early Middle Ages (circa 1325 C.E.). Perhaps because McCrone was so visible and vocal, he drew significant fire from those with honest scientific disagreements as well as those who simply did not want to believe the results. His peers however were impressed and rewarded him with the prestigious National Award in Analytical Chemistry in 2000 for his work on the Shroud. However, the emotionally charged Shroud controversy clearly took its toll on the aging microscopist, and the drain increased with renewed attacks on his Vinland findings.

In the later part of the 1990s, the map case reared its head again, and other analysts presented evidence that indicated that the map might have been authentic. Articles were appearing as late as 2004 on both sides of the issue, but it appears that McCrone's position provides the best explanation. As he neared the end of his life and career, his exhaustion because of the attacks was beginning to show. He wrote:

> Lately ... I find it more difficult to see the humor in these situations. From a scientific point-of-view, these two problems were not difficult to solve. ... No one other than McCrone Associates working on these two fakes used light and electron microscopes. Instead, others looked for traces using good but inadequate and inappropriate trace analysis techniques. These are not intended for problems like VM or the Shroud. I had hoped solving these problems using PLM then using other proper ultramicroanalytical instrumentation for confirmation would help PLM recover its lost position in analytical chemistry. PLM has been cheated out of this recovery and is rapidly sliding into oblivion. This situation is now no longer funny.[3]

While McCrone was correct that polarizing light microscopy was being used less in analytical chemistry as a whole, it remains a critical tool for forensic analysis. Other forms of microscopy never lost their foothold. The first, scanning electron microscopy (SEM) has become the instrument that provides the most analytical and probative bang for the buck. Trace analysts might argue that PLM still holds that title, but none can argue with the ability of SEM instrumentation to magnify and provide unprecedented information about chemical elements present in that sample.

SCANNING ELECTRON MICROSCOPY

The idea behind an SEM is the use of electrons to probe a sample in the same sense photons (light) probes a sample in traditional light microscopy. The ability to see the magnified sample arises from electrons that are scattered off the surface of the sample. The heavier the element, the greater the scattering, and by directing the electrodes into a cathode ray display, a black and white image is created with magnifications of up to a million times. The first inkling that electrons could be employed like light for imaging came in 1926 when it was noted that electrical fields could be harnessed to act like lenses for charged particles in the same sense glass can be used to focus light. Initial work began in Germany shortly thereafter on devices that created electron backscattering with an emphasis on elemental analysis. The concept of an electron-based microscope using this technology took shape in the 1930s, and a prototype was built by Manfred von Ardenne (1907–1997), but it was destroyed in an Allied air raid in 1944.

Wartime improvements in technology proved critical to improving the components needed for electron microscopy to become a viable microscopic tool. The center of research moved to the Cavendish Laboratory in the physics department at the University of Cambridge in the United Kingdom where surplus war equipment was as plentiful as eager graduate students. Among them was C.W. Oatley (1904–1996), considered to be the key person in the development of SEM technology. From the late 1940s through the 1960s, he and others worked to improve the technology and study applications. He also was instrumental in moving the SEM from laboratory to commercial device, although the complexity and expense made for a slow transition relative to techniques such as gas chromatography. It would require the advent of computers, and in particular smaller computers, to make SEM a viable option to forensic labs. Even with this, not all labs can afford one.

The interaction of electrons creates other effects that can be exploited to obtain information about the elemental composition. The most widely used in forensic science is X-ray fluorescence (XRF) in which X-rays are used to eject electrons from atoms. The holes created in the electron structure make the atom unstable, and electrons cascade down to fill the void. In the process, characteristic light is emitted. Detection of this light and its wavelength (or energy) correlates to the element that emitted it.

XRF was conceived shortly after X-rays were discovered, and the credit for building the first X-ray spectrometer goes to English physicist Henry

Moseley (1888–1915). His story is one of the many scientific tragedies of World War I. Moseley was shot through the head and killed at the Battle of Gallipoli in August 1915 when he was only twenty-seven years old. Both sides were aghast at the loss of Moseley, who was praised and admired by the likes of Rutherford and Bohr. At the time of his death, he had published only eight papers, last two of which brought him lasting, albeit posthumous, fame. He did not live to see his data interpreted or used to validate the quantum structure of atoms for which it was essential.

Moseley was personable, warm, and a born experimentalist who appeared to prefer lab to books. He once wrote after lengthy exams and graduation that his mind was "full of cobwebs."[4] In 1912, reports appeared in the literature that X-rays, like visible light, could produce diffraction patterns and lines if passed through the appropriate type of crystal. Moseley focused his attention in this area and constructed a spectrometer with adaptations to X-rays as opposed to light. Working contemporaneously with the Braggs (a father and son team that would give their name to Bragg's law), Moseley used the spectrometer to study X-ray emissions. His contributions to understanding fundamental atomic structure and the accurate determination of atomic number were invaluable. From the forensic point of view, it was his development of X-ray emission as an analytical tool that is of most interest. Moseley volunteered for the war effort, and although he was offered scientific positions on the home front, he requested and obtained the combat assignment he wanted.

MICROSPECTROSCOPY

The union of spectrometry and microscopy has poetic elements for the forensic world. These two instruments constituted all that a forensic lab had available in the late 1800s. A century later, their combination yielded but one of many of the powerful instruments available. Spectrometers characterize composition from the chemical perspective, and coupling them with microscopes has brought chemistry back into the fold of trace evidence analysis.

The idea of combining a microscope with a spectrometer was conceived as soon as instrumentation allowed for it, in the 1940s. The technical limitation is signal intensity. As spectroscopy moved from the visible to the UV and then the IR regions, so did microspectrometry. A UV microscope was reported in the 1940s with IR microscopes soon afterward. These devices were limited to specialized applications, awaiting two technical advances. First was the development of lasers, which can deliver intense light into small spaces. Secondly, in the case of IR microspectrometry, the Fourier transform approach was essential, given its inherent sensitivity advantages. With these two advances in place, the 1990s saw increasing use of microspectrometry, particularly in IR. Forensically, the advantages of micro versus macro instruments were the small sample size and the minimally destructive nature of micro IR.

The first wave of micro IR (late 1980s) was based on a technique called DRIFTS (diffuse reflectance Fourier transform infrared (FTIR)) in which the sample was placed in a small cup underneath the microscope interface. The technique worked well but was quickly supplanted by one that was easier and more versatile. This method, called attenuated total reflectance (ATR) has come to dominate IR instrumentation in forensic labs.

HAIR AND FIBER EVIDENCE

The value of hair evidence was well appreciated by the middle of the 1800s and was mentioned in many medicolegal textbooks such as Tidy's book described earlier in Chapter 8. Microscopy was the one and only method of study of hairs and often essential for locating hairs in stains, on clothing, and associated with other evidence. Hairs are easily differentiated from fibers, and by 1866, authoritative references were available describing these differences. A good reference collection could do the job as well. Presaging some of the controversy to come in hair analysis, Tidy as well as Alfred Swaine Taylor urged that numerous comparisons be done as part of any analysis and that the results not be overinterpreted such as claiming that a hair could unambiguously be assigned to one and only one person.

One of the earliest recorded cases involving hair was recorded in 1851 in which the victim was killed by bludgeoning. The wounds to the head were in the region of the eyebrows, which consisted of stiff white hairs. A hammer was found in a hedge nearby, close to where the suspect worked. The suspect claimed that the hammer was not a murder weapon but rather being used to work with goatskin. Hairs were found on the hammer, and microscope examination revealed them to be consistent with the victim's eyebrow hair. Numerous similar cases involving transfer evidence of hair from victim to suspect or vice versa occurred in the remainder of the nineteenth century.

Fiber analysis was little more than another form of hair comparison until the later part of the 1800s when the first synthetic fibers were introduced. Nylon appeared in 1938. It was not the first manufactured fiber but it was the first synthetic. Cotton and other natural fibers such as wool and silk were common and easily distinguished through microscopic examination and reference sets. Rayon, a reprocessed fiber derived from cellulose, was first made in 1892 as part of the search for silk. Rayon was in fact called artificial silk or other names until 1924. In 1891, the French had made a nitrated version of the fiber reminiscent of guncotton, but the fiber was quickly found undesirable because of its high flammability. Rayon has a shiny appearance and appears smooth relative to cotton and animal fibers and as such did not present too much of a problem for microscopic examinations. Fiber cases were reported in the literature in the 1850s, and in one case in the 1890s, a singed fiber was used as part of a shooting reconstruction to estimate the likely position of a gun when it was fired.

Microscopic comparisons changed little in the twentieth century, although McCrone and others made significant contributions through libraries and atlases. McCrone also described microchemical tests that could supplement observation and simple measurements like hair and fiber diameters. Solubility tests using solvents and acids became more useful as the number of synthetic fibers on the market increased, but a polarizing light microscope was still sufficient to differentiate most synthetic fibers from one another. The most significant advance has been the recent combination of microscopes and spectrometers. Infrared microspectrometry can identify the many synthetic fibers with ease while microspectrometry can quantitate color using visible spectroscopy, removing the issue of color perception subjectivity from color matching and identification.

The ultimate tool for microscopic comparison is the comparison microscope. This instrument consists of two separate but identical microscopes linked to a single eyepiece by an optical bridge. The user places one sample on each stage and can then move and focus the instrument such that images of both are viewed side-by-side. The comparison microscope championed by Dr. Robert Goddard (to be described shortly) became the basis of modern firearms examination, but it never made as many inroads into trace evidence analysis as had been expected. Likely, cost and application factors were responsible.

Goddard's scopes and those used for firearms evidence use reflected light or light supplied from lamps positioned above the sample. This works fine for opaque objects like bullets but not so well for fibers and hairs. Additionally, it is not possible to match fibers or hairs in the same way it is possible to determine that two different bullets were fired from the same weapon. Thus, the utility of a comparison microscope in trace evidence work is not as great as it is in firearms evidence. Trace evidence analysis typically uses transmitted light and often requires polarization. The fledgling FBI laboratory did have a comparison scope in the early 1930s, but it does not appear to have been heavily used. Paul Kirk, the most famous American forensic scientist of the twentieth century, also used a comparison scope for trace work, but it was one tool of many.

FIBER'S FINEST HOUR

The quintessential hair and fiber case of the twentieth century occurred in Atlanta. Starting in 1979, young black males were disappearing in Atlanta, Georgia, and their bodies were later discovered dumped in wooded areas or near highways and streets. Most of the victims died of asphyxiation. The bodies were found with a wealth of fiber evidence that indicated that the victims had all spent the time immediately before and after their death in the same environment. When a local paper published information relating to the fiber findings, the killer began stripping his victims completely or down to their undershorts and dumped some of the bodies into the Chattahoochee River.

This change of pattern led to the arrest of Wayne Williams. During the early morning hours of May 22, 1981, his car passed slowly over a bridge being watched by a surveillance team. A splash was heard as he drove over the bridge. Subsequent searches of his home and vehicles led to the discovery of the probable sources of the fibers and hairs (a family dog) and, most importantly, a greenish carpet fiber with the unusual cross section similar to those found on some of the victims. Additional research eventually led to the probable manufacturer of the carpet and allowed the forensic analysts to estimate that this type of carpet would be found in only one in approximately 8,000 homes in the Atlanta area. When the particular combinations of fibers were considered, the odds of a random match were even smaller. Williams was tried for two of the murders with evidence from ten others introduced, and suspicion remained that Williams killed more. The totality of the fiber transfers and the combination of fibers found on the victims that could be linked to Williams won the conviction.

14

Patterns I: Firearms and Tool Marks

Firearm evidence is a cornucopia. Pulling the trigger drives the firing pin into primer, creating a mark and initiating a tiny explosion. The hot gases pour into the powder, igniting it to create a tidal wave of expanding gases that force the bullet down the barrel as it twists against the grooves machined into it. The bullet emerges, often at supersonic speed, trailing flame, gases, soot, and unburned powder that may travel 18 or more inches before settling if not otherwise impeded. If the bullet strikes home, it deposits most of its energy into the flesh, often creating fatal wounds and damage. Any clothing between flesh and bullet is shredded by its violent passing. A recovered bullet may contain fibers and patterns embossed in the metal. Gunshot residue (GSR) awaits a chemist who looks for barium, antimony, and lead remaining from the primer, copper from the bullet, and, on occasion, organic compound residues of the primer-powder burn event. The firearms analyst studies the marks gouged in metal by other metal created by the firing pin on the primer, the barrel on the bullet, and others depending on the weapon.

By the turn of the twentieth century, it was clear, at least in the United States, that firearms and forensic science would become inevitably linked. The analysis of firearms evidence requires chemistry and microscopy. Bullets and cartridges are studied using microscopy and the analysis of tool marks and patterns. Gunshot residue is analyzed using chemical tests, instruments, and scanning electron microscopes. This combination of pattern and chemical evidence illustrates the areas into which forensic science was moving in the early part of the twentieth century.

COMPARISON MICROSCOPES

Firearms produce two types of evidence. The first is chemical—the residue and products of the propellant burning and moving outward from the gun barrel to deposit on the target as well as the person shooting. The other evidence is *pattern evidence*, the markings created on the bullets and casings when the trigger is pulled: the firing pin makes an impression on the primer; the barrel leaves a pattern of twisting ridges and grooves on the bullet; and the ejector (if present) leaves marks on the cartridge cases. If a bullet or cartridge is recovered from a scene, these markings can be studied microscopically and the results used to classify the evidence. For example, a certain number of grooves and the direction of twist may point to a particular manufacturer or group of possible manufacturers of a weapon, as can a distinctive pattern of firing pin impression. Much more information could be gleaned if a weapon was also recovered and comparison shots could be made.

Thanks to Sam Colt and others, guns came off the assembly line nearly identical to each other and thus created similar markings on bullets and cartridges. If this were the only factor involved, forensic firearm analysis would not be very useful. Fortunately for these analysts, different owners use their guns differently. One owner may shoot regularly and clean religiously, while another might fire infrequently and never clean the weapon. These practices cause changes in the metal and thus in the markings. It is these differences in use and wear that allow for linking of a fired bullet to an individual gun in all but the rarest and most unusual cases.

The use of wear characteristics is now central to all types of pattern evidence (save fingerprints). Analysis of bullets is the earliest instance where the forensic model of successive comparison and classification gelled into a systematic method of analysis. Bullets can be classified by type (lead, copper-jacket, hollow point, and the like), size, and weight using simple tools and visual examination, all of which were available as the nineteenth century turned to the twentieth.

The key evidentiary information sought with bullets was, and remains, linking a recovered bullet to a specific gun.[1] This requires that the analyst examine the markings on the bullet in question and compare them to a test-fired bullet from the weapon in question. Counting the number of lands and grooves assists in classification, but identification (i.e., linking a bullet to a gun) requires microscopic examination of the markings unique to the weapon. Even if two barrels come off the assembly line as nearly identical, subsequent use inevitably creates unique markings. One owner may fire the gun once a year and never clean it, allowing rust to form. Another may use it frequently, causing wear and scratches from cleaning. To find these subtle but telling features, only microscopy will do.

In the early 1900s, the limitation was technical, not conceptual. To compare one bullet to another, say a test-fire to a bullet recovered at autopsy, a

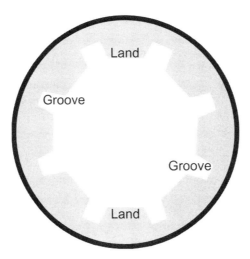

Figure 14.1 The structure of a rifled gun
barrel.

microscope is needed that can compare the two side-by-side under identical optical and lighting conditions. In 1900, this was a tall order. A few
attempts at building comparison microscopes began in the late 1880s and
were based on the optical bridge design. The role of the bridge was to
link the images from two separate microscopes in a single field of view so
that the microscopist could see and manipulate both images at once.
Credit for the first generally goes to Alexander von Inostranzeff, a Russian
mineralogist, who developed a system in 1885. Albert S. Osborn (1858–
1946), a pioneer in the analysis of questioned documents and inks, developed the first forensic comparison scope. In 1908, he announced the
color microscope which he designed and Bausch and Lomb Optical company built. Osborne's was used to examine inks. Other companies followed with different designs in the next few years.

Comparison microscopy entered the forensic mainstream in 1915 when
Emile Chamot began working with it and published reviews and methods
in 1915 and 1922 in *Handbook of Chemical Microscopy*. He also noted that
polarized light could be incorporated in the comparisons, which would
prove valuable when comparing fiber evidence. Chamot published the
first report on the use of comparison microscopy in firearms identification in 1922. By the end of that decade, Dr. Calvin Goddard (1891–1955)
and Philip O. Gravelle (1891–1955) had described the use of comparison
microscopy for the comparison of bullets and cartridge cases. Both men
were employed by the private Bureau of Forensic Ballistics in New York
founded by Charles E. Waite (1865–1926). They were joined by John Fisher
who had worked at the Federal Bureau of Standards but was "currently
a gentlemen of leisure with a substantial income."[2] Waite convinced him

to come to New York to join the group. Gravelle was a photographer and microscopist who had designed the comparison scope, but he left the Bureau in 1925. Waite died soon after, leaving Goddard in charge. He was the one to popularize the use of the comparison microscope in forensic firearms analysis. In the short time between the initial use in 1925 and 1931, several commercial models were available and the technique was being widely used in Europe.

The analysis of firearms evidence was brand new and uniquely forensic. It was based on patterns imparted to bullets and cartridge cases as a result of being fired from a weapon. Rifled barrels were standard by the late 1800s, and different manufacturers adopted different rifling patterns. All consisted of ridges (called lands) and grooves machined into the barrel with a twist. When the bullet passes over these, it is hot and slightly soft. The lands and grooves grasp the bullet and impart spin, greatly increasing accuracy over nonrifled barrels. When the firing pin strikes the primer embedded in the base of the cartridge, a mark results. Automatic weapons can also employ some of the hot gas to eject cartridges, a process that also can generate markings on the casings. Most of the early work focused on the bullets.

The first publication in the United States to recognize the different markings on bullets because of firing from different weapons was a report published in 1900 by Dr. Albert L. Hall in a medical journal. Little came of it, and Hall moved on to other topics. In 1907, investigators working at the U.S. Army arsenal conducted a study and demonstrated the ability to link cartridge cases to specific weapons based on marking patterns. They were also able to classify bullet markings but did not link specific bullets to specific guns. There were a few early studies in Europe as well, but Goddard had little to work with when he began his studies.

CALVIN GODDARD

Goddard was a retired army physician and professed gun enthusiast who had risen to the directorship of the Johns Hopkins Hospital in Baltimore, Maryland. In 1925, he joined the Bureau of Forensic Ballistics, which owed its existence to the famed Stielow case, which had played out a decade earlier. In 1915, a double murder occurred involving a pistol. Charles Stielow was a hired helper on the farm where the crime took place. A recent immigrant, he did not speak English well, nor was he particularly bright, a fact that would be used against him. He was arrested and interrogated, using questionable practices (at best), and eventually confessed. He never signed a written confession and retracted the oral version in court.

The firearms evidence was weak to begin with and made weaker by the testimony of a self-anointed firearms expert, Albert Hamilton. Hamilton's resumé was interesting fiction, including his doctorate degree. He began his career, poetically enough, as a patent medicine salesman and embellished his expertise from there. He testified at the trial that a gun Stielow kept in his shack fired the bullets recovered from the victims. That and the confession were sufficient for a guilty verdict and a death sentence. The court remanded Stielow to death row at Sing Sing prison where he endured a harrowing trip to the electric chair halted by a last-minute reprieve.

A prison guard took up Stielow's cause, convinced that the man was too simple-minded to have committed the crime. Later, word leaked out that two other prisoners might have been involved; one even confessed to it, although he later recanted. Word of the unfolding debacle finally reached the governor, who set up an independent investigation, which set to work in 1917. Charles Waite worked for a New York State prosecutor and quickly became involved in the investigation. Waite initiated another firearms examination, this time using a police detective who had, unlike Hamilton, actually studied firearms. Eventually the bullets were examined microscopically, and it was quickly and unequivocally shown that the patterns of lands and grooves in the bullets could not possibly have been made by Stielow's weapon. Stielow was immediately pardoned and released.

Waite had found his calling. After World War I ended, he began collecting data on firearms from manufacturers such as Colt and Smith & Wesson. He traveled to Europe and did the same. Within a few years, he had an extensive collection. In 1924, he founded the Bureau of Forensic Ballistics and hired Goddard. Waite's premature death ended his role in the evolving story but not his influence. Goddard was a World War I veteran and a physician by training. His passion was firearms, and in 1924, he met Hamilton to discuss becoming an independent consultant. He apparently knew a rat when he smelled one and contacted Waite.

For his part, Goddard barely had time to acclimate to the new job when another famous firearms case came his way. On April 20, 1920, a robbery took place in South Braintree, Massachusetts, in which five men robbed a paymaster, killing him and the guard. A month later, two men, Nicola Sacco and Bartolomero Vanzetti, were charged with the crime. A .38 pistol was recovered from Vanzetti, but it could not be conclusively tied to any of the evidence. From the bodies, .32 ACP (Automatic Colt Pistol) bullets were recovered, and Sacco had a .32 pistol in his possession when arrested. Numerous experts, including Goddard, testified. The trial was controversial from the start, and the convictions instigated a worldwide spate of protest and demonstrations. The two, who were Italian immigrants, became symbols in the age in which anarchy and communist were emerging. Charges of false imprisonment and political overtones were rampant, but despite the upheaval, both were executed. Later review of the forensic work upheld the conclusions.

Because of his growing reputation, Goddard was called to examine evidence of the infamous St. Valentine's Day Massacre in Chicago in 1929. During the coroner's grand jury inquest, he was able to show that two Thompson submachine guns had killed all the murdered men. Some of the jurors in that case later raised money to establish a forensic laboratory at Northwestern University in Evanston, Illinois, called the Scientific Crime Detection Laboratory. It was not the first forensic laboratory formed but one of the most influential. Goddard served as the first director and stayed until 1932. The laboratory moved to Chicago and became the Chicago Police Department laboratory in 1938. Goddard also assisted the FBI in establishing a firearms analysis capability at their new lab, inaugurated in 1932.

In France, Victor Balthazard (1872–1950) played a significant role in firearms analysis. He was the medical examiner for the city of Paris and a contemporary of Edmond Locard. His initial exploration came in 1912 when he studied enlarged photographs of bullets recovered from homicide victims in an attempt to find distinguishing characteristics. He recognized the importance of lighting in the photography and the need to photograph multiple angles. The procedure was too lengthy and difficult for routine use, but it set the precedent for modern microscopic photographing and lighting. Balthazard was the first to publish a report of a lead bullet picking up the imprint of the weave of a fabric that it passed through. Outside of Paris, the Germans were also active in early firearms investigations. Goddard cited a German paper by the team of Metzger, Heess, and Hasslacher as pioneer in work with cartridge casings. He was so impressed that he had the work translated and republished in his journal, *American Journal of Police Science* in 1932.

In the United Kingdom, chemist A. Lucas was studying the chemical analysis of projectiles and gunshot residue (GSR). Lucas was one of the first chemists to call himself forensic. His official position was the Director of the Government Analytical Laboratory and Assay Office in Cairo, Egypt. In his 1921 book entitled *Forensic Chemistry*, Lucas described in detail methods of dissolving and testing bullets for tin and antimony using digestion, selective precipitation, and titration. He mentioned enlarged photographs of bullets and cartridges as useful and noted that it was often possible to determine if a cartridge was fired from a revolver or automatic based on marking on spent cartridges. In the second edition of the book (1931) he included a definition of forensic chemistry:

"Forensic Chemistry is often confused with Forensic Medicine; thus one writer states[3] that one of the most valuable functions of the Medical Profession is the detection of poison, blood, and other matters by chemical examination," and again, "Chemical analysis is in fact a special branch of medical jurisprudence . . ." This, however, is no [sic] the case and "the detection of poison, blood and other matters by chemical examination" is manifestly purely chemical and in no way medical, though it is convenient that the specialist undertaking such work should possess, as he often does, a medical as well as a chemical qualification so that he may combine the two subjects of Forensic Chemistry and Forensic Medicine.[4]

The statement summarizes the divergence occurring in forensic science in the early twentieth century.

Once microscopy and pattern matching became the standard for firearms analysis, there were few technological advances save photography. Then in the 1990s, databasing and cataloging of firearms data became common practice. The national system, called NIBIN (the National Integrated Ballistics Information Network) is currently administered by the Bureau of Alcohol, Tobacco, Firearms, and Explosives (ATF) and, like the CODIS system for DNA, consists of a network of linked databases that agencies can search. The ATF supplies the equipment (microscope and data system, called an IBIS for Integrated Ballistics Identification System) to participants who then link into the NIBIN network.

GUNSHOT RESIDUE (GSR)

Chemical analysis for the residue produced by firing a weapon relies on the old (color-based presumptive tests) and the new—scanning electron microscopy which was devised in the late 1940s but not generally available to crime labs until relatively recently. The chemical components of gunshot residue are residual unburned powder, chemical residues of nitrates, nitrites, and barium/antimony/lead particles that originate from the primer. The detection of nitrates and nitrites has a bit of a notorious history marked by a tendency to overinterpret results. The most abused was probably the dermal nitrate test (also called the paraffin test) in which the hand of a suspected shooter was dipped in warm wax and the cooled cast carefully peeled away and tested for the presence of nitrates. Theodoro Gonzales of the Mexico City Police Department first described the test in 1933. The color tests used to detect the ions were based on dye-forming reactions using compounds such as diphenylamine or the Griess test (name for the dye chemist introduced previously). The problem and controversy was not the chemistry per se but rather the source of nitrates found. The nitrate ion is a common ingredient in cosmetics, fertilizers, and other consumer products. Finding it on someone's hand is not always damning evidence, although it was sometimes interpreted that way.

The best method to identify material as gunshot residue is by scanning electron microscopy (SEM). Earlier attempts were based on the older elemental analysis techniques of atomic absorption and for a time, neutron activation analysis. The SEM identification is based on the shape of the residue (roughly spherical) and the composition, a combination of barium, antimony, and lead. These materials originate from the primer and the high explosive used, such as lead styphnate, not from the bullet or the powder. When ignited, the primer burns rapidly generating sufficient heat to vaporize the metals present. As these cool and condense, they form roughly spherical, smooth particles. Finding particles with this morphology and chemical composition is now considered definitive for GSR, although not all labs have access to SEM.

In 1959, H.C. Harrison and R. Gilroy proposed the first chemical test to identify the three ingredients. For this test, the hands were swabbed and the collected residues tested with two reagents in succession: first, triphenylmethylarsonium iodide (for antimony) and then, after drying, sodium rhodizonate for lead and barium. This method had the advantage of being accessible to any forensic lab. One technique that was not nearly as accessible was neutron activation analysis (NAA). NAA is a powerful elemental analysis technique that required only a nuclear reactor to perform. Clearly, it presented a bit of a problem. A few cases were tested using NAA in the brief period from the late 1950s to the 1970s, with the first court application coming in 1958 in Canada. NAA was also used in one of the early tests of Napoleon's hair for arsenic (1961) and to test the bullet fragments recovered from the Kennedy assassination. Atomic absorption techniques were also introduced in the 1970s and worked fine for lead but lacked the ability to detect antimony and barium at low levels. A host of other procedures were published in this period, but none fit the needs of routine forensic analysis.

The fundamental problem with these procedures is that there was no way to isolate individual particles and determine if some combination of the three characteristic elements were found in one, as characteristic of GSR. A person could conceivably have lead and antimony on their hands, one element from one source and one from another and neither attributable to having fired a weapon. The Metropolitan Police Laboratory in London was the first to begin large-scale testing and evaluation of SEM for GSR in 1968 with publications appearing in the early 1970s. Later in the decade, the FBI began comparative studies of NAA and SEM, and the initial results were published in 1977. The definitive article in the area by G.M. Wolten and others appeared in 1979 in the *Journal of Forensic Sciences*. Other reports followed in quick succession, establishing the technique as the standard for GSR.

15

Patterns II: Measuring and Mismeasuring Man

All of the forensic disciplines described so far, with the exception of bullet comparison, are derivative. For example, death investigation and toxicology are associated with medicine and derived from chemistry and biology. The first uniquely forensic disciplines are those associated with identification such as fingerprints identification and pattern evidence such as firearms identification. If not for guns and their use in crimes, there would be no need to study firearms identification and bullet markings. If not for crime, there would be no need to identify criminals and no need for criminal identification science. Thus, it is not a coincidence that the emergence of a distinct and recognizable discipline of forensic science is intimately associated with pattern identification.

Fingerprinting and its precursors are derivative in less obvious ways. Even less obvious is their derivation from biology. Aristotle started it with his obsession for classification, the essential element of modern forensic science. He attempted to define a natural classification system that would link all things, living and nonliving, in the natural world. This work laid the foundation for *taxonomy*, the biological science devoted to classification and description of the biological world. The Arab scholars continued the traditions of classification through the Dark Ages. In the West, biology stagnated and strayed little from basic agricultural sciences. Newton's passion with systematic study of natural phenomena spilled over into the biological sciences during the seventeenth century and beyond. Among the most notable classifiers was the Swede Carl von Linne (1735–1758, also known as Linnaeus) who, like Aristotle, modestly claimed to have developed a classification system applicable to all life. Linnaeus' key contribution to taxonomy was to start at the bottom—the species level—and move up. Prior to his work, most taxonomists started at the top (animals vs. plants, for example) and worked their way down to smaller groups. The latter is more common in forensic practice where evidence is usually divided into successively smaller groups. Regardless of where the process starts, biologists were among the first scientists to practice systematic classification in the guise of taxonomy. Today's trace evidence analysts often speak of the taxonomy of fiber evidence, echoing these roots.

Aside from the concept of classification, the forensic importance of this was indirect but critical. The study of taxonomy and classification led ultimately to Darwin's work in evolutionary theory. The process of classification and the keen observation demanded by it led to the early inklings of how species are related and how, in many cases, the differences were subtle. The role of Charles Darwin (1809–1882), greatly simplified, was to enunciate an explanation for the observed differences through evolution and natural selection. He published his famous work, *The Origin of Species by Means of Natural Selection, or the Preservation of Favoured Races in the Struggle for Life*, in 1859. It is no coincidence that interest in fingerprinting traces to this period. Unfortunately, other misguided ideas did as well.

THE ATAVISTIC TYPE

Measuring physical features of human beings was the prelude to classifying those features. In some cases, it was also the prelude to categorizing the human beings bearing those features. Evolutionary theory also gave rise, in the late 1800s, to the concept of the *atavistic criminal personality*. Some Darwinists held that there were some people who had missed the evolutionary train and whose personalities were stuck somewhere back in evolutionary history. These people, given their primitive state, were thought to be naturally predisposed to criminal behavior.

Darwin's writings added to the problem. In his book *The Descent of Man* (1871), he put forward the ideas of what would become social Darwinism, a philosophy that believed natural selection and evolution extended to intelligence and even morality. By this thinking, those failing to subscribe to social norms of behavior were subhuman and worthy of contempt, a mode of thinking that led to all manner of ills and tragedy in the twentieth century. Worse, Darwin held that because criminality was related to evolution, it therefore must also be related to physical appearance and characteristics. A person with heavy or unbalanced facial features, such as big ears, or odd behavior, such as homosexual tendencies, was automatically suspect since these were "ape-like" characteristics.[1]

For the forensic community, such thinking led to attempts to measure and classify people such that atavistic criminals could be easily identified and segregated. In other words, "[b]orn criminals differ so radically from lawful people that scientists can identify them by their physical and mental abnormalities, just as physical anthropologists can identify members of different races by their physical characteristics."[2] These ideas gelled in a thankfully short-lived discipline called *criminal anthropology.*

A vocal champion of criminal anthropology was Cesare Lombroso (1835–1909), an Italian physician. He held a professorship in forensic medicine at the University of Turin and, in 1906, added chair in criminal anthropology to his title. One of the ideas he set out to prove was that animal behavior was innately criminal and, therefore, an atavistic person was by definition innately criminal. Even criminal language and slang was evidence of criminal and animal traits. He said, "They speak like savages, because they are true savages in the midst of our brilliant European civilization."[3]

From the forensic perspective, Lombroso's role in its history was to influence the first scientists working in the field of forensic identification. One of those who held to Lombroso's philosophy was Alphonse Bertillon (1853–1914), who was the first to systematically measure criminals (literally) to identify them. Although Lombroso and others were strongly influenced by Darwin, Darwin himself had no direct forensic connection. He did come from a family of naturalists, including his cousin, Sir Francis Galton (1822–1911), who did have a significant role in the history of forensic science.

Galton's interest in fingerprints was initially linked to his work as a naturalist. He collected print patterns from humans as well as primates and this work led to his observation that these biological patterns appeared to be unique to each individual rather than common to species or related individuals. However, Galton was a relative latecomer to fingerprints, and fingerprinting was a latecomer to the broader field of forensic identification which began much more humbly.

CRIMINAL IDENTIFICATION

Criminal identification (more broadly, forensic identification) is an art and science that hovers between police work and forensic science. Whether its practitioners are scientists or technicians is a debate that has been going on for as long as the two have coexisted. One of the first to propose a systematic approach to criminal identification was the Frenchman Alphonse Bertillon who designed, used, modified, and defended a system called anthropometry (Bertillonage). Bertillonage was based on a system of bodily measurements stored on file cards. Mainly on the strength and reputation of Bertillon and his steadfast (some would say stubborn) defense, the system insured its dominance, even over fingerprinting, until after his death.

Bertillon started with the assumption that after the age of twenty, skeletal measurements are essentially constant and thus could be used to unambiguously identify a person. He estimated that the combination of measurements he used would be unique down to about one person in every 300 million. He recorded the body measurements on a card called a *portrait parle,* which included a photo, physical descriptors, such as eye color, and eleven measurements, such as:

- left arm length, elbow to tip of the middle finger;
- width of the outstretched arms;
- sitting and standing heights;
- length of right ear;
- length of the left foot;
- length of the left middle and little finger; and
- length, width, and diameter of the skull.

Bertillon began to develop the system in 1879 in Paris. At the time, he was an assistant working in the Paris criminal identification bureau. The cutting edge of criminal identification technology in the late 1800s consisted of lineups and memorization or primitive photography. Photography had been quickly adapted to police use, and by 1867, it was being used to document some crime scenes. However, it was a cumbersome process, and when applied to criminal identification, the disadvantages were painfully obvious. It was simple to change one's appearance or wear a convincing disguise that easily fooled anyone viewing a picture of it. Bertillon saw the limitations first hand and was able to obtain permission to work on his idea of measurements. The idea of measuring and anthropometry was not new, but its application to criminal identification was. It took years and some pressure, but eventually Bertillon got his chance and the police permitted a ninety-day trial run, which proved a success. The system was officially implemented in 1883.

The greatest drawbacks to Bertillonage were measurement errors and inconsistencies and the time required to gather the measurements. Regardless of the cumbersome nature, the system quickly spread around the world, including the United States. The system was widely accepted and its brief heyday lasted from around 1890 to 1920. Bertillon worked in the period when fingerprinting was the rising star of forensic identification. He resisted its use, although he did add space to his data cards for the inclusion of fingerprint data from the right hand of the individual being cataloged.

Ironically, despite his reluctance to accept fingerprinting, Bertillon was the first forensic scientist in Europe to use it to solve a case. In October 1902, he used fingerprints left at a crime scene to identify the murderer, a convicted swindler whose prints had been taken and cataloged on his Bertillon card. The man later turned himself in and confessed.

Bertillon's continued lack of enthusiasm for fingerprints worked against him in a later, more famous case. When the Mona Lisa painting was stolen in 1911 from the Louvre Museum in Paris, Bertillon was unable to identify the suspect even though he left prints on the glass covering the painting. Unfortunately for Bertillon, these prints were from the left hand and his cards stored prints only from the right, so even an exhaustive search of his data cards was in vain.

What was to prove the fatal blow to the Bertillon system had come in 1903, where two men in Leavenworth Penitentiary were found to have nearly identical Bertillon measurements but different fingerprints. Will West, an African American, arrived at the prison, where staff thought they recognized him. A review of Bertillon cards found another inmate with identical Bertillon measurements named William West. Although the men claimed to have been unrelated, subsequent research indicates that they might well have been estranged twin brothers. Regardless, while their measurements were identical, their fingerprints were not. This undeniable fact eventually convinced most agencies to switch to fingerprints. By 1920, Bertillon was gone and the system he championed left with him.

Bertillon is usually remembered for his ultimately failed identification system, but that sells his contribution to forensic science short. He was instrumental in directing the evolution of what amounted to specialization of photographic studios into identification bureaus, focusing on his system of body measurements. Although not a crime laboratory in the modern sense, his identification bureau led to further improvements and expansion into other areas of crime science and criminalistics. He also advanced work in the fields of questioned documents and crime scene photography.

FINGERPRINTING

As a mark of individuality, fingerprints have a long history. Ancient cultures such as the Babylonian and the Chinese cultures used them as a signature, although it is not known if the ancients recognized that fingerprints were unique to each individual. Modern interest in fingerprints as an aid to law enforcement (also called *dactyloscopy*) traces back to the middle of the nineteenth century. In 1858, the chief administrative officer of the East India Company, Sir William Herschel, faced problems of impersonations among native workers. To combat this, he adopted the ancient traditions and began to use handprints as a form of identifier on documents. Shortly he moved to using only the fingerprints from the last joint to the tip. By 1877, he was using the same procedure to identify prisoners.

In 1880, Scottish physician Henry Faulds published an article in *Nature*, a respected scientific journal, concerning the identification of criminals based on the uniqueness of fingerprints. Herschel sent a reply, pointing out his success with the practice. This led to further advances in the new field, and in 1892, Sir Francis Galton (previously introduced) published a book entitled *Finger Prints*. In 1894, Scotland Yard adopted fingerprints to go along with the Bertillon system of body measurements (anthropometry) used at the time for criminal identification. Across the Atlantic, Juan Vucetich (1858–1925), an Argentinean police official, was maintaining a large catalog of fingerprints. In 1892, the first case in which a fingerprint was used to solve a crime was recorded. A mother had murdered her two children and blamed a neighbor, but finding her bloody fingerprints on a doorpost was enough to elicit her confession. The children had apparently presented a barrier to her marrying her lover. Vucetich would later develop a fingerprint classification system that is still used in much of South America. Through his efforts, Argentina was the first country to adopt fingerprints as a means of identification.

The new century saw increasing interest in and acceptance of fingerprints in law enforcement. In 1900, Sir Edward Richard Henry of the Metropolitan Police Force (London) published *Classification and Use of Fingerprints* based on the ideas put forth by Galton eight years earlier. The work formalized these ideas into a system of fingerprint classification that has come to be known as the Henry system, variations and extensions of which are used in the United States, Europe, and elsewhere. By 1902, the United States had begun to adopt fingerprinting for identification with the New York Civil Service, followed in 1903 by adoption at Sing Sing prison. The military soon followed.

The William West case in 1903 sent fingerprinting into a rapid ascendancy. By 1915, the first professional society in the area of fingerprinting, the International Association of Identification (IAI) was formed. In 1923, the International Association of Chiefs of Police established the National Bureau of Criminal Identification (NBCEI) at Leavenworth. The next year, the Identification Division was established at the Bureau of Investigation, the precursor of the FBI, and they merged in the NBCEI collection with theirs to create a national centralized repository for fingerprint information. This collection, now housed within the FBI, is the largest in the world. In the late 1960s, the FBI began research into the use of digital and computer technologies to assist in fingerprint classification and identification, with the first operable reader available in 1972. This technology continued (and continues) to evolve to the current system of automated fingerprint identification (IAFIS, Integrated Automated Fingerprint Identification System).

ECHOES OF THE FUTURE

Fingerprinting and, to a lesser extent, the sciences of personal identification, represent the greatest accomplishments, the greatest failures, and the greatest dangers associated with forensic science. As will be described in a later chapter, fingerprinting is not the panacea it appeared to be in the middle of the twentieth century. Its shortcomings became known only with advances in other areas of forensic biology and DNA typing. DNA typing became possible only recently and required biologists and chemists to plow through other methods of identifying and typing the substance most associated with forensic science—blood.

Blood: Forensic Biology Arrives

Forensic biology emerged from forensic chemistry much as forensic chemistry emerged from forensic medicine. The focus of forensic biology is the identification and classification of blood and body fluids. The discovery of blood group systems allowed for typing, and DNA methods allowed for linking a specific person to a specific biological sample, within the bounds of a set uncertainty. Before any of this could even be attempted, some basic questions about biological evidence had to be answered. In the forensic tradition, any potential biological evidence has to be classified using a series of comparative tests. The first test answers the most fundamental of these questions.

IS IT BLOOD?

Blood is emblematic of forensic science. It is one of a group of materials referred to as *body fluids*, a collection that includes saliva, semen, vaginal fluid, sweat, urine, and tears—essentially any liquid that can be excreted or extracted from a body. Of these, forensic interest focuses on those that carry or can carry the most information about the person who excreted it. Such information is carried by cellular and genetic materials; you are what you excrete. The initial step is to identify the body fluid as blood, saliva, or something else. This story gets going in the late 1800s.

The first question was identification of a substance as blood. The problem is more complex than might be at first imagined. Fresh blood is unmistakable, but dried, weathered, aged, and decomposed blood may look nothing like the instantly recognizable coppery crimson substance that

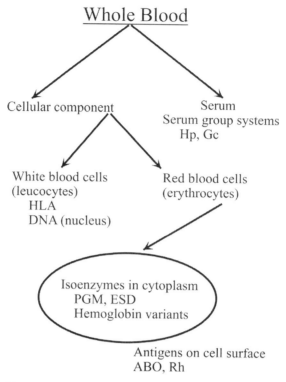

Figure 16.1 The components in blood that can be and have been analyzed and typed using techniques of forensic biology.

flows from a fresh wound. Once a substance or stain is identified as blood, the next question that arises is from whom it came, a human or an animal. Human blood constitutes one of the most complex sample types faced by forensic scientists. It is an aqueous system in that the primary constituent is water, but add to that a mixture of salts (electrolytes), fats, proteins, and cellular components, and the difficulty of working with it becomes clear. Screening or presumptive tests for blood target hemoglobin because it is present in high concentrations, is relatively stable, and occurs only in blood.

"I have found a reagent that precipitates haemoglobin and by nothing else," proclaimed Sherlock Holmes in *A Study in Scarlet* (1887). Sir Arthur Conan Doyle's writings came at a time when people were searching in earnest for such a test. There are hints that work on bloodstain identification was proceeding at the French Royal Academy of Medicine as early as 1828. Soon after (in 1853), Ludwig Teichmann (1823–1895) described a test that produced distinctive microcrystals in the presence of blood. The test was used into the later part of the twentieth century. The first color change test came in 1862 when Izaak van Deen (1804–1869) described the guaiacum test, also known as the van Deen or Antozone test. That was the extent of the repertoire when Doyle penned *A Study in Scarlet*. It is not that hemoglobin is such a difficult material to target; rather it is the difficulty in finding a reagent that reacts with it alone, something that is yet to be accomplished.

The earliest test known for blood was called the Schonbein test for the German chemist who described in 1863. This is the same chemist who discovered how to make guncotton. He had noted that when hydrogen peroxide (H_2O_2) comes in contact with hemoglobin, it reacts violently as it decomposes into oxygen and hydrogen gases (O_2 and H_2). The activity is classified as *peroxidase activity*, for the enzyme action that catalyzes the reaction and causes it to occur so quickly. Many substances contain peroxidases, so this test, while extremely sensitive, was not specific to blood.

The chemical basis of all of the presumptive tests for blood commonly used since the 1800s is a color-change reaction catalyzed by the iron-hemoglobin complex. The reaction in question involves a peroxide such as hydrogen peroxide and a substrate that is oxidized in its presence. The role of the iron-hemoglobin complex is to catalyze the reaction so that it occurs quickly. The guaiacum test was the first such reported and resulted in the substrate (guaiacum) turning blue in the presence of hemoglobin. The late 1800s and early 1900s saw the introduction of many of these tests, once the underlying principle was understood. Alder and Alder introduced one of the best substrates, benzidine (p-diaminodiphenyl), in 1904. Benzidine was found to be a human carcinogen in the 1970s, and its use was phased out. Other tests introduced in this period were the Kastle-Meyer phenolphthalein test (1901), and leucomalachite green (by the Adlers, 1904). Other tests appearing in this century involved o-tolidine (which also proved carcinogenic) and, as a replacement for benzidine and o-tolidine, tetramethylbenzidine.

One addition was particularly noteworthy, that of luminol (3-aminophthalhydrazine). This compound was recognized as a good substrate for peroxidase-like reactions in the 1930s, but it was not commonly used for blood testing until later in the century. The chemical concept is the same as for the other tests, except that instead of a color change reaction, a chemiluminescent reaction occurs, resulting in the emission of light. The reaction is quite sensitive, particularly for trace amounts of blood and blood that has been cleaned up as far as the eye can see. The disadvantage is that the area has to be dark to see the emitted light. Luminol has the added advantage of not interfering with subsequent blood analysis. By the turn of the twenty-first century, toxicity concerns have all but eliminated benzidine and o-tolidine from the repertoire, leaving phenolphthalein and luminol as the workhorses of presumptive testing for blood.

There was a period of about eighty years from the late 1800s to the mid 1900s when microchemical methods were used for confirming the presence of hemoglobin. As mentioned above, Teichmann introduced a crystal test in the 1850s in which hemoglobin forms a characteristic crystal in the presence of acetic acid and a halogen ion such as chloride. The crystals, called hemin (ferriprotoporphyrin), are brownish parallelograms. Takayama introduced a second crystal test in Japan in 1912 in which hemochromogen crystals (pyridineferroprotoporphyrin) are formed by hemoglobin in the presence of the organic solvent pyridine and glucose and sodium hydroxide. The crystals are feathery with multiple arms extending from a central point. Others were described, but these two were the most commonly used. The Takayama test proved more robust and sensitive, and variations of crystal tests are still used in some laboratories.

From the outset, the value of presumptive and crystal tests was debated and the problems of false positives and false negatives recognized. Hemoglobin is not the only material with peroxidase activity. Several vegetable-based materials can also catalyze color-change reactions. Both the color- and crystal-based tests work with any hemoglobin, not just that found in human blood. As Sherlock Holmes noted, determination of the species of origin of blood is the next logical step, although a simple color test that can do both still eludes forensic biologists.

IS IT HUMAN?

In 1891, German immunologist Paul Uhlenhuth (1870–1957) began research that would lead to species tests for blood evidence. He noted that serum isolated from the blood of an animal caused an immunological reaction when injected into rabbits. The work demonstrated that the serum of one species of animal contained some unknown component that reacted with the serum of other species. These reactions presaged development in immunology—or immune reactions. For the next century, immunological reactions would form the core of the emerging field of forensic serology. For purposes here, immunology will be considered at its most basic level, that of the reactions of antigens with antibodies.

By 1901, Uhlenhuth had progressed to the stage of understanding the concept of antiserum. When the rabbit was injected with human serum, the rabbit's immune system responded by producing antibodies to the components in the human serum recognized as foreign. If the rabbit survived the introduction of human serum, then its serum contained a complex of antibodies collectively labeled as "antihuman serum." Uhlenhuth had also realized that the strength of antiserum varied widely. One rabbit might react strongly, another less strongly, leading to less reactivity. Uhlenhuth noted this problem in 1901 and cautioned that in forensic casework, antiserum should be pretested to determine how strongly it would react. Like Orfila sixty years earlier, Uhlenhuth understood that forensic science and quality assurance had to go hand in hand.

Once antisera were available, application to casework was straightforward. If the analyst managed to tentatively identify substance as blood using a presumptive test, the next step was to classify that blood as human or not. The likely alternatives are domestic animals such as cow (bovine), cat, dog, horse, and other assorted domesticated or farm animals. If relatively fresh, a bloodstain should contain active antigenic material characteristic of its species of origin. When an extract of the stain was mixed with the proper antiserum, an immunological reaction (or lack of one) would tell what species the blood could or could not have come from. These reactions were visualized as *precipitin reactions*, in which antigens and antibodies combine to form a cloudy solid or precipitate. Besides Uhlenhuth, Wasserman and Schuetze (working independently but nearly simultaneously) had developed techniques for visualizing these reactions around 1901.

The first two methods were simple and relied on diffusion of the antigens and antibodies toward one another in a small test tube. The ring test, if positive, would show a milky ring at the junction of two layers (a sample extract and an antiserum). In practice, several tubes using several antisera were needed. If the stain were human and only human blood, a white ring would appear in the tube with antihuman serum but not in the tubes with anti-dog, anti-cat, or anti-bovine.

Later in the century, two other variants of the procedure were introduced. In 1949, Orjan Ouchterlony (1914–2004) introduced a method using a shallow petri dish containing a thin filling of agarose gel. A small hole is punched in the center of the gel and several other holes encircling the original. Extract of the sample is placed in the center well and the different antisera in the surrounding holes. The solutions diffuse radially outward and encounter each other in the region between the outer ring and the center well. A white arc in the gel is a positive reaction. The test can also be done in miniature on a glass slide. The test is convenient but requires time for the diffusion to occur. The second variant, introduced by Brian Culliford in 1967, used the same concept but used electrophoresis and electrical fields to speed up the process. He called the protocol *crossed-over electrophoresis*.

BLOOD TYPES AND BLOOD GROUPS

The early work of Uhlenhuth and others in forensic applications of immunology led to rapid and dramatic developments in immunology. The most famous of these came in 1901 when Karl Landsteiner (1868–1943) discovered the first blood types (A, B, and O). A fourth type, AB, was identified in 1902. The linkage to genetics and the idea that a person's blood group was inherited was proposed in 1908. By the mid 1920s,

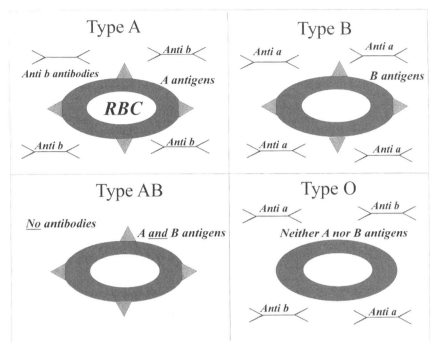

Figure 16.2 The composition of antigens and antibodies in the ABO blood group systems.

immunologists thought that each parent contributed one codominant allele (A, B, or O) to their child.

That blood from different people had different characteristics had been known for some time. The knowledge came from the observation that blood transfusions had a poor success rate. Physicians and scientists were puzzled to note that sometimes transfusions worked perfectly, while in other cases, a transfusion caused a fatal reaction to occur in the recipient. This had been Landsteiner's motivation, but the forensic applications were immediate and obvious. After some initial confusion over naming and designation, the ABO system became the first blood group antigen-antibody system. Because a person's ABO blood type is inherited and thus genetically determined, ABO was the first genetic marker system. Put another way, your blood type is a marker that directly reflects your genetic code, even though the specifics of that underlying code were unknown in Landsteiner's time. Because the ABO gene from the parent has many possible types (A, B, or O), the system is polymorphic (literally, having many forms).

Max Richter is credited with the first attempts to apply the ABO genetic marker system to criminal cases in 1902. However, the primitive typing techniques then available were designed for liquid blood, which contained whole red blood cells. Stains, in which the cells were broken (lysed), were not typable using these procedures. Another decade would pass before reliable procedures for typing stains appeared. For his part, Landsteiner won a Nobel Prize in 1930. He was just getting started in making contributions to serology and immunology.

As with most extensions of new technologies to forensic casework, it is the nature of the samples that slows the pace of application. Exploitation of blood groups provides a perfect example. Typing freshly drawn blood is a simple matter; the ABO antigens are located on the surface of red blood cells. A person who gets the gene encoding for A from both parents has a genotype AA and type A blood. If one parent contributes an A gene and one a B gene, the child will have type AB blood. Type O blood means that a person has no antigens on the surface of his or her red blood cells.

To type a fresh liquid blood, the analyst first separates it by centrifuge such that the cells are isolated from the serum portion. Next, the cells are divided into two portions. To one, a serum containing anti-A antibodies is added and to the other, a serum containing anti-B antibodies. A person whose blood is type A has A antigens on the surface of his or her red blood cells. These antigens will react with anti-A antibodies but not with anti-B antibodies. The reaction, clumping or *agglutination* of cells, is easily visible under low magnification. Agglutination is what caused the transfusion deaths Landsteiner sought to understand and stop.

Unlike drugs or fibers, biological evidence such as blood begins to degrade the moment it is spilled. As blood dries, the cells burst (lyse) and disperse the antigens throughout the stain. The simple test no longer works because there are no longer whole red blood cells that can be made to clump. Leon Lattes (1887–1954) of the Institute of Forensic Medicine in Turin, Italy, offered a solution. Trained in medicine and physiology, Lattes left Italy prior to the Second World War and spent a significant part of his career in Argentina, working as a serologist in Buenos Aires. He returned to Italy in 1946 and worked in Pavia until his death. His interest in forensic science complimented an interest in criminology and a discipline referred to as criminal anthropology. He believed that crime had an anthropological (i.e., racial) component, but it would be unfair to color his contributions with too broad a stroke. He considered many criminals as "an unhappy brother, needing comprehension and charity and help for redemption, and, in any case, worthy of being treated, for a necessary social defense, with humanity devoid of vengeance."[1] Lattes' compassion stands in stark contrast to that of criminal anthropology and its followers.

One of Lattes' first cases was a domestic dispute in which a wife accused her husband of cheating. The conflict raged for weeks until the husband finally sought help in clearing his name. As evidence, Lattes had only two small reddish stains on the lower portion of the man's shirt. The wife suspected another woman was the source and implied that the blood was menstrual blood. A mutual female friend had been in the house recently and admitted to having her period at the time, but she steadfastly denied any improper behavior. The man insisted he was faithful to his wife and offered two other possibilities—his own blood spilled by accident or animal blood from a butcher shop. Lattes agreed to try and sort out the situation, knowing from Max Ritcher's work that only fresh stains were likely to be typable.

Lattes obtained blood from the man and the two women. He typed both, determining that the man and female friend were type A, and the wife was type O. Lattes tried a new approach to type the stains and was able to exclude the wife as a source. The stains did not show any cellular material that might have indicated menstrual blood, clearing the female friend, but opening the hapless husband to accusations of other unknown lovers. Since Lattes could not exclude the man as a source of the stains, he attempted to offer an alternative hypothesis that would explain how the man might have stained his own shirt. Lattes calmed the situation by finding that the man had prostate trouble that frequently resulted in blood in the urine. In one of the more whimsical scientific papers published, Lattes reported that his results "restored peace to the family."[2] For how long, he did not say.

This case convinced Lattes that a viable method to type stains was critical and he continued working on the problem. In the period, 1915–1916, he managed the feat. Lattes designed his *Lattes Crust test* to detect the antibodies in the stain indirectly rather than directly on the surface of the cell. He demonstrated the forensic value of the test in a case where he was able to clear an accused murderer based on an analysis of bloodstains on the suspect's coat. Although a giant step forward, the test still required relatively fresh and large stains.

Lattes continued to work on his technique, with an interruption during the First World War in which he served. In 1923, he published a textbook on blood typing and was a full professor of forensic medicine at the University of Turin. He had refined his technique so that it could be performed on relatively small stains using a glass slide, and he periodically worked on criminal cases and testified. Word of his successes spread to Germany, then a leading center of forensic science, helping to spread the technique of ABO typing using the Lattes method.

Crucial to forensic work was another finding in 1925 by Japanese scientist Yamakami and, shortly thereafter, Landsteiner. The discovery was of genetically controlled secretion of blood group antigens in body fluids other than blood. Approximately 75 percent of the population is secretors, meaning that they secrete ABO and other genetic marker system materials into their body fluids, notably semen, saliva, and vaginal fluid. In 1928, Japanese forensic serologists were able to determine blood type from semen evidence in a rape and murder case. This discovery of secretor status extended the reach of typing systems to body fluids. It also complicated interpretation where mixed fluids occurred, such as in rape.

Using methods and knowledge provided by Landsteiner and others, immunology expanded and advanced rapidly. By the 1970s, nearly 400 blood group antigen-antibody systems had been identified. However, only a few are typable in stains, and for most cases, ABO type classification was by far the easiest and most frequently used.

In Austria, a young man named Franz Joseph Holzer (1903–1974) dove into research on improving Lattes' typing method. At the time, Holzer was at the Institute of Forensic Medicine at the University of Innsbruck and was familiar with the crust test as well as its limitations. In the late 1920s, Holzer worked to develop an alternative that would allow typing on smaller and older stains. His idea was not new, but he was apparently the first to get it to work on stains. The idea was straightforward: If a bloodstain came from a person with type A blood, then the blood contained A antigens on the surface of the red blood cells and anti-B antibodies in the serum. Even though the cells lyse when the stain dries, the A antigen remains in the stain. What, Holzer wondered, would happen if the stain were extracted and mixed with two solutions, one containing anti-A antibodies and one containing anti-B?

If A antibodies were present, the strength of the anti-A antiserum would decrease, since some of those antibodies would react with the A antigens. The strength of the anti-B antiserum would be unchanged since there are no B antigens present. The change in strength could be determined by testing the antisera before exposing them to the stain extract and then again after exposure. The technique became known as the Holzer absorption test, later absorption-inhibition for the inhibition of the activity of the antisera. Holzer took the idea further by using not two antisera but one: serum from a person with type O blood. Such blood contains both anti-A and anti-B antibodies. He made his work public in 1929 at a German forensic medicine conference. It caught on immediately.

In 1933 and 1934, Holzer left Europe to venture to the United States at the invitation of Landsteiner. Landsteiner, now a Nobel laureate, was working at the Rockefeller Institute. Holzer participated in a research with Landsteiner and Levine that led to elucidation of subtypes of the A blood group (eventually called A_1 and A_2) and of another blood group system, MN, and a related P factor. Holzer eventually was able to type the MN system in some stains, but it would never be widely used in forensic serology. Other breakthroughs of that decade were the introduction of luminol in 1937 and initial attempts to type other body fluids. In 1939, an important case in England involving Bernard Spilsbury and serologist Roche Lynch revolved around saliva evidence from a cigarette.

The case involved a vicious rape and murder of an eleven-year-old girl named Pamela Coventry. A few hours after disappearing on the way to school, her body was found in bushes. She was nearly naked, with her legs tightly bound to her chest with wire. In the space between her legs and chest, a cigarette was found. Spilsbury collected it and gave it to Lynch. The serologist knew of secretor status and was aware of attempts to type body fluids. Since the techniques were relatively new, Lynch spent a great deal of time studying and practicing before turning his attention to the evidence.

Meanwhile, solid detective work had narrowed the suspect list to one strong suspect. Unable to compel the man to give a blood sample, detectives obtained a search warrant for the suspect's house, hoping to (literally) find dirty laundry that would include used handkerchiefs. Lynch felt certain he could type the hankies using the techniques he had practiced and mastered for the cigarette. During the search, investigators found that and more, including a bloodstained raincoat, wire, and tape that were consistent with those used to bind the victim. Unfortunately, Lynch was unable to type the saliva on the cigarette since, as it turned out, the suspect was a nonsecretor. The suspect was eventually freed; however, an important forensic precedent had been set.

Karl Landsteiner returns to the picture in 1940 with the discovery of the Rh blood group system. Despite many efforts, Rh typing never played a significant role in forensic work. The same can be said of many other blood groups discovered around the same time. These genetic marker systems, with names like Lewis, Kidd, and Duffy, proved difficult to impossible to type in bloodstains. Subtypes of ABO and Rh were also identified but were rarely applied to forensic casework. All found extensive applications in paternity testing since liquid blood was available for such purposes.

In the United States, the person generally credited with pushing ABO typing into the realm of routine forensic use was Dr. Alexander Weiner, who worked in the New York City medical examiner's office under Dr. Thomas Gonzales. Appointed to his position, Weiner had worked with Landsteiner, as had so many of the pioneering forensic serologists. Weiner was also the first to use body fluids other than blood for typing and, more importantly, to have the results lead to a confession and conviction. In March of 1943, a woman was murdered in New York City. The key evidence was sweat-stained garments that Weiner was able to type as B, the same as the suspect. Faced with this evidence and other information, the man confessed.

The period after World War II but before the advent of DNA typing saw incremental improvements in typing procedures. In 1960, Stuart Kind (1925–2003), a noted forensic scientist in the United Kingdom, published a paper on absorption inhibition and a new variant, the absorption-elution procedure, in the journal *Nature*. Kind qualifies as one of the first modern forensic scientists who lived through the War years and who was instrumental in bringing new technologies into forensic science. His generation was probably the last of the generalists, forensic practitioners, who could move from discipline to discipline as the case demanded. A child of the Great Depression, Kind left school at an early age, a decision he later regretted. His first encounter with death came at age sixteen when he responded to heavy German bombing attacks. At age eighteen, he joined the RAF and trained as a navigator. One of his brothers, also in the RAF, bailed out into the English Channel one night in 1943. His body was never found.

After the War, Kind returned to Nottingham and studied chemistry and biology, and in 1952, he accepted a temporary position with the forensic science service that lasted the rest of his life. Seven years later, he founded the Forensic Science Society (FSS), which became one of the most influential professional forensic societies in the world. He moved among the FSS labs, and in 1978, he assumed the post of director of the Home Office Research Establishment in Aldermaston, a facility renowned for forensic research. One of his most famous cases was that of the Yorkshire Ripper, captured in 1980. The Ripper was a serial killer who murdered thirteen women in Northern England, starting in the 1970s. Using skills he had acquired as a navigator, Kind plotted the location and time of all the killings and postulated where the murderer probably lived based on the results. He turned out to be right, and it was the first known use of geographical profiling.

In forensic biology, Kind is remembered for his methods of typing stains. The techniques were adopted by London's Metropolitan Police Laboratory (MPL) which became an international hub of forensic serology. One more significant advance in that field was forthcoming—the typing of serum proteins and isoenzymes using electrophoresis. These techniques would also emanate from MPL, but it would be the last forensic breakthrough before the DNA juggernaut eclipsed serology. Typing these proteins required a technique called electrophoresis, which went on to become the core instrumental component of DNA typing to follow.

ELECTROPHORESIS

Methods of separation using gel became the basis for a host of techniques used in biochemistry and forensic chemistry and biology. Gels are hydrated porous structures usually made of a cellulose starch framework. Because the molecules have to wend their way through the pores, gels slow the progress of large molecules but do not stop them completely. As such, gels are the ideal media for separating large molecules. Early work in what would eventually be called gel electrophoresis began, as did work in the related separation techniques of chromatography, in the late 1800s using "U-shaped" tubes and jelly-like packing. Landsteiner had done experiments in U tubes with blood serum and noted that when an electrical field was applied, moving boundaries were seen in the gel. By the late 1800s, scientists knew that hemoglobin moved in an electrical field.

Proteins such as those in hemoglobin are enticed to move using electrical fields, and for this, the watery gel was essential. Proteins are chains of amino acids, and as acids, individual acidic sites can exist as charged or neutral entities ($HA \leftarrow \rightarrow H^+ + A^-$). When the pH is acidic, the neutral form is favored, and when the pH is basic, the ionic (charged) form is favored. An analogous situation applies to the amino sites. Proteins have both acidic and basic sites (the amino groups), and as a result, the pH of the solution dictates how many sites are charged and how many are neutral. When the protein is charged, it is mobile in an electric field. Because it is charged and free to move, it does so, migrating to the electrode having the opposite charge. The watery gel conducts the charge and provides some resistance to movement, allowing time for proteins to separate based on their relative sizes and charges. The only technical limitation is the heat generated in the process, which tends to dry gels.

Chemists and biologists dabbled in electrophoresis for the next few decades, but little concrete progress occurred until the 1930s. In 1937, Swedish chemist Arne Tiselius (1902–1971) described the first reliable electrophoresis apparatus, a monster instrument nearly 20 feet long and 5 feet high. By comparison, modern DNA electrophoresis requires a tube a few centimeters long, and a diameter of ten human hairs. Regardless of its size, Tiselius' device effectively separated complex protein mixes in a way not previously possible while minimizing the heat problems using a cooling system. The detector employed a special photographic technique that targeted shadows, since the proteins themselves are colorless. The result was a pattern of bands that characterized protein size and charge. The work earned Tiselius the 1948 Nobel Prize in chemistry and sparked a revolution in molecular biology and, by association, forensic serology and forensic biology.

Although it led to many fundamental breakthroughs, the Tiselius instrument was the biological equivalent of a particle accelerator and about as accessible to most researchers. For a time, only the privileged few were able to use it or similar devices. This began to change in the late 1940s, when companies began making more affordable instrumentation, but forensic applications would have to wait another decade. In 1955, Oliver Smithies (1925–) reported on the use of slab gel for electrophoresis. In this approach, a thin slab of gel (a few millimeters thick) is made by pouring the hot gel into a mold and scraping the excess away. When dry, this leaves a thin gel slab, the size and thickness of which depend on the mold used. The approach caught on quickly, and by 1958, the slab technique had been used to separate enzymes. Slabs were much easier to work with than the U tubes, and the entire apparatus fit on a small bench top. The remaining advances were more refinements than revolutions, and forensic applications to serum proteins (described in the next section) followed quickly. The variations of forensic interest were the development of acrylamide gels, which provided better control over pore sizes, and isoelectric focusing (IEF).

An elegant concept underlies IEF. The idea that proteins are always charged and mobile in an electrical field is an oversimplification. Proteins have many sites on their molecular skeleton that can carry a positive or a negative charge. Whether or not a given site is charged depends on the pH of the solution. At a pH called the characteristic isoelectric point, the molecule's charged sites are equally positive and negative. The molecule is no longer charged and thus immobile. Isoelectric focusing exploits this by running the separation in a gel that has a pH gradient. At a given point in the gel, the pH might be 6.3 and a millimeter to the left 6.4, for example. In principle, IEF can produce sharper separation than the slab gel technique. The tradeoff is cost. The powders and gels needed to create a reproducible pH gradient are costly. During the 1970s and 1980s, there was some forensic exploration and use of IEF, but it never competed on a large scale with the slab gel method. Had DNA not appeared when it did, IEF would likely have played a much larger role in forensic biology. Timing is everything.

SERUM PROTEINS AND ISOENZYMES

Once electrophoresis had proven itself as a viable and reliable technique for molecular biology and separation of large molecule, the stage was set for the next significant developments in forensic serology. The flood began in 1950s with identification of additional genetic marker systems, this time found in the blood serum rather than associated with the cells. Once again, the Metropolitan Police Laboratory in London took the lead in bringing these systems to the forensic community.

Collectively called serum proteins, these systems added greatly to the discrimination power provided by ABO typing. These proteins are polymorphic, have inherited types, and are thus, like ABO typing, genetic marker systems. Brian Culliford and Brian Wraxall (1943–), forensic serologists working for the Metropolitan Police Department in Britain in 1967, reported the first system, haptoglobin (Hp). The next system, PGM (phosphoglucomutase) came the following year and is classified as an isoenzyme system. These systems became the best known, probably due to a combination of their resiliency compared to other systems in degraded samples and the ability to type and subtype the samples. Culliford perfected a technique for typing isoenzymes using a thin gel, paving the way for widespread forensic use.

By 1969, the PGM system was being used in forensic cases in the United States on a small scale. In 1971, Culliford wrote a procedure manual describing blood typing procedures under a federal grant. The manual—*The*

Examination and Typing of Bloodstains in the Crime Laboratory—became the standard in the United Kingdom and the United States. This was important in a broader sense because it represented one of the first generally accepted and shared manuals of standard procedures in forensic science. In 1978, Wraxall and Mark Stolorow (1946–) introduced the starch gel procedure that could type more than one isoenzymes system at a time.

The use of ABO typing and starch gel electrophoresis dominated forensic serology from the 1970s into the late 1980s and early 1990s. Although some labs could type as many as fifteen different systems, four were commonly used: PGM (polyglucomutase), AK (adenylate kinase), EAP (enzyme acid phosphatase), and EsD (esterase D). While powerful, the isoenzymes systems were often difficult to type in older stains.

In most labs, serologists typed each system separately, each requiring a new sample, new gel, and additional times. The profusion of methods and media further added to the confusion. In response, the U.S. government commissioned a study that included Wraxall and B. Grunbaum and Robert Shaler[3] from the United States. In 1978, the group issued a report and recommended techniques that could type more than one system with each electrophoretic run. This approach was referred to as a multisystem in which the systems were broken into three groups. Group I included PGM, EsD, and GLO I (glyoxylase I); Group II included ACP and AK and Group II permitted typing of Gc (group-specific component) and Hp (haptoglobin). After a period of review, the methods were well established in most U.S. and U.K. labs. The FBI in the United States and the Home Office in the United Kingdom took the lead in researching IEF applications, adding them to the mix. The confusion led to the Starch Wars, a whimsical name for a period of intense and often bitter debate within the young forensic biology community. The conflict presaged the DNA wars to come.

With the sudden abundance of available methods came the inevitable arguments about which were the best and why. The Starch Wars and related issues, in what would prove to be a preview of what was to come with DNA, bled over into the courtroom with experts favoring one methodology over another, squaring off against each other in admissibility hearings. During the period from 1923 to 1993, the primary rule governing the admissibility of scientific evidence was the *Frye* rule. Under the Frye criteria, courts based their acceptance of a new scientific method or procedure on acceptance by the relevant scientific community.

Unlike the DNA battles to come, here it was easy to define the relevant scientific community as the forensic science community, and the battles played out, for the most part, outside of the public spotlight. Privacy did not make the battles any less vicious or painful for the scientists involved, and many of the wounds were just healing when DNA appeared. The need for common procedures and quality assurance would play out on a much larger scale in just a few years. In the interim, forensic serology enjoyed a brief golden age of its own, from about 1960 to 1986 when DNA would pull the rug out from under it and make the Starch Wars seem as trivial as the cinematic name deceptively suggested.

17

DNA: The Genetic in Genetic Markers

With acceptance and widespread use of isoenzyme systems in forensic serology, the goal of individualization based on a biological fluid stain was closer but still tantalizingly out of reach. Biologists, including forensic biologists, knew that individuality lie in the genes. However, ABO and isoenzyme typing indirectly measured an infinitesimal fraction of possible gene expressions, and not very distinctive ones at that. By the late 1980s, isoenzymes and blood group typing was a mature technology with little ahead except fine-tuning. Any forensically significant advances were contingent on dramatic breakthroughs, and none were on the horizon. There were forays into white cell antigen typing and even talk of typing blood using the constellation of disease-based antibodies present, but none ever made the transition to forensic labs.

If blood group types and isoenzyme systems are all that is available, the indirect snapshot they provide of the underlying DNA will never be sufficient to link a sample to one and only one person. That is not to say the results are useless, but it does mean that the best that can ever be expected is inclusion or exclusion. In the best scenarios in the Starch War days, combining ABO with isoenzyme types could reduce the pool of potential donors of a given stain to about 1 in 10,000 or about 0.01 percent of the population. In the United States, this would correspond to roughly 285,000 people and in a city such as New York City, about 800 people. Nothing to dismiss, but nothing that alone could break a case. As a result, much of the evidence produced from ABO and isoenzyme typing was exclusionary in the sense that the analysis showed that a person could not have been the source of a stain. Linking a specific stain to a specific person

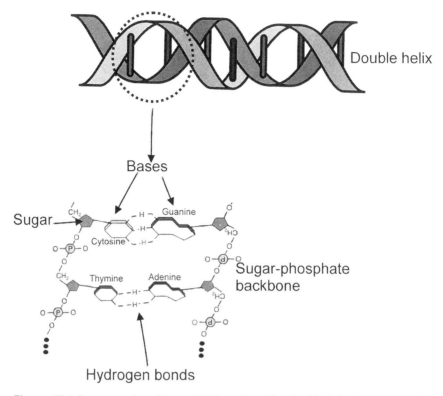

Figure 17.1 Terms used to discuss DNA typing. The double helix is composed of two strands of linked sugar-phosphate groups. The bases are adenine (A), guanine (G), cytosine (C), and thymine (T). A associates with T through hydrogen bonds (shown), while G associates with C.

with a reasonable degree of scientific certainty necessitated another leap in serology, akin to those of Landsteiner. To get there, forensic serology itself would have to cede domination to forensic genetics and DNA.

DNA

By now the story of the discovery of DNA and its self-replicating structure in 1953 are well known. As Landsteiner had, Watson and Crick won a Nobel Prize in 1962 for their work unraveling the structure of DNA, and they, like Landsteiner, could not have foreseen how their work would upend forensic science. Identification of DNA's structure and replication mechanism, along with the realization that DNA carried the genetic code, carried the promise of true individualization. It was only a promise though, given the analytical difficulties the task posed.

First, forensic biologists had to find regions in DNA that differentiate one person from another. The regions had to be variable and have several different types spread throughout the population, and they had to be clearly inherited, independent from any other regions or genes, with decipherable and predictable rules of inheritance. Next, as in the case of electrophoresis, analysts needed reliable procedures and methods to type those regions. Such revolutionary protocols would be nothing like what forensic serologists were doing at the time. Third, labs would need a database of the population. Forensically, it does no good to type a bloodstain as type A without knowing that 45 percent of the population has type A blood. These population frequencies provide the context for meaningful interpretation.

There are advantages to DNA as a forensic tool. Unlike ABO antigens, DNA is found in any cell with nucleus. Red blood cells lack a nucleus, but all other cells have one. Anywhere there is cellular material, there will be DNA. Secretor status is irrelevant since everyone sheds DNA. As medicine was the parent of forensic serology, molecular biology was the parental discipline of forensic DNA analysis. By the 1970s, it was a recognized part of biology, combining aspects of biology, chemistry, biochemistry, and genetics.

Two techniques from molecular biology were adapted to DNA typing. The first, *Southern blotting*, named for its inventor and not the region, provided a simple method for transferring DNA pieces from a gel to a firmer and more robust support. E.M. Southern described the technique in 1975. There is a similar technique named Northern blotting for RNA, christened so for no obvious reason other than fun, demonstrating that molecular biologists have a sense of humor.

The next important step was discovery of special kind of variation in DNA called generically VNTR (variable number of tandem repeats) first reported in 1980 by White and Wynan. In such cases, the variation is the number of times that a sequence of amino acids repeats itself, not variations in the sequence itself. Consider a simplified example: The location of a sequence of bases may contain the sequence of AACCT. A person's mother might have five repeats of that sequence (AACCT- AACCT- AACCT- AACCT- AACCT), while the father might have ten repeats of the same sequence (AACCT- AACCT- AACCT- AACCT- AACCT- AACCT- AACCT- AACCT- AACCT- AACCT). The child in this example would have a type of 5–10 at this location.

Using Southern blotting, White and Wynan confirmed variable number of repeats, established inheritance rules, and demonstrated at least eight different numbers of repeats (eight alleles) existed at the locus they studied. They noted that if a person is homozygous (same number of repeats from mother and father), the result is a single band, while someone who is heterozygous will show two bands, as would be the case in the example above. In their work, detection relied on radioactive labeling of the bands once they had been transferred to a nylon membrane. After the transfer step, they placed the membrane next to an X-ray film to record radioactive decay events. The film was exposed wherever there was labeled DNA, and the result was an X-ray film with a pattern of bands often referred to as a barcode, although the bands were never as neat or clear as a barcode. The fuzzy boundaries of bands emerged as one of the problems associated with early DNA typing methods.

Restriction fragment length polymorphisms (RFLPs) describe the broader group of polymorphisms to which VNTRs belong. Simplified, the RFLP technique relies on a molecular probe that includes the same bases (ATGC) as DNA but assembled in such a pattern as to recognize a specific sequence on DNA. For example, a probe with the sequence AAT will recognize a string of TTA on DNA since the base A compliments T and vice versa. The actual sequences exploited in DNA typing are much longer, but the principle remains the same. When DNA is unzipped in the presence of enzymes that incorporate these probes, the probes align with the recognition sites. The recognition sites define the boundaries of the region of tandem repeats (VNTR). In practice, the repeating sequences used in RFLP are quite long (thousands of base pairs). One distinct advantage of the RFLP techniques was that most of the loci are hypervariable, meaning that there are many variants in the population as compared to a genetic marker system such as ABO and its four variants (A, B, O, and AB).

By the mid 1980s, biologists had described two variants of RFLP, the first occurring at a single locus and the other at multiple loci. At about this same time, forensic serology had more or less settled the Starch Wars, adopted a set of methods and markers, and amassed population databases. Just as serologists were settling into the routine, molecular biologists were poised to throw it into chaos. The missing spark was the right case.

THE WORLD TURNED UPSIDE DOWN

The right person was Dr. Alec Jeffreys (1950–) working at the University of Leicester. The right case was the rape and murder of two young girls nearby. As with so many, he did not consider himself a forensic scientist but rather a molecular biologist working on regions of DNA that were variable from person to person. Although the case (described later) would bring Jeffreys and DNA to the public's attention, his analysis of the evidence was a natural extension and application of work he had been doing since the late 1970s. Jeffreys had come to the University of Leicester in 1977 with a keen interest and skills in molecular biology and a desire to apply those skills to human genetics. He wanted to take the study of genetic markers to the next logical level—detection of inherited and predictable variations in the DNA itself.

Jeffreys then zeroed on regions of the DNA referred to as short tandem repeats or STRs, also called minisatellites. The path to humans and forensic application trod an unlikely path through grey seals and the British Antarctic Survey office located in Cambridge. Jeffreys was working on a related project at the time, seeking the structure of the gene that encodes for the protein myoglobin, which carries oxygen in muscle tissues. Since grey seals produce more myoglobin than humans do, it provided an easier place to begin the hunt. Jeffreys retrieved seal meat from the Survey office, went about finding the seal gene, and then moved on to the human counterpart. In the human gene, he found a repetitive segment.

The serendipitous discovery led to the realization that portions of the repeating section were similar to sections found in other minisatellite regions that had been found, which at that time were very few. This hinted at some underlying similarity shared by some of the minisatellite regions in human DNA. Jeffreys created a molecular probe to search DNA for this characteristic core sequence to ferret out other minisatellite regions encompassing similar cores. To investigate if these varied between people, he applied the probe not to one person's DNA but to that taken from several people. Jeffreys described the results as a *eureka moment*.

Perhaps the naturally modest Jeffreys is prone to understatement. The year was 1984. Jeffreys published the work in the journal *Nature* in 1985 and the paper ("Hypervariable 'minisatellite' regions in human DNA") marked the beginning of the end of forensic serology. Not only was biological evidence changed but because of the legal drama to come, so too did the nature and practice of all forensic disciplines. It is still playing out. As for Jeffreys, he had one major role to play in the forensic arena before returning to his research and being knighted by the Queen.

FORENSIC APPLICATIONS AND LEGAL REACTIONS

The cases that pushed Jeffreys into the spotlight involved the rape and murder of two fifteen-year-old girls who died within miles of Jeffreys' lab at Leicester. The killings were three years apart but similar enough that investigators believed that both died at the hands of the same man. They had a suspect, a young man named George Howard of limited mental capacity, who eventually confessed to accidentally killing one victim. The physical and serological evidence was unconvincing, and they had no link to the other killing.

Investigators asked Jeffreys to test blood from Howard as well as semen found on the clothing of the two victims. Prophetically, the first forensic DNA test exonerated an innocent man and debunked a false confession. Police released Howard in 1986 and the investigation stalled. At the time, the number of human DNA profiles in population databases was zero. Having clear results from the case samples was of little investigative information without such data. Thus, Jeffreys had data without context, and investigators had nothing.

The solution, collection of samples from all men in the area, proved prophetic as well. It was the first *biological dragnet*. Police began collecting blood samples and eventually had 4,000-plus nonmatching samples. No one was particularly surprised; it was hard to imagine the killer happily turning over blood that would prove his guilt. This realization led indirectly to his capture. A group of people sitting in a pub overheard a conversation in which one man said that he had given his blood in place of another. The man skipping the test was Colin Pitchfork. Police found Pitchfork and obtained a sample for Jeffreys to complete the analysis that was eventually used to convict Pitchfork and sentence him to two life terms. Without the DNA evidence, George Howard would likely have been in his place until Pitchfork killed again.

The forensic community quickly embraced DNA typing, but it was not a smooth transition. The first application in the United States occurred in 1987, but the late 1980s and early 1990s were a time of controversy, contradiction, and courtroom drama. An important chapter occurred in New York City in 1989, involving another double murder and another confession. In this case, someone had stabbed a woman and her two-year-old daughter in their apartment. One of their neighbors, a man named Castro, was the suspect, and a drop of blood found on his watch was the key piece of biological evidence. Lifecodes, a private company, did the DNA work using techniques similar to Jeffreys. The type of blood on the watch matched one of the victims. At the trial (*People v. Castro*, 144 Misc. 2d 956 545 N.Y.S. 2d 985, Sup. Ct. Bronx Co. 1989), the defense pointed to the lack of standardized procedures to question the work and the results. The head-on collision of science and the law embodied in *Castro* was an important milestone in several respects.

First, the court permitted the scientific experts from both sides to meet as a group to discuss the science involved in DNA typing. The meeting went well by all accounts, with one participant—Richard Roberts— noting, "It was comparatively straightforward in the absence of the lawyers."[1] Roberts was a molecular biologist and an expert testifying for the prosecution. Eric Landers, a human geneticist, represented the defense. There were eight experts in all, four of which attended the meeting. They emerged with a two-page consensus report that stated that in effect, an admissibility hearing was the wrong place for scientific peer review, and that the adversarial nature of such a proceeding was incompatible with scientific peer review method. In *Castro*, there was no body of precedent for the judge to fall back on, so the Lifecodes results were not allowed. The prosecution's case evaporated. Castro later confessed to the murders, a vindication of sorts for the science. However, the need for procedural controls was set in concrete by the document written by Roberts and his colleagues.

The bigger impact of *Castro* was the recognition that DNA was a powerful method but that set procedures and strict quality assurance and quality control procedures would have to be agreed upon by the forensic science and the broader molecular biology communities before such evidence could expect routine acceptance. The FBI was already moving in that direction, and the National Research Council (NRC), a body representing the National Academy of Sciences, was working on a comprehensive report regarding DNA evidence. The first, *DNA Technology in Forensic Science*, appeared in 1992. It generated significant criticism.

A follow-up appeared in 1996, *The Evaluation of Forensic DNA Evidence*, that addressed some of the contentious issues. The first arguing point was populations and how to define them. Suppose a suspect is Hispanic. The frequency of types found in that person is best evaluated in the context of population data from all Hispanics. However, a person of Hispanic origin may come from Mexico or Puerto Rico or be a second or a third generation American with marriages between. This is an example of substructure in populations, and it turns the population question on its head. One approach was to use the highest frequency for any group as a ceiling. For example if a given type is found in 10 percent of the Caucasian population, 12 percent of the Hispanic, and 15 percent of the African American population, then using the 15 percent figure would always err on the conservative side. This practice gave any benefit of the doubt to the defendant while often decreasing the probative weight of the evidence. By 1997, the data available had grown significantly, and the problems became less of an issue but never went away. Other issues discussed in the NRC book were laboratory quality assurance, testing, and how results should be stated. However, as with serology a decade before, the RFLP methods were about to have the rug pulled out from under them. This specific debate was self-limiting.

Richard Roberts, one of the authors of the *Castro* document, seemed discouraged by his experience at the intersection of science and law, noting, "We all did so much better when we sat down without the lawyers, and had a reasoned scientific discussion. Perhaps it's time the system changed." It did, but perhaps not in the way Roberts had meant. Rather, even before the law could get its feet planted firmly on RFLP methods, science and technology swept them out again.

PCR AND STR

One of the problems associated with the RFLP methods used by Jeffreys and Lifecodes related to how gels were prepared and read. The resulting data, a barcode-like pattern in gel, is hard to read. The bands are neither sharp nor discrete. Unlike a line written on paper, bands that form in gels are subject to shifting and other phenomena that make interpreting the patterns difficult. The results cannot be converted into a discrete number or digitized. Finally, the amount of initial sample needed was relatively large. The Castro case brought many of these concerns to the surface, and for a time, enthusiasm for DNA evidence cooled a bit while thoughts were gathered and procedures designed and refined.

The lull turned out to be a short one. The problems with reading gels quickly became, like RFLP, outdated by other events. The next steps came in quick succession and addressed a fundamental limitation with RFLP methods. RFLP targeted relatively large sequences. The longer the sequence, the more fragile it is and the likelier it is to degrade. Given the condition of most forensic samples, RFLP was bound to fail when evidence degraded or aged. The solution lie in targeting smaller repetitive regions called *single locus polymorphisms*, sometimes abbreviated as SLPs or more recently as STRs (*short tandem repeats*). STR loci are similar to VNTR loci in that they have the replication of the same sequence. The variability is, like VNTRs, in the number of repeats, not the sequence itself. The difference is size; STRs are much shorter than VNTRs and, as such, more robust and less prone to damage during analysis. While each STR loci has fewer variants than the VNTRs that have been used, several loci can be typed and combined just as different blood group types could be chained together to increase discrimination.

The technical catch was again quantity. Although STRs resist degradation far better than RFLP, effective typing of small samples was still difficult or impossible; simple extraction did not provide enough DNA. An elegant solution came quickly. In 1983, Kary Mullis and colleagues developed a technique called *polymerase chain reaction* (PCR). He published the results in *Nature* in 1986, and seven years later, he took home a Nobel Prize for the work. Mullis is an unlikely scientific hero, a California surfing enthusiast who conceived the idea of PCR during the late 1970s and 1980s while riding his motorcycle along the Pacific Coast highway. His bachelor's degree is in chemistry and his Ph.D. in biochemistry with the thesis entitled "The Cosmological Significance of Time Reversal," a topic somewhat removed from DNA replication.

Like most brilliant discoveries and ideas, in retrospect, it was a classic *"Why didn't I think of that?"* discovery that revolutionized many aspects of biotechnology including forensic DNA analysis. In PCR, the analyst extracts DNA and places it in a tube. Molecular probes locate and isolate the regions of interest along the DNA strand. Gentle warming unzips the DNA at those points. The solution contains free bases (ATGC or adenine, thymine, guanine, and cytosine) that attach to the unzipped areas, pairing up as per the usual rules. As the solution cools, the DNA reforms, except there are now two copies of the target loci. Each time the cycle repeats, the number of copies doubles. Thus, a tiny sample can yield enough DNA for typing. The drawback of the technique is related to this exquisite ability to reproduce even small amounts of DNA; contamination is a constant concern.

The first locus studied forensically was the DQα system in the late 1980s, and by 1990, a commercial kit was available through Cetus. Other systems followed, including applications to VNTR markers. The impact of PCR technology spread to forensic applications in the 1990s, both in the United States and Europe. The FBI worked on amplified fragment length polymorphism (AMFLP) loci such as D1S80, and some of these were also used in Europe for a time. One of the more interesting developments during this period was the introduction of commercially available testing kits that simplified and made routine, to some extent, the DNA analysis protocols. It was a two-edged sword. Forensic labs had an affordable gateway into forensic DNA typing that serologists easily mastered with proper training. The time to do each case fell and efficiency increased; investigators got a flood of data to work with compared to the ABO days. The downside, which would manifest itself later in the decade, was that the kits available dictated which loci were to be tested. In effect, this put vendors and suppliers in the position of being able to influence, if not dictate, which loci were tested. For better or worse, a partnership of scientists, law enforcement, and private industry was born. As databasing emerged near the turn of the century, the inevitable limitations of this approach became more apparent.

While DNA typing became more familiar to the forensic community and more analysts became skilled in the procedures, work continued on selecting which methods and loci to use. Debate and discussion in the forensic community revolved around how robust (i.e., reliable to be extracted from old and degraded samples) the loci were, how much sample was needed (less of a problem since PCR but still significant), and how variable the location is across the population. In recognition of problems with reading VNTR gels, the results had to be numerical and quantitative rather than fuzzy gels read by visual means. This reduced subjectivity and more importantly facilitated databasing.

By the mid 1990s, the community zeroed in on STR loci, which were short repeating sequences of three to five bases, the total length of which was around 300 bases, versus thousands for the RFLP regions. Initially, loci were grouped into what were called multiplexes that contained three or four different loci each, reminiscent of the Group I and Group II approach to isoenzymes and serum proteins. This is not coincidence; it reflects the necessity in the forensic world of getting the most information per analysis. As the decade wore on, the debate moved on as to which loci to use. In the United States, thirteen loci became the standard. These include the amelogenin locus, which allows for determination of sex. European countries settled on a slightly different list, but there is enough overlap to allow for meaningful exchanges of data across the Atlantic.

CODIS

The history of DNA typing as a forensic science is incomplete without a discussion of the databases created to store the data. DNA typing also evolved in the age of the personal computer and linked networks of information. In the United States, the idea for a national database was recognized early, and in 1989, the FBI made such a proposal. The system was called the combined DNA index system (CODIS), and it was eventually designed and implemented such that it could include data from the earlier SLP and AMFLP tests as well as the current standard of thirteen STR loci. The system allowed the submitters to retain control over their own data, but data from across North America was pooled to provide a larger population for comparisons. The first European databases appeared in the United Kingdom in 1995, followed by the Netherlands, Germany, Austria, Finland, Norway, and others.

If creating a database were all that was involved, it would be no more noteworthy than the fingerprint databases nearly a century old. What makes DNA databasing a more interesting and thorny proposition is the type of data stored in those databases. Data in CODIS includes type information at the thirteen CODIS loci along with identifying information such as name. In this sense, it is hardly different from a database of fingerprints. What is unique is the type of samples that are collected to obtain DNA and how those samples are treated. The STR locations are not genes and, as far as is now known, do not code for any expressed traits. This is critical; if they did, they would be subject to evolutionary and selective pressures that would make them less variable and less forensically valuable. The types also reveal nothing about the person, just as having a whorl as a base fingerprint pattern reveals nothing intrinsic about that person.

Now back up a step. A fingerprint comes from a finger whereas DNA comes from cellular material collected from blood or a cheek swab. A finger is rolled in ink and then on paper to collect the print and is then returned (hopefully) to the owner. A typical swab contains much more cellular material than is needed for typing, and the remainder of that material can be preserved for later use. Therein is the heart of the promise and the peril associated with DNA typing and DNA databases.

First, an example of the promise. The Green River Killer—Gary Ridgeway—pled guilty in late 2003 to forty-eight murders in the Seattle area that began in the early 1980s and ended in the late 1990s. The victims were predominantly young prostitutes. Ridgeway had been a person of interest in the case early on. Police arrested him for prostitution-related crimes in 1982. In 1987, investigators obtained hair and saliva from Ridge-way when police questioned him after he was seen with victims shortly before they disappeared. The first attempt at DNA testing yielded inconclusive results. Worse, a good portion of the sample was consumed. The saliva sample was frozen, awaiting better technologies. By 1991, the investigation had stalled, and the Green River Taskforce was comprised of one investigator. Another victim was found in November of 1999 and was identified using DNA typing. She had last been seen in 1983. In 2001, the Washington State Patrol began reexamining the evidence using DNA testing, including the frozen saliva sample. The results led to Ridgeway's arrest and plea bargain that spared him from the noose. Skeletal remains are still being recovered around Seattle.

The forensic value of DNA databases and archived samples for investigation, conviction of the guilty, and exoneration of the innocent is beyond question. The peril of archived samples and databases is the potential for misuse and abuse. As with drug abuse, the definition of abuse is a social rather than a scientific one. For example, a person's CODIS types are inherited analogously to the ABO blood type. As such, types of siblings and other relatives are similar. This fact was invaluable in assisting in identification of remains in the aftermath of the attacks of September 11, 2001. This fact has also been used to identify relatives of suspected criminals. For example, a CODIS search of a given type from a rape case may not reveal a perfect match but can flag close matches. Questioning these people may lead to relatives that did commit the crime. Is this a violation of privacy or an acceptable trade-off? These questions lie at the heart of the controversy. Forensic science can only contribute to the discussion.

DNA typing is the first type of forensic evidence to involve the rules of admissibility in a fundamental and inseparable way. How the courts handled the new DNA methods created ripples that will affect forensic laboratories for decades to come. Consequently, the history of this aspect of science is incomplete without a foray into the associated legal history.

18

Admissibility and the Trilogy

DNA rattled the scientific and legal foundations for forensic science. The technique came of age when industry and government laboratories of all kinds were embracing *quality assurance and quality control*. These have always been important in analytical work, but formalized systems began to take shape after the Second World War. Laboratories had access to standard methods and procedures such as Culliford for isoenzyme typing, but there was no systematic framework supporting the forensic science laboratory as a routine analytical laboratory. One of the pillars of such a framework is standard methods and protocols. The hearings associated with the *Castro* case emphasized that, ready or not, such standardization was coming to forensic science. The simultaneous legal wrangling taking place in this and myriad other cases involving scientific evidence led to a reevaluation of scientific evidence and the rules governing its admissibility.

THE FRYE DECISION

The law is a decidedly cautious beast, while science embraces change with childlike exuberance. Prior to the Renaissance, it was easy for the law to keep pace with science since the pace of the latter was no faster than the former. Once science ignited, its speed of propagation quickly outpaced that of the law and legal practices. In this context, it comes as no surprise that the first significant legal ruling of the Modern Age[1] came in 1923, some eighty odd years after Orfila broke the scientific ground for modern expert testimony.

The ruling, made by the Court of Appeals in the District of Columbia in 1923, related to the validity of the newly invented polygraph machine (lie detector).[2] The case was *Frye v. United States* (293 F.1013). The essence of the decision is summarized as *general acceptance*, meaning that the court would defer to the scientific community and generally allow the admission of scientific techniques and procedures if they had won general acceptance in the relevant scientific community. The decision read in part, "Just when a scientific principle or discovery crosses the line between the experimental and demonstrable stages is difficult to define. Somewhere in the twilight zone the evidential force of the principle must be recognized, and while courts will go a long way in admitting expert testimony deduced from a well-recognized scientific principle or discovery, the thing from which the deduction is made must be sufficiently established to have gained general acceptance in the particular field in which it belongs."

The court opted out of the scientific debate and expressly left the job of judging the value of scientific evidence to the scientific method and peer review. In this particular case, the court rejected the argument that the lie detector as then practiced was a sound technique because of the lack of general acceptance by psychologists. While the scientific and legal communities generally applauded the decision, it hinted at some of the flaws that would lead eventually to a much different ruling to come in sixty years.

The Court of Appeals rejected the lie detector based on the lack of general acceptance in the relevant scientific community, here psychologists working in the area of deception. At the time, the number of such reputable scientists was limited to perhaps a dozen at best. How the court weighed and considered their opinions was not clear, nor was the exact reason for the rejection of the technique clearly specified. It might have been the underlying theory; it might have been the device; it might have been the qualifications of the expert; or it might have been the operation of that device. Finally, and perhaps most damning, how is the reliability of such an instrument measured when measuring the error rate of a polygraph test is as much a philosophical question as a scientific one?

If a person successfully beats the polygraph, how would anyone know? What constitutes a control experiment? In most forensic analyses, this is trivial. If a red substance is blood, it will respond in specific ways when tested with specific reagents and it is simple to design a positive control. All that is needed is a known sample of blood. If the material is catsup, it will not respond in those ways. Creating a negative control is equally simple. However, if someone lies purposely as a positive control for a polygraph, there are unknowable variables. There are no long-term stakes associated with a laboratory test, and so, presumably, little emotion is attached to the lie. If a person lies when there is no consequence, how does that differ from a person lying under police questioning where much is at stake? The *Frye* decision opened a door but barely crossed over the threshold.

Frye was a crucial decision, but as a practical matter, little changed relative to scientific evidence and admissibility until after World War II. Courts employed the *Frye* standard primarily to exclude deception testing and rarely applied it to exclude scientific testimony and evidence more broadly defined. The upsurge of science and technology that accompanied the War and the immediate aftermath was a driver of change, as was the formation of a network of local, state, and federal scientific and forensic laboratories as discussed in the next chapter. As more scientific evidence became available to the courts, they increasingly called upon *Frye* as precedent to decide its admissibility. By the 1950s, the legal and forensic community viewed it as the most important decision regarding this topic. The increased volume of scientific evidence caused judges to be more involved in screening and evaluating the merit of scientific evidence and testimony. Over the next thirty years, the *Frye* standard crept over into civil cases as well.

The same factors that brought *Frye* into the mainstream of legal thought also accented its limitations. Forensic laboratories increasingly divided into specialties, further fracturing and subdividing the world of the relevant scientific community. Scientific and technical advances were now coming with such speed that it was difficult for those on the leading edge to keep pace, let alone forensic scientists and the legal community. A natural lag developed between innovative research and forensic application, typified by DNA's crossover from seal myoglobin to STRs.

The next significant development occurred in 1975, when federal government adopted the *Federal Rules of Evidence*. Although the rules differed significantly from the *Frye* concept, they embodied the evolving practice of judges playing a more active role in screening expert testimony and scientific evidence. Rule 702 states in part, "If scientific, technical, or other specialized knowledge will assist the trier of fact to understand the evidence or to determine a fact in issue, a witness qualified as an expert by knowledge, skill, experience, training, or education, may testify thereto in the form of opinion or otherwise."

Absent is the mention of general acceptance; missing are the guidelines to assist the judge in his or her gatekeeper duties. However, Rule 702 gave judges more latitude in defining what constitutes scientific and technical evidence. Notably absent was an explicit rejection of general acceptance. Many courts interpreted the absence of such a statement as tacit approval of general acceptance as a foundation for admissibility. Using this reasoning, Rule 702 was best applied after general acceptance was established.

The ambiguity led to increasing arguments at a time when scientific expertise was becoming more important, particularly in civil litigation. Incidents such as drug side effects and environmental disasters such as Love

Canal and Times Beach raised the scepter of mega lawsuits that would rest almost exclusively on scientific evaluations and opinion. Defendants facing huge judgments understandably wanted the most stringent controls possible on admissibility. This desire to make admissibility more stringent came just as forensic scientific evidence such as DNA was providing a cornucopia of investigative information and greatly increasingly the odds of just convictions and acquittals. Understandably, pressure developed to admit more of the novel and powerful scientific evidence. The two forces pressed against each other, insuring that when the right case came along, the dam would break. It happened in 1993.

THE TRILOGY

The case, the first in what was anointed as the Daubert trilogy, was a civil case concerning a drug called Benedictin, which was used to control nausea in expectant mothers. The plaintiff's name was Jason Daubert, a child whose mother had taken the drug. The plaintiffs charged that the drug, made by Merrell Dow Pharmaceuticals, caused birth defects. The scientific challenge was to prove that the drug was directly and unambiguously to blame. No matter what, there was going to be room for argument and differing interpretation of data. Clearly, the verdict would depend on which scientific evidence the court deemed admissible and which it did not.

The plaintiffs produced three types of scientific evidence. The first were chemical analyses that pointed out the molecular similarity of the drug to other compounds already known to cause birth defects. The second type was a reevaluation of existing data that supported a correlation between taking Benedictin and birth defects. Third, the plaintiffs presented other studies that were conducted and pointed to the same correlation. The court ruled these studies inadmissible based on a *Frye*-like argument because the scientific work was done specifically in the context of the case. As such, there had been no review by the scientific community and thus no general acceptance. The court ruled against Daubert.

The plaintiffs appealed based on the argument that the Federal Rules of Evidence had superseded the *Frye* standard and, therefore, disallowing admissibility of the evidence on this basis was unfounded. The case made its way to the U.S. Supreme Court and a ruling was handed down in *Daubert v. Merrell Dow Pharmaceuticals* (113 S. Ct. 2786; 1993). In it, the Court formalized the concept of the judge as the gatekeeper and provided a list of considerations to assist in doing so. One of these factors remained general acceptance, but the Court added other considerations for judges to ponder such as testability, peer review, known error rates, and existence of standards to judge performance. This created a new type of proceeding called a Daubert hearing that judges could employ to determine the admissibility of scientific evidence.

Two important points need to be emphasized. First, a gatekeeper judge is responsible for admissibility. The task does not fall to a jury. The gatekeeper function exists in the spirit of protecting the jury from spurious or unreliable testimony and information. The judge filters and selects what the jury will hear. In most criminal cases, scientific evidence is part of a larger milieu. However, in many civil cases, like the so-called toxic tort cases, the scientific attribution of cause and effect is often the heart of them. In the Daubert case, science had to show that taking Benedictin was directly and solely responsible for Jason Daubert's birth defects. Little else was relevant to reach a just decision. In such situations, the outcome depends heavily on what happens during admissibility hearings, even before the trial starts. Second, although Daubert standards are now common, they are not universal even within the United States, and some jurisdictions still rely on *Frye* or related standards.

General Electric v. Joiner (522 US 136; 1997) was another Supreme Court decision applied to a civil toxic tort case. The plaintiff, an employee of the company, developed cancer and charged that workplace exposure to PCBs and related compounds was the cause. The trial court rejected the testimony of experts, while an appellate court reversed that decision. The Supreme Court sided with the trial court, supporting the discretion of the trial court in such matters when appropriate. This decision also encouraged judges to take advantage of the advice of appointed neutral experts in evaluation of evidence. The Federal Rules of Evidence (2004) Rule 706 codifies this, stating, "The court may on its own motion or on the motion of any party enter an order to show cause why expert witnesses should not be appointed, and may request the parties to submit nominations. The court may appoint any expert witnesses agreed upon by the parties, and may appoint expert witnesses of its own selection. . . . Nothing in this rule limits the parties in calling expert witnesses of their own selection."

The final case of the trilogy was the Supreme Court decision in *Kumho Tire Co., Ltd. v. Carmichael* (119 S. Ct. 1167; 1999). The issue was the cause of a tire blowout and a resulting fatality. At the trial, the judge excluded the testimony of an engineer based on *Daubert* criteria. The reasoning was that an engineer's testimony did not qualify as scientific testimony under *Daubert* standards. The appeals court rejected that argument and said that all expert testimony could be considered. The U.S. Supreme Court upheld the appellate decision, emphasizing that the key criteria for admitting or excluding such testimony were relevance and reliability rather than if the testimony qualified as scientific testimony. The effect of *Kumho* was to apply *Daubert* standards to all expert testimony, not just strictly scientific expert testimony.

The guidelines set forth from *Frye* to *Kumho* currently dictate how courts in the United States rule on the admissibility of expert testimony. However, there is no uniform standard of which is applied when and where. It is important to remember that the trilogy were all civil cases in which scientific attribution of cause and effect was at the heart of the matter, and admission or exclusion of certain evidence literally made or broke the cases in question.

A criminal case, where forensic science mostly lives, rarely falls into that category. It is probably fair to state that the core idea that now guides most admissibility considerations can be paraphrased as the two Rs, *reliability and relevance*. The latter is reasonably easy for a judge to decide, the former more difficult. DNA evidence was the first form of new scientific evidence to have to navigate the legal system with the trilogy as the backdrop. This had enormous consequences for DNA and forensic science. Crossing the river meant there was no going back.

19

Profession and Personalities

The forensic profession crystallized around strong personalities such as Orfila, Spilsbury, Norris, McCrone, Bertillon, Galton, Kind, Helpern, and others. Many stumbled into the spotlight; others chased it. Where crime, blood, and murder are the subjects, there is no lack of audience. As the century progressed, governments worldwide established systems of forensic labs. Educational programs appeared separate from the schools of legal medicine that dominated forensic training in the 1800s. Forensic science moved from avocation and sideline to profession, complete with professional organizations, journals, accreditation, and certification.

Until the twentieth century, there is no lineage that forensic science could call its own. The chemists have one, the biologists another, and the medical examiners and toxicologists yet another. Once forensic science/criminalistics condensed around the early practitioners, the first men (for there were no women) who could be called forensic scientists appeared. In the forensic tradition, they borrowed and integrated existing science, technology, and techniques into the new field. Calvin Goddard epitomized this pattern by bringing microscopy to bear on firearms evidence. Men such as Goddard and his ilk were not pioneers in the sense that Orfila was, but that is not to minimize their importance. Many of today's forensic scientists can trace their professional lineage to one or more of these men, and many have become famous in their own right. Some of the forensic celebrities have already been introduced, including Spilsbury, Bertillon, Goddard, Osborn, Helpern, and Kind. Almost all have some connection to each other, even if indirect.

FORENSIC SCIENCE CELEBRITIES

Hans Gross (1847–1915) was an Austrian Renaissance man—a lawyer by trade and forensic generalist in the best of that tradition. He coined the label *criminalistics* for the comparative analytical science he practiced. He was an investigator for the legal system in Graz, Austria. Gross viewed forensic science holistically and believed that experts from diverse fields would contribute to the analysis of physical evidence and solving crimes. He understood the value of biological evidence, soil, dust, and many other types of transfer and trace evidence.

One of his most important contributions was to the literature of forensic science. He first penned a compilation of scientific methods and techniques translated as *Handbook for Examining Magistrates* to share what he had learned with other investigators. It was significant in that it was the first forensic book to include many topics—geology, chemistry, blood, pathology, toxicology, and others—in one volume. In 1893, he published the first textbook in forensic science, which was translated into English under the title of *Criminal Investigation*, and he started a journal called *Kriminologie*, which is still published. Gross was a pioneer in the field, and he exerted a strong influence on his contemporaries including other pioneers in the field such as Edmund Locard. Gross also reportedly enjoyed the Sherlock Holmes stories, a common thread among the forensic scientists of this time.

In the neighboring Germany, Dr. Georg Popp had established a laboratory and was making a name in trace evidence analysis, microscopy, and geology. Popp trained as a chemist, and his laboratory was an analytical one, not specifically a forensic one. However, in 1900, he joined the forensic world. An investigator who had read Gross' book sought out Popp in Frankfurt and asked if he could examine a spot found on a pair of pants. Popp was hooked and became a central figure in European forensic science.

In 1904, he faced his most famous case. He examined a handkerchief left at the scene of a murder. The victim, Eva Disch, was killed in a field by strangulation. Popp found coal dust, snuff, and mineral bits embedded in the mucus on the handkerchief. The police had identified a suspect who worked in both a local gravel pit and a coal works. Popp found coal and mineral bits under his fingernails, not probative by itself. More damning, Popp found soil that was consistent with the murder scene and the path that the suspect would have taken to leave the scene. The suspect confessed when advised of Popp's findings. Popp went on to work many cases, and he is considered the first practitioner of forensic geology.

The French, so active in the early development of forensic science, remained in the thick of things well into the twentieth century. Edmond Locard (1877–1966) was trained in law and medicine, which he had studied under Alexandre Lacassagne at the University of Lyon. Like Popp, Locard had read some of Gross' works as well as some of the Sherlock Holmes stories. Locard formed the first dedicated forensic laboratory in 1910. Comprising a couple of attic rooms, it was not glamorous or well equipped. Despite this, Locard was able to establish a reputation and increase the visibility of forensic science in Europe. The fifteen years from 1910 to 1925 saw many labs founded, including those in Germany, Switzerland, and Sweden.

Locard was interested in microscopic evidence, particularly dust, and believed that such trace evidence was crucial in linking people to places. Although he apparently never used the exact term himself, he is famous for *Locard's exchange principle*, a concept that evolved from his studies and writings. The principle is stated as a version of "every contact leaves a trace" and reflects his belief that every contact between a person and another person or a person and a place results in the transfer of materials between the entities involved. Locard wrote in 1930, "Yet, upon reflection, one is astonished that it has been necessary to wait until this late day for so simple an idea to be applied as the collection, in the dust of garments, of the evidence of the objects rubbed against, and the contacts which a suspected person may have undergone. For the microscopic debris that covers our clothes and bodies are the mute witnesses, sure and faithful, of all our movements and all our encounters."[1]

Most of this transfer evidence, such as dust, is microscopic and transitory. In Locard's view, a forensic scientist's charge is to find those traces and use them to establish the link. Popp's work in the murder of Eva Disch was the perfect example. The success of Locard's laboratory and methods encouraged other European nations to form forensic science laboratories after the conclusion of the First World War. Like Gross, Locard contributed to the early forensic literature and was the editor of *Revue Internationale de Criminalistique* which started publication in 1929. In Lyon, he founded and directed the Institute of Criminalistics located at the University of Lyons, and he remained a dominant presence in forensic science into the 1940s.

In the United States, the medical examiner system was successful, but it took longer for forensic scientists to diverge from the medicolegal sphere of forensic investigation. One of the first disciplines to emerge in the United States was questioned document (QD) examination. Questioned document analysis was not new, nor was it exclusively American in origin. A French sourcebook on document examination appeared in 1609, and as early as 1810, the Germans were using scientific examination in forgery cases. Given the German penchant for chemistry, it is not surprising that they emphasized ink analysis.

The drawback to chemical ink analysis, especially in the eighteenth century, was that the analysis was destructive and took far too much of the sample to be practicable. Emphasis shifted to other aspects of document examination. The reemergence of QD in the United States is associated with Albert S. Osborne (1858–1946). In 1910, Osborn authored a textbook (*Questioned Documents—A Study of Questioned Documents with an Outline of Methods by Which the Facts May Be Discovered and Shown*) that is still considered a foundational work and source of reference in the field. He also was a founding member of the American Society of Questioned Document Examiners (ASQDE) and served as its first president from 1942 until 1946, the year of his death. Osborn's sons continued in the field, and both he and his son were involved in the Lindbergh kidnapping case.

KIRK AND AMERICAN CRIMINALISTICS

While the ME system flowered in the East Coast of the United States, criminalistics thrived in the West. The early applications centered on microscopy and questioned documents but quickly expanded to other fields. A key figure was August Vollmer (1876–1955)[2], who was elected as Town Marshall in Berkeley in 1905 and moved to Chief of Police in 1909. He was not a scientist, but he was resourceful and understood that emerging science could aid his department. He also had the good fortune of being Chief of Police in a town that was home to the University of California at Berkeley (UCB), one of the strongest science universities in a strong state system. He recruited faculty members to assist in casework, calling on those in the medical school and the chemistry and biology departments, among others. Vollmer launched a school of criminology that covered police procedures, practices, and physical evidence. It ran as a summer program at first, although Vollmer had aspirations of making it part of UCB. That did not occur until 1937, when a biochemist named Dr. Paul Kirk (1902–1970) became involved as an advisor to the criminology program.

Kirk was not the first criminalist at Berkeley, but he is considered to be the founder of American criminalistics. Working with Vollmer's encouragement, Kirk established the criminalistics program in 1937, and by 1948, it was a department under the university's School of Criminology. Like many before him, his initial involvement in casework led to a lifelong career in forensic science. Kirk was active in research in many areas of evidence including trace, hair, and fibers as well as in teaching and casework. He authored a pioneering textbook, *Crime Investigation*, in 1953 and its second edition in 1974. The 1950s were Kirk's most active years. In 1955, he analyzed crime scene evidence from the Sam Sheppard case, in which Sheppard had been accused of murdering his wife, Marilyn. The famous case would later become the basis of the television show and the 1994 movie both entitled *The Fugitive*. Kirk's controversial analysis concluded that Sheppard was not guilty of the crime. The Sheppard case was to the 1950s what the O.J. Simpson case was to the 1990s. It was widely publicized and discussed, and the publicity brought forensic science to the public's attention. In this instance, blood typing and blood spatter, not DNA, stole the show.

Kirk was a forensic science generalist in the sense that he believed forensic scientists should have a broad scientific education and knowledge of many aspects of physical evidence. He considered individualization the primary skill and distinction of forensic science. Criminalists, in Kirk's view, were tasked with finding common sources and linking evidence to its source. Locard had voiced the same philosophy. In this view, identification of evidence is secondary to individualization. The important question is not "Is this hair?" but rather "Could this hair come from this person or is this person excluded as a possible source?"

Berkeley disbanded the criminalistics program in 1955, but by then, many of the next generation of leaders in the field had trained there under Kirk, and his legacy continues to be central to forensic science in the United States. He published an article in *Science* in 1963 that defined the science and profession of criminalistics as he viewed it. Reflecting a complaint voiced to this day, he stated, "Criminalistics is an occupation that is poorly understood by the great majority of people, including the scientific public. It is generally assessed in terms of high-grade detective work rather than in terms of a serious and very demanding type of applied science."[3]

CENTRALIZED (GOVERNMENT) FORENSIC LABORATORIES

Locard gets the credit for the first forensic lab, but many labs that became forensic labs started out with an emphasis on public health, safety, commerce, and taxes. Beginning in the late 1700s and early 1800s, English laws specified how to measure the strength of alcoholic beverages. The English government formed the Excise and Inland Revenue Laboratory in 1842 for this reason. Responsibilities grew and the lab became the Laboratory of the Government Chemist. By 1850, laws specifying purity of tobacco were in place, and the medical journal *The Lancet* was publishing lists of companies and individuals that were adulterating products. This was the direct result of the work of the forensic chemist O'Shaughnessy introduced earlier. The post of Public Analyst was created in 1866 with increasing scope and authority, eventually to focus on food and drugs, loosely similar to the Food and Drug Administration in the United States. Similar developments occurred in Europe at about the same time but came later in the United States.

In the Americas, Dr. Wilfrid Derome formed the first forensic laboratory in Montreal in 1909. Derome had studied in Paris, obtained a degree in legal medicine, and visited Locard's laboratory while there. He returned with an enthusiastic report as was able to convince the local Attorney General to fund a similar facility. The lab, called the Laboratorier de Recherché Medico-Legales opened in 1914. As Locard's lab had served as a model for Derome, his lab would later serve as a model to an American named J. Edgar Hoover. The second government laboratory opened in Canada in 1932 in Ontario. The Royal Canadian Mounted Police established a forensic science laboratory service in 1937. One of the first hair examiners there recalled the problems of working in a nation that had so many remote areas. The examiner, Lance Corporal James Robinson, attempted to collect reference specimens from different areas and received the following response to one of his requests: "I am not able to fill the fourth request as the women I know well enough are not in the settlement at the present time."[4]

To the south, Hoover and the FBI were not the first to open a forensic lab in the United States, nor was Washington, D.C., to be the geographic center of early forensic science in the United States. Vollmer trumped everyone by forming a lab in 1916 with Albert Schneider as the director. Vollmer had previously established a small school of criminology (not to be confused with criminalistics) near the University of California campus in town. This facility would become home to Kirk and would be the nexus of American forensic science into the 1950s.

In 1929, Roy Pinker took over as head of Vollmer's lab as Prohibition began. Previously, Pinker had worked as a chemist in a lab in Los Angeles, becoming chief chemist in 1929. Interestingly, he was one of the first to doubt the utility of the paraffin test for gunshot residue and conducted a demonstration in 1932 to prove his point. When he assumed the lead in Vollmer's lab, alcohol and the analysis of beverages became a primary focus of law enforcement and forensic science. Pinker embraced the work and extended chemical analysis to other kinds of evidence. In the 1940s, he did extensive work with blood alcohol determinations and went on to be a founding member of the California Association of Criminalists that would eventually be critical to establishing national certification of forensic scientists. Pinker also became the radio world's equivalent of Sherlock Holmes and *CSI*, the two fictional forensic science realms that bracketed his time. Although he did not play himself, there was a scientist named Pinker in the popular radio show *Dragnet*.

At the federal level, the United States Bureau of Investigation founded the Technical Laboratory. Early examinations focused on firearms and questioned documents. The laboratory moved to the Department of Justice building in Washington, D.C. The Technical Laboratory was the largest laboratory in the United States and evolved into the single most influential national source of forensic analysis and information. The organization of the lab served as a model for many other state and local facilities formed in subsequent years.

Later in the same decade (1935), the Bureau became the Federal Bureau of Investigation. Also in 1935, the FBI National Academy was opened and became a center for the training of law enforcement officers from all over the country and, eventually, all over the world. By 1943, the laboratory had become a division within the FBI. During the war years, the Technical Laboratory contributed in intelligence operations and was active in the field of cryptography (making and breaking codes). In 1950, the now famous *Ten Most Wanted* list was born. In 1974, the FBI moved, along with the laboratory, to the new J. Edgar Hoover Building in downtown Washington. Currently, the laboratory provides forensic services in many diverse areas including chemistry, DNA typing, firearms and tool marks, explosives, visual and audio recordings and image enhancement, fingerprints, questioned documents, and trace evidence. In 1981, a research and training facility was established in Quantico, Virginia, in association with the National Academy. The facility hosted training courses for forensic scientists in its premises, which also was a center of forensic science research. In 2002, the FBI laboratory moved to a new facility in Quantico.

Other federal agencies followed the FBI in forming forensic labs specific to their needs. The Revenue Laboratory, the precursor to the Bureau of Alcohol, Tobacco, Firearms, and Explosives, created one of the earliest in 1887. In 1914, the lab added drugs to alcohol as their main charge. The United States Postal Inspection Service formed their first lab in 1940, a system that now includes five laboratories. The Drug Enforcement Administration added laboratories in the 1970s, and the Food and Drug Administration formed a forensic center in 1989, a successor to their Elemental Analysis Research Center (EARC). In 1982, the EARC was instrumental in analyzing the cyanide powders found in Tylenol and, based on those profiles, tracing the poison back to the manufacturer.

A similar pattern of laboratory evolution played out in the United Kingdom. In 1902, the Cardiff Police Department began a lab that worked with fingerprints and photography. By the 1930s, other labs had sprung up and were integrating chemistry and biology into their repertoire, and by 1938, a national tiered system was in place. Police departments concentrated on the fingerprint/photography aspects and simple scientific testing. Small regional labs had more capability and scientific staff, while larger labs were located in different regions and were funded independently of police labs. Arguably the most famous and respected forensic lab was founded in London in 1935 as part of the city police, better known as the Metropolitan Police or the Scotland Yard. In 1949, the lab moved to the famous Scotland Yard location, and the Aldermaston Central Research Establishment (CRE) facility was built in 1967. The Home Office Forensic Science Service merged with the MPL in 1996, creating a national forensic science service, distinctly different from the American model, in which, federal, state, and local entities can establish independent forensic science laboratories.

PROFESSIONAL MATURITY

There are labs, and there are forensic scientists, but is there a profession called forensic science? Forensic scientists themselves will still argue over what their profession is and what makes it different from medicine or science. This raises the question of what defines something as a profession. A reasonable definition is that a profession is the practice of similar skills by a group of people who are paid to do so. To take it a step further, a profession is differentiated from a job in that there is a governing body that oversees, regulates, and insures that practitioners of the profession adhere to standard guidelines and meet certain minimum requirements. In a true profession, this regulation is derived internally, not imposed by an outside entity that does not practice the profession. The American Medical Association dictates how medicine is taught and practiced. The AMA works in concert with medical schools, hospitals, and governments, but fundamentally, doctors dictate how doctors work and what the public can expect from physicians. A profession requires the existence of professional associations, which have a recognized and accepted authority within that profession.

The earliest professional societies trace back to the 1600s. The French Academy of Sciences formed in 1666 and the English counterpart, the Royal Society, coalesced about the same time. The role of early societies was to promote discussions and share results, which quickly formalized through the publications. These transactions and journals were the first to institutionalize peer review of scientific work, a foundation of modern scientific practices. The Royal Society issued Volume 1 of its journal, *Philosophical Transactions*, in 1665. Robert Hooke, so instrumental in development of microscopy, was curator of the instrument collection of the Royal Society in London. The early societies were eclectic, emphasizing combinations of physics, chemistry, and biology. Later groups became more specialized; currently the largest scientific society is the American Chemical Society with nearly 160,000 thousand members.

In the forensic world, professional societies formed much like isolated droplets of mercury joining into larger aggregates. Among the oldest is the American Society of Questioned Document Examiners, founded by Albert Osborn in 1942, but with informal beginnings in 1913. Two years later, the International Association for Identification (IAI) took shape. It is fitting that the first exclusively forensic societies related to fingerprints and document examination since at the time, these were the only identifiably distinct forensic disciplines.

The largest forensic science association was formed in 1947 as the American Academy of Forensic Sciences (AAFS). Appropriately, its history parallels that of its discipline by beginning with medicine and physicians. Dr. Rutherford B. Gradwhol, then director of the St. Louis Police Department laboratory, called the first meeting. A group of about 150 forensic scientists descended on the city and formed AAFS with Gradwhol as its first president. As of 2005, the Academy had over 5,000 members divided among sections such as criminalistics, toxicology, questioned documents, pathology and biology, and jurisprudence. One of the key roles of societies such as AAFS is the publication of scientific journals that are disseminated to their members and beyond. AAFS launched the *Journal of Forensic Sciences.*

Six years after the Academy was born, Stuart Kind in the United Kingdom formed The Society of Forensic Science and ran it from an office in his house. The official charter approved in 1959 changed the name to the Forensic Science Society (FSS). Their journal is entitled *Science & Justice.* Others to follow suit in this period were the Canadian Society of Forensic Science formed in 1953, the Association of Firearm and Tool Mark Examiners (AFTE, 1969), and the Society of Forensic Toxicologists (1973).

QUALITY ASSURANCE AND QUALITY CONTROL; CERTIFICATION AND ACCREDITATION

DNA and the legal issues of the late 1900s accelerated the advance of quality assurance (QA) and quality control (QC) into forensic laboratories. As a systematic procedural approach, QA traces to the post-World War II years and to applications in the military and engineering. Quality management often has a business orientation, but the philosophy is applicable to laboratory work. The International Standards Organization (ISO) states, "Quality management means what the organization does to ensure that its products or services satisfy the customer's quality requirements and comply with any regulations applicable to those products or services." In a forensic context, the organization is the laboratory, the products and services are analytical data, and the customer is the justice system.

The practices and procedures used within a forensic laboratory are often referred to as total quality management or TQM. TQM consists of the protocols used by the lab and involves everyone from the bench analyst through management. The structures and protocols within a TQM system are often adopted or adapted from external standardization and quality assurance entities. The international body mentioned above, ISO, was formed in 1947 as a voluntary organization consisting of member groups. The American National Standards Institute (ANSI) is the U.S. representative in ISO. Within ANSI, the American Society of Quality (ASQ) oversees issues of quality management. These organizations do not regulate, and they are not industry or product specific.

Within the analytical and forensic communities, specific guidance for methods and procedures are provided by groups such as ASTM (American Society of Testing and Materials) International and professional organizations including the American Academy of Forensic Sciences (AAFS), the Society of Forensic Toxicology (SOFT), and the American Society of Crime Laboratory Directors (ASCLD). ASTM develops procedures called standards that are applicable to specific industries and processes. The organization was formed by engineers and chemists in 1898 and has grown to cover everything from amusement rides to wood. Committees of professionals in their field develop standards. Committee E30, currently with about 300 members, drafts and approves forensic science standards.

Unlike ANSI and ISO, NIST (National Institute of Standards and Technology) is an agency of the U.S. government. Founded in 1901, it is part of the Department of Commerce, but it does not have any regulatory functions. Rather, the role of NIST is to promote the standardization of weights and measures to serve the needs of industry, commerce, science, and technology. Forensically, one of the most important functions of NIST is the creation, maintenance, and supply of standard reference materials (SRMs). There are several types of SRMs, including certified SRMs (CRM).

Generically, QA/QC applies to two parts of the forensic enterprise—the analyst and the laboratory. In this parlance, the analyst is *certified* and the lab is *accredited*. These reflect the practices and procedures brought into sharp relief by the DNA debates of the 1990s, but the move toward certification and accreditation began much earlier. The National Institute of Justice funded the formation of the Criminalistics Certification Study Committee in 1975. The group worked through 1979 and offered a plan that was rejected by most of the forensic scientists asked about it. The issue was dead from 1980 until 1989 when microscopist Walter McCrone organized a meeting of the committee to revisit the issue. In attendance were members of the California Association of Criminalists (CAC), which turned out to be important. California had an organized system of labs in 1931, the year before the FBI lab was organized. In 1953, analysts in the state formed the California Association of Criminalists as a professional society and source of education and support. The CAC was the first forensic professional organization to offer certification of analysts based on a comprehensive written examination, and this occurred prior to the McCrone meeting in 1989.

In December of that year, the American Board of Criminalistics (ABC) was formed as an umbrella organization that would tackle analyst certification, and within two years, the American Society of Crime Laboratory Directors (ASCLD) and the criminalistics section of the AAFS had joined. In 1993, certification finally went national when ABC offered the first round of testing. The initial written test, called the General Knowledge Examination, covers a wide range of topics in forensic science. Passing this examination gives the analyst "diplomate" status designated as D-ABC. To advance to "fellow" status (F-ABC), the analyst must take and pass a second written examination in a specialty area as well as a laboratory proficiency test. Currently, specialty tests are available in DNA typing, trace evidence analysis, drug analysis, and arson analysis. These technical specialist exams, which include proficiency testing, were added in 1998.

In late 2005, the ABC announced that the testing process would change in 2007, with exams more attuned to individual specialties. The process will retain the philosophy that all forensic scientists should master forensic basics that span across the different specialties. In the field of forensic toxicology, analyst certification and laboratory accreditation is overseen by the American Board of Forensic Toxicologists (ABFT), formed in 1975. Like ABC, other organizations such as AAFS send representatives to this umbrella organization.

The beginnings of laboratory accreditation in the United States go back to the 1970s. In 1973, thirty laboratory directors were invited to Quantico, the site of the FBI Academy and forensic science training labs. This organization grew to become the Association of Crime Laboratory Directors (ASCLD). The purpose was to form an umbrella organization for laboratories that would work toward accreditation and certification of labs and analysts. The charter was approved in 1974 after a long, painful, and heated debate. The next significant development was a set of laboratory accreditation standards first applied to the Illinois State Police laboratories in 1982. The accreditation arm of ASCLD, called ASCLD/LAB (for Laboratory Accreditation Board), oversees the process, and as of March 2004, 259 labs had been accredited. The process is moving toward international ISO standards.

THE OTHER TRIAL OF THE CENTURY

Forensically, the trial of the nineteenth century was the LaFarge case. For the twentieth century, there are many contenders. Certainly, the O.J. Simpson case had significant impact but was perhaps overemphasized in the larger context because it remains fresh in memory. The forensic scientists took some comfort from the acquittal in that the defense did not attack the results of DNA testing procedures. This demonstrated acceptance of the science. What was attacked were the protocols and procedures used to collect and store the evidence, among other things. Secondly, the trial was the most public exhibition of DNA evidence to date, playing out on national TV for weeks. The trial also highlighted problems of scientific communication and the ability to explain DNA typing results to a jury. In that sense, it parallels the LaFarge trial, which also enthralled the public while raising awareness of forensic toxicology. However, the Simpson case was not the first to bring forensic science to the attention of the American public, nor was it the first to involve a celebrity. That distinction goes to the Lindbergh case.

Charles A. Lindbergh became a national and international hero in 1927 after flying the Atlantic alone in the Spirit of St. Louis. He later married Anne Morrow, and their first child, a son named Charles Jr., was twenty months old when he was kidnapped around 9:30 P.M. on March 1, 1932. The kidnapper spirited the boy from his nursery located on the second floor of the Lindbergh's home in Hopewell, New Jersey. The kidnapper left a homemade ladder at the scene that would later provide critical evidence, but first responders and investigators failed to document or preserve footprints also left at the scene. A ransom note, one of fourteen eventually sent by the kidnapper, demanded $50,000 in ransom for the boy's safe return. Mailed notes all had postmarks from the New York City area.

The investigation by the New Jersey State Police was headed by Colonel Norman Schwarzkopf, father of the general who would later lead coalition forces to victory in the 1991 Gulf War. The case took many bizarre turns and became the subject of worldwide media frenzy. An elderly retired teacher named John Condon became the intermediary between Lindbergh and a man who called himself "John," and eventually a ransom of $50,000 was paid. Most of the payment was in gold certificates, which were used as currency at the time. Serial numbers of the bills were recorded before the money was delivered. Sadly, the body of the child was found a month later in the woods close to the Hopewell home. The cause of death was listed as a skull fracture, most likely the result of an accidental fall from the ladder during the kidnapping. Because a forensic pathologist or medical examiner did not conduct the autopsy, the conclusion has been questioned. It is possible that the kidnapper killed the boy shortly after the abduction and dumped the body near the home. The kidnapper was never seen or heard from after the ransom was paid.

In 1933, President Roosevelt ordered that all gold certificates be exchanged for standard currency. Law enforcement agents still working the case hoped for a break, anticipating that the kidnapper would have to turn in a good portion of the ransom money, most of which had not yet surfaced. That which had been spent was all in the New York City area, allowing law enforcement to concentrate efforts there. The break came in September 1934 when an exchange bank received a $20 gold certificate from a man that matched the description of the kidnapper. More importantly, a license plate number had been written on the bill, which was quickly traced to a truck belonging to Bruno Richard Hauptmann who lived in the Bronx. He was arrested and a subsequent search of his garage uncovered a gun and several thousand dollars of the ransom money in gold certificates. Hauptmann at first denied all knowledge of the money but soon changed his story, claiming that a friend had given him the money. The friend had previously returned to Germany and died there, making it impossible to investigate that claim.

During the time between the kidnapping and murder of the child and Hauptmann's arrest, forensic investigations were undertaken on the physical evidence. This included the ransom notes, trace evidence, psychological and psychiatric studies, and, perhaps most damning for Hauptmann, analysis of the ladder. Albert Osborn, the document examiner, performed analysis of the handwriting found in the ransom notes. Arthur Koehler, a wood expert employed by the Forest Service undertook a meticulous evaluation of the ladder, including the wood, construction techniques, and tool marks found on the wood. Eventually, he was able to trace the lumber used to a lumberyard and mill located in the Bronx. Marks made by planers on the wood in the ladder matched a planer at the yard. A search of the attic above Hauptmann's apartment revealed a missing floorboard. Nail holes and tree ring patterns from a rail of the ladder lined up perfectly where the floorboard had been. Furthermore, Koehler was able to demonstrate this at the trial as well as show how the planer marks from the ladder matched Hauptmann's planer. Hauptmann was convicted and after a series of appeals and reviews, including one by the Supreme Court, he was executed on April 3, 1936. Like any case that captures the public's imagination, conspiracy theories persist, but the consensus among forensic scientists that have reviewed the case is that the analyses were sound and that Hauptmann was justly convicted.

FORENSIC SCIENCE FICTION AND CONSEQUENCES

Forensic science fiction is not a modern or even a Western phenomenon. The Chinese were fond of detective fiction. One favored theme, seen around 1700, was murder by nails. In a story, a magistrate had to exhume a body and, after shaving the head, found a nail driven deeply into the brain. The heroes of these stories were the magistrates who unfailing had brilliant detection skills, unflinching courage, and unimpeachable character.

The Sherlock Holmes stories influenced Locard and Gross, and the *Sherlock Holmes effect* on forensic science and criminal investigation predates the *CSI effect* by a century. Before that, one could identify the *Orfila effect* that drew countless would-be toxicologists to study with the master in the 1840s. What is interesting and different about the recent incarnation is the role of the mass media and the fact that books, magazines, TV shows, and movies reach a much larger audience much faster than Doyle's short stories did.

One of the first post-Holmes writers to delve into forensic topics was Dorothy L. Sayers (1893–1957) who named her detective hero Wimsey. She began publishing the series in 1923 and had a penchant for poison, used as frequently in real life, as a plot device—mushrooms (*The Documents in the Case*, 1930) and arsenic (*Strong Poison*, 1930)—to dispose of an inconvenient suitor. Sayers' work was characterized by detailed research and the use of chemists and scientists as characters and heroes. One such character was Sir James Lubbock, a master of all forensic disciplines, from chemistry to autopsy. The popularity of Sayers' works during the 1930s and 1940s coexisted with the continuing popularity of Sherlock Holmes but updated the chemistry. Commenting on the obvious reason for her success, she wrote in 1934 that death seemed "to provide the mind of the Anglo Saxon race with a greater fund of innocent enjoyment than any other single subject."[5]

Others in the detective story genre continued the tradition, notably P.D. James with books such as *Death of an Expert Witness* (1977). Other authors such as Agatha Christie wrote similar fiction, which had a softer form of forensic science that was usually incidental to the plot rather than central. This began to change in the late 1970s. A landmark was the movement of forensic science to television and the show *Quincy, ME*, which ran from 1976 to 1983 on NBC. Although hardly gritty by today's standards, the show centered on the work of a medical examiner character loosely based on Los Angeles ME Dr. Thomas Noguchi. Noguchi was a forensic celebrity himself, the *coroner to the stars*, and performed autopsies on people such as Natalie Wood and John Belushi. Noguchi was a technical advisor to the show.

Grittier still were the serial novels that came a few years after the show ended, beginning with trendsetter Patricia Cornwell and the Kay Scarpetta series (1990–). Another notable entry into the genre is Kathy Reichs and her forensic anthropologist heroine. Forensic science is center stage in these books, written by women with experience in the forensic field; Reichs continues to practice forensic anthropology. In 2005, the TV series *Bones* debuted on FOX, based on the same character. The success of the *CSI* franchise on CBS (the original and the Las Vegas, the Miami, and the New York flavors) embodies the public fascination with forensic science.

Popularity is decidedly a two-edged sword. In a large-scale replay of what occurred after the LaFarge case, students are flooding forensic science programs, which are springing up in colleges and universities across the United States. Many have nary a forensic scientist on the faculty. Inevitably, many will collapse when the realization hits the job market. Forensic labs cannot possibly absorb everyone who will graduate with some form of forensic science degree. To address the burgeoning number of forensic science programs, the Forensic Education Program Accreditation Commission (FEPAC) took shape in the early 2000s to evaluate and accredit programs. The accreditation process began in 2003 for undergraduate and graduate programs.

The other aspects of popularization of forensic science that will have lasting impact are the public expectations that arise. Anecdotal stories are circulating in legal and forensic circles of juries expecting scientific evidence even when it may not be necessary, cogent, or feasible. This undercurrent of increasing demand for scientific evidence comes, ironically, at a time when science education in the United States is in a sorry state and most legal professionals and jurors are unlikely to have had any science courses since high school. Perhaps one problem will help solve another, though. Several groups are working to develop forensic science labs, curricula, and workshops that can exploit student interest in forensic science as a means to encourage and improve science education in general. The situation is likely not one foreseen by Sir Arthur Conan Doyle, but the link is there.

20

Professional Immaturity

Like any discipline, forensic science has dark corners and scandals. In the late 1990s, the FBI laboratory came under intense national scrutiny as a result of allegations made by one of its senior explosives chemists, Frederic Whitehurst, who joined the FBI in 1982 and moved to the laboratory in 1986. He began filing complaints soon after, charging that work was sloppy and testimony misleading, and his complaints resulted in retaliation. His criticisms involved some of the biggest cases of the 1990s including the first World Trade Center bombing in 1993 and the Oklahoma City bombing in 1995.

Because of the controversy, the Department of Justice Office of the Inspector General launched an investigation and issued a report in 1997. The report was critical of the laboratory personnel and procedures and initiated a wave of reform as well as increased media attention. Another scandal erupted in 2004 concerning FBI practices related to the analysis of bullets using elemental analysis techniques. The National Academy of Sciences Press in 2004 published *Forensic Analysis: Weighing Bullet Lead Evidence* that was critical of the statistical analysis methods used to interpret the results. The FBI requested the evaluation after a prominent metallurgist in the Bureau raised questions about the practice.

An FBI analyst admitted to false testimony in a Kentucky case related to bullet lead analysis and resigned. An FBI DNA analyst resigned in 2002 with several cases under scrutiny. Perhaps the worst laboratory scandal to date involves the Houston Police Department laboratory in which DNA evidence has been brought into question. The scandal erupted in 2003, but the problems may go back much farther. Agencies in West Virginia and other places have dismissed and disciplined analysts for false testimony and poor analysis. The forensic system in the city of Houston was in shambles from the late 1990s to the early 2000s.

Fingerprinting is also under fire. The most recent and devastating instance is the Brandon Mayfield case. It occurred in 2004 and was associated with the terrorist bombing of commuter trains in Madrid on March 11, 2004. Mayfield spent fourteen days in prison as a material witness to the attack based on a fingerprint. Spanish investigators provided the FBI with an image of a partial print found on a plastic bag recovered from the scene. Investigators suspected that the attackers had handled it. Search of the IAFIS system provided a list of potential matches, and evaluation by experts led to an identification of Mayfield, whose prints were on record because he had served in the army. The fact that Mayfield had converted to Islam and had acted as an attorney for a person Portland accused of operating a terrorist training camp added fuel to the fire, even though the matter he acted on was an unrelated child custody case.

Spanish investigators expressed misgivings about the identification and eventually linked the questioned fingerprint to another suspect. Mayfield was released, and the FBI issued a press statement and apology in May 2004, promising to review procedures and practices. The problems were ultimately blamed on poor quality of the digital image, even though several examiners looked at the print and believed it to be a match to Mayfield. The case will likely have far-reaching consequences for fingerprints and pattern identification, although it will take years for it to play out.

The criticisms and challenges to pattern evidence owe their short history to the evolution of DNA evidence and the Daubert trilogy of court decisions. DNA evidence is presented to a jury in probabilistic terms based on genetic frequencies in the population. Not everyone on the planet has been or ever will be typed for the thirteen DNA loci in use, just as not everyone will ever be typed for their ABO blood group. The frequency of types across a population can be extrapolated from a smaller subset using mathematical relationships as long as the loci are not linked to each other. The type of statistics used and how they are presented are direct results of the DNA controversies of the late 1990s; now the courts and defense lawyers are asking the same be applied to fingerprints. The contrast between DNA evidence, what lies behind it, and how the courts vet it via *Daubert* and similar standards stands in stark contrast to fingerprint evidence.

First, there are no widely accepted databases of frequencies of fingerprint features. Second, there are no generally accepted statistical models that specify how to apply them. As in the Mayfield case, a fingerprint is usually presented as either a match or not a match, that is, a probability of 100 percent or 0 percent. There are no agreed upon measurements or methods to gauge error in classification or identification. The concept of proficiency testing of methods and analysts involved DNA analysis is accepted as necessary, although debate continues on how to implement and express it. In fingerprinting, the hurdle is defining and measuring the error rate.

As the Mayfield case so clearly illustrated, that error exists is beyond dispute. The problem is how to express and address it. What befalls fingerprinting in the next few years will impact pattern evidence generally, but the trend is clear. Like it or not, agree with it or not, the emerging standard for forensic evidence is the DNA-*Daubert* model. Data will have to be quantitative and probabilistic with supporting evidence, peer review, standards, error measurement, and testing behind it. Every forensic practice, no matter how well entrenched, will face the same scrutiny. The history of forensic science in the twenty-first century will undoubtedly be intimately related to how science and the law deal with it.

CURSE OF COMPLEXITY

As the scope and technical sophistication of crimes and criminals increase, so must the sophistication of the technologies used to combat them. Huge databases of fingerprints, firearms, DNA types, and footwear are used to store and screen evidence and test results, speeding and improving an otherwise tedious human search and comparison procedure. Although most people do not fret about the pattern of their favorite shoe being in a database, the prospect of their DNA profile being there is another matter. As always, issues of individual rights and privacy struggle in the face of increasing government actions designed and implemented to protect society.

What sets the modern debate apart from its predecessors is the complexity of the issues, both scientific and social. The CODIS (Combined DNA Index System) database administered by the FBI does not, as many people believe, contain a person's genetic blueprint. Rather it contains typing information for thirteen different loci (locations on the genes). The DNA in these regions is sometimes called *junk DNA*, although the function of these sequences is still unclear. It is not conceptually much different from having a blood type (ABO) in a medical file or a fingerprint in the FBI's centralized files. This does not mean the data does not warrant protection; however, the core issue and debate should center on the issues of whose profiles are entered, under what circumstances they are entered, and to whom they are accessible.

A disturbing corollary is that as the technical complexity of forensic science races ahead, it becomes increasingly difficult to explain results and interpretations to a jury, judge, and lawyers who, on average, will have a year, or at the most, two years of high school science. If a person does not understand the basics of a scientific procedure, it is impossible for them to fairly judge its outcome or weigh its importance. Juries may discount such arguments and weigh more heavily on eyewitness testimony and emotional response, the very things forensic science is supposed to replace. Credible arguments have been made that jury nullification played a role in the O.J. Simpson criminal trial and verdict in 1994. However, evidence of the *CSI effect* creeping into the courtroom remains elusive and anecdotal.[1] If it ever does occur on a wide scale, the courtroom reverts to that of the Greeks, Romans, and their predecessors in which sworn oaths, statements, and affirmations carried the day regardless of the physical evidence.

Another aspect of the new age of forensic science is an emphasis on the ability to positively identify an individual. In an era in which lives are labeled by barcodes and numbers, obtaining false identification is a matter of paperwork, and the crime of identity theft is booming. Fingerprints, the mainstay of forensic identification, are under new legal scrutiny, much of it the result of the lessons learned during judicial review and acceptance of DNA typing.

It is conceivable that fingerprints will eventually go the way of Bertillonage. As DNA typing technology improves and can be applied to smaller samples, it may be possible to obtain a DNA type from a fingerprint. Conversely, this approach may be used to provide the scientific underpinning that many argue is missing from fingerprinting. One of the foundational disciplines within forensic science—fingerprinting—has entered the twenty-first century on the brink of an upheaval reminiscent of the demise of Bertillonage a century earlier.

21

Let Us Return to the Scene of the Crime

The general opinion of those gathered there was that the man outside had been the first one wounded and had died from his injuries. The man inside was though [*sic*] to have committed suicide after that. The officials, considering that both men were injured and that no valuables were involved, declared it to be a cause of mutual homicide. One inquest official alone said, "That is not so. If we use circumstances to measure circumstances, making it out that two killed one another, then that would be possible. But the knife wounds on the right side of the back of the head of the man inside are suspicious. How could he have inflected such wounds on the back side [*sic*] of his own head? This would not be easy to do." Within a few days, a man was apprehended who had hated the two men and killed them. The unsolved case was clear.

—Sung Tz'u, circa 1247 c.e.[1]

This history of the science of circumstance has come full circle, returning to the stage where forensic science performs. The key to crime scene investigation has always been observation and documentation. What have changed are the methods used for each task. For most of recorded history, some form of paper and pen constituted the required tools for translating observation into documentation. Police agencies and death investigators adopted crime scene photography in the late 1800s. Another critical tool in recreating the circumstances of a violent crime is bloodstain pattern analysis. These two stalwarts—photography and blood spatter analysis—are scientifically mature although continually updated by new technologies such as digital imaging and crime scene mapping.

A forensic scientist such as Locard, sitting in his laboratory in Lyon in 1900, might have looked forward into the next century and predicted that forensic science depends on advances in chemistry. Broadly speaking, he would have been correct. Had Locard been sitting at the same desk in 1999, the horizon would have looked to belong to biology. Even discounting DNA, the early part of the twenty-first century is witnessing a biological boom analogous to the chemical boom of the early twentieth. Nowhere is this more apparent than at the crime scene. Anthropology, archaeology, entomology, and botany have come of age as crime scene tools in the last few decades, but all rely on observation and documentation.

DOCUMENTING DEATH

Aside from judicial death investigation such as the one described in the quote at the beginning of this chapter, formalized crime scene investigation was not common until well into the twentieth century. Because a death scene is rarely a crime scene, one of the tasks assigned to death investigators, coroners, and medical examiners has been determination of the nature of the death. Both cause and circumstance of death must be questioned before a forensic inquiry is called for. Crime scenes are often devoid of a body even though violent acts may have occurred there. Some crimes create more than one scene. For example, a person could kill his or her victim in an apartment (the primary crime scene), wrap the body in a sheet and place it in a car trunk (a secondary scene), and then take the body to a burial site in a remote abandoned field (another scene and a clandestine grave). Recognizing each as a scene and linking them together calls upon Locard's principle and all the forensic skills.

Aside from questioned death scenes, police or other law enforcement officials practiced various levels of crime scene investigation. Documentation using early photography, particularly daguerreotypes (also informally called tintypes), was tedious and not well suited to the transitory nature of crime scenes. The method was used for criminal identification, with one of the earliest known mug shots being daguerreotypes from Belgium taken in 1843.[2] The method of tintyping had been made public only four years earlier (1839), indicating that in Europe, the gap between development of a technology and forensic application was narrowing. By 1854, the Swiss had also used mug shots. Once simpler methods using negative plates were developed and commercialized, crime scene photography was used, but not universally. Few of the earliest and more famous examples were crime scene photos taken in London in 1888 as part of the Jack the Ripper case. Legal acceptance of photographic evidence from crime scene to photomicrographs occurred in the late 1800s in Europe and in the United States.

The man most responsible for the early adoption of forensic photography was Professor Rudolph A. Reiss (1875–1929), who was a professor at the University of Lausanne in Switzerland. Previously, he had studied under Bertillon who used photography as part of his Bertillonage criminal identification system. In 1902, Reiss taught a course in what he called *judicial photography*. Reiss' efforts and interest in forensic science led to formation of the Lausanne Institute of Police Science. This was the first known university program devoted to forensic science, as opposed to the institutes of legal medicine dotting Europe by that time. The school was renamed School of Criminal Sciences, which remains a hub of forensic science education in Europe.

SPATTER VS. SPLATTER[3]

A violent crime usually creates a chaotic and bloody crime scene. The bloodstains capture the moment and, when properly analyzed, can reveal much about the circumstances of the attack and afterward. Bloodstain patterns on clothing, skin, and weapons are also information-rich, but it is analysis of stains at the crime scene that has proven invaluable in many cases. By the 1840s Alfred Swaine Taylor noted the importance of bloodstains as part of the milieu of circumstantial evidence in death investigation. He devoted several pages of his text on medical jurisprudence to the evaluation of bloodstains, bloody footprints, and arterial blood and the use of the size and shape of blood droplets in determining their point of origin. He discussed at length how bloodstains were useful for determining if a victim had been moved or how he or she had been moved once injured. His discussion also included the importance of color and clotting and pointed out that he believed clotted blood could only have originated from a living person rather than the dead. One case he related described how he had used bloodstain patterns to discern the order of the attack on a female victim found dead at the bottom of a staircase:

> At the top of the stair, and at a height of four or five feet above the level, several spots of blood were observed upon the brick-wall. These were rendered very evident by the wall having been whitewashed. The spots took and [*sic*] oblique direction from above downwards, were of pale red colour at the upper part, but dark red below; terminating in a point consisting of the fibrin and the greater part of the red colouring matter. Their form and regularity proved they ad [*sic*] proceeded from a small artery, and that the wounded individual could not have been very distant from the wall, while their shining luster rendered it probable that they were of recent origin, and their well-defined termination in a firm coagulum showed that they had proceeded from a living blood-vessel. The deceased had died from a fracture of the skull and vertebral column by a fall from the top-strain; one branch of the right temporal artery was found divided, and this wound could not have been produced by the fall. It was therefore evident that a murderous assault had been made upon her at the top of the stair.[4]

In a time before fingerprints, Taylor urged investigators to look for bloody hand marks on a victim's skin, paying particular attention to marks in places the victim could not have made them. Taylor cited a case in which the bloody imprint of a left hand was found on the left hand of a victim and noted the conundrum this presented.

From 1850 on, bloodstain patterns were discussed frequently in European literature. Dr. Eduard Piotrowski of the University of Vienna published the first comprehensive treatment in 1895. His book, translated as *Concerning Origin, Shape, Direction, and Distribution of Bloodstains Following Blow Injuries to the Head*, covered theoretical concepts and described the results of numerous experiments. Hans Gross joined the discussion in 1904 by including information about documenting and interpreting bloodstain patterns in his textbook.

In 1939, Victor Balthazard presented another landmark paper, this one describing in detail how the geometry (length and width) of a blood drop could be used to estimate impact angles. His research produced what are today called stringing techniques in which the length and width of a drop are used to estimate angle of impact. Investigators anchor a string to the spot and hold it at the appropriate angle to estimate the trajectory of the blood before the impact. Stringing several spots in a stain pattern results in the strings converging in an area in space where the blood must have originated.

The definitive modern study of bloodstain patterns began in the 1960s, led by Dr. Herbert L. Macdonell. He differentiated appearance (size and geometry) of stains based on the speed at which the blood was traveling when it impacted the target. A slow drip from a bloody nose became a low velocity impact pattern, a stain resulting from a punch (smaller drops) resulting from a medium velocity impact, and a gunshot usually creates tiny spots from high velocity impact. Macdonell studied how drops elongated based on angle of impact and demonstrated how simple trigonometry can be used to locate a point (or region) of origin of stain patterns. Such information is essential in re-creations such as related by Taylor earlier. As evidence of forensic maturity, The International Association of Bloodstain Pattern Analysis was formed in 1983. The International Association of Identification now offers certification in this specialty.

From bloodstain pattern analysis through taphonomy and botany, crime scene investigation is embracing new integrative techniques with a biological flavor. In the best forensic tradition, the science was not developed for forensic applications but, once available, was quickly adapted to it. The application of archaeological and ecological techniques to crime scenes like clandestine graves illustrates the intermarriages that are expanding the scope of forensic science. The more unexpected the combination, the more interesting the result. Consider one of the newest avenues in drug analysis, the domain of the forensic chemist for over a century.

Forensic biologists are using DNA typing to differentiate samples of marijuana, not for legal or courtroom procedures, but to provide investigative information to law enforcement. Another example of how a hybrid of biology, chemistry, and medicine has proven its worth for both investigation and prosecution.

ECOLOGY OF DEATH

Emblematic of new integrative directions in forensic science is the discipline of entomotoxicology that unites elements of death investigation, time of death, and toxicology. The use of insects (the study of which is called entomology) in death investigation was recorded in 1247 in Sung Tz'u's text mentioned earlier, *The Washing Away of Wrongs*.[5] In the case recounted in the book, a sickle used in a murder was located from among a large collection of worker's tools by placing all of them in an open field and seeing which one attracted blowflies. These tiny flies are the first to arrive at a death scene, sometimes within minutes of the death and, anecdotally, even just before death. Even today, the exact chemical trigger for this fatal attraction is unknown.

The road from dust to dust passes through a stage in which the body becomes the nexus of a microenvironment complete with succession through generations of inhabitants, predators, and prey. Blowflies seek out the dead as an ideal place to deposit their eggs. Decaying flesh and blood provided a veritable banquet to emerging maggots. In turn, the maggots and hatchlings provide food for beetles and other successive generations of predators that arrive on scene. Forensic entomologists use their understanding of populations and succession to estimate a time of death. The biggest variable that makes these estimates rather than firmer windows is the environment itself. Temperature and humidity in particular dictate who shows up when and in what numbers.

Despite the limitations, the skills of forensic entomologists are about all that is available once a body passes through initial decomposition stages. Chemical tests, stomach contents, body temperature, rigor mortis, and lividity can only be gauged in the early postmortem stages that range from hours to days. Insects also are agents of decomposition as well as its beneficiaries. Orfila, besides being a preeminent toxicologist, was a forensic investigator of the first order. In this role, he attended exhumations and wrote in the 1830s of his observations of maggots and how their presence accelerates decomposition and skeletonization. An early biologist noted that three flies could destroy a horse just as fast as several lions.[6]

Orfila was apparently not the first to use insect succession to estimate the time of death. That honor goes to a French physician named Bergeret in a case from 1850. The deceased was a child found buried in a tenement. The circumstance of the death was in question, as was the time of burial since several people had occupied the structure in the years after the recovery of the body. He concluded that two generations of maggots had called the body home and that the postmortem interval was about two years. If the body had been buried close to the time of death, he reasoned, then death had probably occurred in 1848; if the decomposition was farther along or the body dry, then death probably occurred in 1849. Interestingly, Bergeret referenced the work of Orfila in his report. Bergeret himself was referenced in an 1878 case report by Paul Camille Hippolyte Brouardel regarding the mummified body of a child. Brouardel, who would later become the president of the French Society of Forensic Medicine, estimated when the child had died based on moth larvae that inhabited the body.

Another physician, German H. Reinhard, published the first known study specifically devoted to forensic entomology in 1881. Another French doctor, Jean Pierre Megnin, began publishing what would become a series of papers and manuscripts in 1886 culminating with the book *La Faune des Cadavres* in 1894. The book crossed the Atlantic where Canadians Wyatt Johnson and Geoffrey Villeneuve summarized their comprehensive research on insects and human corpses in 1895. The concept of a cadaver forming the base of an insect ecosystem had become common by the 1920s, and by the beginning of the 1950s, forensic entomology had established itself as a small but distinct arm of forensic death investigation, practiced by an eclectic mix of physicians and biologists.

Chemists and toxicologists entered the picture in the 1970s, via environmental studies. This decade saw an explosion of research related to environmental problems as well as the birth of the Environmental Protection Agency. The forensic implications were twofold. First, environmental laws and regulations became the basis for legal action, civil and criminal. The trilogy case described in a previous chapter, *G.E. v. Joiner*, was an example of a case derived from environmental concerns. Second, there is significant overlap between criminal toxicology and forensic toxicology; a person can be poisoned purposely or accidentally by exposure to environmental toxins. Typically, the difference is in dose and timeframe. Environmental toxicology usually involves chronic exposure to low levels of toxins over a long time. Forensic toxicology usually (but not always) involves acute exposure to a large dose of a toxin.

In the late 1970s, papers appeared in the literature showing how insects could accumulate metal poisons from the environment just as fish, for example, concentrate metals such as mercury in their bodies. If the insect's environment and food source happens to be a dead body, then metals in the person's tissue are transferred to the insects in proportion to the amount consumed. Mercury levels in insects were utilized in a case in Finland in 1977: A decomposed female body was found in advanced decomposition and with a thriving insect population. Analysis of the insects revealed only trace levels of mercury, indicating that the woman had lived in an area where the food and environment was low in mercury contamination.[7] In 1980, insects associated with a decomposing body were analyzed and found to contain barbiturates, supporting suicide as a manner of death. These cases illustrate the advantage of entomotoxicology; the techniques can be applied when decomposition has destroyed or compromised the tissues and fluids needed for traditional toxicological analyses.

Continuing research has revealed the limitations of using insects as toxicological matrices. First, there are too many variables to allow for direct correlation between concentrations found in the insects or larvae and a dose or doses taken by the deceased. Second, just as drugs and poisons have adverse effects on people, so they do on insects. Larvae dining on morphine and cocaine may be happier than the average larvae, but they certainly do not grow the same. This affects estimates of the postmortem interval and further complicates linking concentrations found in their bodies to concentrations in the deceased. In the worst cases, the insects may consume lethal doses of drugs or poisons.

STILL FUNDAMENTALLY FORENSIC

Paul Kirk or Edmund Locard could not have predicted the direction that forensic science has taken, but they doubtless would have been pleased. The body of scientific knowledge has ballooned such that the true forensic generalist is profession of the past. However, the same goals can be achieved by combining forensic specialties together creatively to generate ideas such as entomotoxicology. The heart of it remains the fundamental and distinctly forensic arts of comparison, classification, observation, and documentation. From that creative synthesis, born at the intersection of science and the law, circumstance was, and continues to be, revealed.

Notes

CHAPTER 1

1. Quoted from P.L. Kirk, "Criminalistics," *Science* 140 (1963): 367–370, quote on p. 368.

2. Birth and death years, where available, were obtained or confirmed online from the *Biography Reference* database, available by subscription through academic libraries.

CHAPTER 2

1. From a report published online by the United States Department of State that summarized the work of a multiagency panel convened after September 11. URL: http://usinfo.state.gov/gi/Archive/2005/Nov/22-525320.html. Last accessed April 27, 2006.

CHAPTER 6

1. From F. Szabadvary, *History of Analytical Chemistry* (Oxford, UK: Pergamon Press, 1966), p. 6.

2. Quoted in D.T. Burns, "Highlights in the History of Quantitation in Chemistry," *Fresenius' Journal of Analytical Chemistry* 337 (1990): 205–212, quote on p. 205.

3. From F. Szabadvary, *History of Analytical Chemistry* (Oxford, UK: Pergamon Press, 1966), p. 22.

4. From R. Morris, *The Last Sorcerers: The Path From Alchemy to the Periodic Table* (Washington, DC: John Henry Press, 2003), p. 30.

5. From Curtis Klaassen, ed., *Casarett and Doull's Toxicology: The Basic Science of Poisons*, 6th ed. (New York: McGraw-Hill, 2001), title page.

6. From B.T. Moran, *Distilling Knowledge: Alchemy, Chemistry, and the Scientific Revolution* (Cambridge, MA: Harvard University Press, 2005), p. 100.

CHAPTER 7

1. An element in the natural state, unbound to any other elements, is in what chemists call "the elemental state." The elemental state of mercury is the liquid found in thermometers and is symbolized as Hg. Elemental arsenic (As) is a dull gray powder. The elemental state is not necessarily the commonest form that an element is found in. Arsenic is common as an ingredient in minerals such as As_2O_3. A similar case is iron, which is most commonly found as Fe_2O_3 or rust.

2. Quoted in I.A. Burney, "Testing Testimony: Toxicology and the Law of Evidence in Early Nineteenth-Century England," *Studies in History and Philosophy of Science* 33(2) (2002): 289–314.

3. From Jürgen Thorwald, *The Century of the Detective*, translated by C. Winston and R. Winston (New York: Harcourt, Brace, and World, 1964), p. 289.

4. Ibid., p. 290.

5. Quoted in I.A. Burney, "Testing Testimony: Toxicology and the Law of Evidence in Early Nineteenth-Century England," *Studies in History and Philosophy of Science* 33(2) (2002): 289–314, quote on p. 307.

CHAPTER 8

1. From Sung Tz'u, *The Washing Away of Wrongs*, translated by B. McKnight, in *Science, Medicine, and Technology in East Asia*, vol. 1, edited by N. Sivin (Ann Arbor, MI: The University of Michigan Press, 1981), pp. 116–117. Original edition, 1247.

2. Quoted in D.M. Lucas, "CAC Founder's Lecture: The Development of Forensic Science in Canada," *Science & Justice* 37(1) (1997): 47–54, quote on p. 50.

3. Quoted in E. Fee and T. M. Brown, "'A Doctors' War': Expert Witnesses in Late 19th-Century America," *American Journal of Public Health* 95(Suppl. 1) (2005): S28–S29, quote on p. 28.

4. Quoted in W.Q. Sturner, "The Wit and Wisdom of Milton Helpern: A Glimpse in Time," *The American Journal of Forensic Medicine and Pathology* 19(3) (1998): 288–290, quote on p. 289.

CHAPTER 9

1. From I.A. Burney, "Testing Testimony: Toxicology and the Law of Evidence in Early Nineteenth-Century England," *Studies in History and Philosophy of Science* 33(2) (2002): 289–314, quote on p. 298.

2. Quoted in I.A. Burney, "Testing Testimony: Toxicology and the Law of Evidence in Early Nineteenth-Century England," *Studies in History and Philosophy of Science* 33(2) (2002): 289–314, quote on p. 306.

3. Quoted in W.A. Campbell, "The History of the Chemical Detection of Poisons," *Medical History* 25(2) (1981): 202–203, quote on p. 202.

4. Quoted in N.G. Coley, "Alfred Swaine Taylor, MD (1806–1880): Forensic Toxicologist," *Medical History* 35(4) (1991): 409–427, quote on p. 409.

5. Quoted in A.G. Christen and J.A. Christen, "The 1850 Webster/Parkman Trial: Dr. Keeps Forensic Evidence," *Journal of the History of Dentistry* 51(1) (2003): 5–12, quote on p. 7.

6. Ibid., p. 8.

7. Ibid., 5–12.

CHAPTER 10

1. Both quotes from F. Szabadvary, "Chapter XI: Optical Methods," in *History of Analytical Chemistry* (Pergamon Press: Oxford, UK, 1966), pp. 330 and 332.

2. Quoted in H.A. Laitinen and G.W. Ewing, "Chapter III: Analytical Spectroscopy," in *A History of Analytical Chemistry*, H.A. Laitinenand and G.W. Ewing, eds. (York, PA: The Maple Publishing Company, 1977), pp. 103–243.

3. The equation is A = εlc where A = degree of absorbance of light of a given wavelength; ε = molar absorptivity, a measure of how efficiently a molecule absorbs light of the wavelength being studied; l = path length; and c = concentration.

4. Quoted in M. Gorman, "Sir William Brooke O'Shaughnessy, F.R.S. (1809–1889), Anglo-Indian Forensic Chemist," *Notes and Records of the Royal Society of London* 39(1) (1984): 51–64, quote on p. 57.

5. Quoted in M. Gorman, "Sir William Brooke O'Shaughnessy, F.R.S. (1809–1889), Anglo-Indian Forensic Chemist," *Notes and Records of the Royal Society of London* 39(1) (1984): 51–64, quote on p. 58.

6. Ibid.

CHAPTER 11

1. Cited in P.F. Brain and G.A. Coward, "A Review of the History, Actions, and Legitimate Uses of Cocaine," *Journal of Substance Abuse* 1(4) (1989): 431–451, quote on p. 436.

2. From C.S. Smith, "Nearly 100, LSD's Father Ponders His Problem Child," *The New York Times*, January 7, 2006. URL: http://query.nytimes.com/gst/fullpage.html?res=9505E3DB153FF934A35752C0A9609C8B63&scp=1&sq=LSD&st=nyt.

CHAPTER 13

1. Quoted in F. Szabadvary, "Chapter VII: Further Developments in Quantitative and Gravimetric Analysis," in *History of Analytical Chemistry* (Oxford, UK: Pergamon Press, 1966), p. 188.

2. Quoted in J.G. Delly, "The Microchemical Bench," *Microscope* 47(1) (1999): 13–28, quote on p. 15.

3. From the McCrone Research Institute Web site. URL: http://mcri.org/home/section/63-64-293/the-latest-shroud-update. Last accessed February 23, 2008.

4. Quoted in J.L. Heilbron, "The Work of H.G.J. Moseley," *Isis* 57(3) (1966): 336–364, quote on p. 338.

CHAPTER 14

1. This section focuses on handguns as firearms evidence. The same principles apply to rifles, but shotguns are somewhat different in that the projectiles (pellets) do not acquire markings the same way bullets do.

2. From C.H. Goddard, "A History of Firearms Identification to 1930," *The American Journal of Forensic Medicine and Pathology* 1(2) (1980): quote on p. 160.

3. Lucas attributes this quote to W.R. Donough in *Principles of Circumstantial Evidence, Calcutta* (1918), p. 131. This is all the information Lucas provides about this reference; it may be a first edition of the book entitled *Principles of Circumstantial Evidence Applicable to British India* published in 1922 by Thacker, Spink, and Company of Calcutta.

4. From A. Lucas, *Forensic Chemistry*, 1st ed. (London: Edward Arnold & Co., 1921), p. 11.

CHAPTER 15

1. G. Bergman, "Darwinian Criminal Theory: A Tragic Chapter in History," *Rivista di Biologia/Biology Forum* 98 (2005): 47–70, quote on p. 53.

2. N.H. Rafter, *Creating Born Criminals* (Chicago, IL: University of Illinois Press, 1997), p. 110.

3. Quoted in G. Bergman, "Darwinian Criminal Theory: A Tragic Chapter in History," *Rivista di Biologia/Biology Forum* 98 (2005): 47–70, quote on p. 56.

CHAPTER 16

1. From G.V. Giusti, "Leone Lattes: Italy's Pioneer in Forensic Serology," *The American Journal of Forensic Medicine and Pathology* 3(1) (1982): 79–81.

2. From Jürgen Thorwald, "Chapter I: At the Limits of Detectability: Forensic Serology," in *Crime and Science* (New York: Harcourt, Brace, and World, 1966), p. 42.

3. Dr. Shaler, of the New York City Medical Examiners Office, was in charge of identification of the victims of September 11, 2001.

CHAPTER 17

1. From R. Lewin, "News & Comment: DNA Typing on the Witness Stand," *Science* 244 (1989): 1033–1035.

CHAPTER 18

1. The focus will be on U.S. law.

2. While the court set a legal precedent in the case relative to the admissibility of new scientific techniques and the associated expert testimony, the controversy over the polygraph continues to this day. The only state that allows admission of polygraph evidence is New Mexico, but the technique is still widely used for investigative purposes.

CHAPTER 19

1. Quoted from M. Houck, "Introduction," in *Mute Witness* (San Diego, CA: Elsevier, 2001), p. xix.

2. Some references spell the name Volmer; the spelling Vollmer is used by the Berkeley Police Department and will be used here.

3. From P.L. Kirk, "Criminalistics," *Science* 140 (1963): 367–370, quote on p. 367.

4. From D.M. Lucas, "CAC Founder's Lecture: The Development of Forensic Science in Canada," *Science & Justice* 37(1) (1997): 47–54.

5. Quoted in P.D. James, "Murder and Mystery: Medical Science and the Crime Novel," *Proceedings of the Ordinary Meeting* (1999): 45–53, quote on p. 45.

CHAPTER 20

1. M. Houck, "CSI: Reality," *Scientific American* 295(1) (2006): 84–89.

CHAPTER 21

1. From Sung Tz'u, *The Washing Away of Wrongs*, translated by B. McKnight, edited by N. Sivin. Vol. 1, *Science, Medicine, and Technology in East Asia* (Ann Arbor, MI: The University of Michigan Press, 1981), p. 67.

2. A.A. Moenssens, ed., "The Origin of Legal Photography," *Fingerprint and Identification News* (1962). Available online at Forensic-Evidence.com. URL: http://forensic-evidence.com/site/EVID/LegalPhotog.html. Accessed February 23, 2008. His online article is an edited reprint of the same article he published in *Fingerprint and Identification News* in 1962.

3. Practitioners of the interpretation of bloodstain patterns prefer the term bloodstain pattern analysis or blood spatter analysis. Blood splatter is generally not used and is avoided here, although popular accounts often do use it.

4. A.S. Taylor, *Medical Jurisprudence*, 4th American from the 5th and improved London ed. (Philadelphia: Blanchard and Lea, 1856), p. 21.

5. The source of much of the information in this section is an article from the journal *Forensic Science International* (vol. 20, 2001, pp. 2–14) titled "A Brief History of Forensic Entomology" by Mark Benecke. The sources he draws on include a large body of translated French and German works that would otherwise be difficult to access.

6. Paraphrased from the previous reference, p. 3.

7. An excellent summary of the brief history of entomotoxicology and the primary source for this section was an article in *Forensic Science International* (vol. 120, 2001, pp. 42–47) by Introna, Campobasso, and Goff.

Bibliography

BOOKS

Aromatico, A. 2000. *Alchemy: The Great Secret.* Translated by J. Hawkes. New York: Harry Abrahams. Original edition, 1996.

Baker, J.H. 2002. *An Introduction to English Legal History.* 4th ed. London: Butterworth. Also available at LexisNexis.

Beavan, C. 2001. *Fingerprints: The Origins of Crime Detection and the Murder Case That Launched Forensic Science.* New York: Hyperion.

Bing, D.H. 1997. "DNA Typing Methods for Forensic Analysis." In *More Chemistry and Crime.* Edited by S.M. Gerber and R. Saferstein. Washington, DC: American Chemical Society.

Cole, S.A. 2001. *Suspect Identities: A History of Fingerprinting and Criminal Identification.* Cambridge, MA: Harvard University Press.

Culliford, B.J. 1971. *The Examination and Typing of Bloodstains in the Crime Laboratory.* Washington, DC: U.S. Government Printing Office.

Emsley, J. 2005. *The Elements of Murder: A History of Poison.* New York: Oxford University Press.

Franklin, J. 2001. *The Science of Conjecture: Evidence and Probability Before Pascal.* Baltimore, MD: Johns Hopkins University Press.

Golan, Tal. 2004. "Epilogue." In *Laws of Nature and Laws of Men.* Cambridge, MA: Harvard University Press.

Houck, M. 2001. "Introduction." In *Mute Witnesses.* Edited by M. Houck. San Diego, CA: Elsevier.

Kelly, J. 2004. *Gunpowder: Alchemy, Bombards, and Pyrotechnics: The History of the Explosive That Changed the World.* New York: Basic Books/The Perseus Book Group.

Kiely, T.F. 2001. *Forensic Evidence: Science and the Criminal Law.* Boca Raton, FL: CRC Press.

Kind, S., and M. Overman. 1972. *Science against Crime*. New York: Doubleday & Co., Inc.

Klaassen, C., ed. 2001. *Casarett and Doull's Toxicology: The Basic Science of Poisons*. 6th ed. New York: Mc Graw-Hill.

Laitinen, H.A., and G.W. Ewing. 1977. "Chapter III: Analytical Spectroscopy." In *A History of Analytical Chemistry*. Edited by H.A. Laitinen and G.W. Ewing. York, PA: The Maple Publishing Company.

Le Couteur, P., and J. Burreson. 2003. "Nitro Compounds." In *Napoleon's Buttons*. New York: Jeremy P. Tarcher/Penguin.

———. 2003. "Phenol." In *Napoleon's Buttons*. New York: Jeremy P. Tarcher/Penguin.

———. 2003. "Silk and Nylon." In *Napoleon's Buttons*. New York: Jeremy P. Tarcher/Penguin.

———. 2004. *Napoleon's Buttons: 17 Molecules That Changed History*. New York: Jeremy Tarcher/Penguin.

Lucas, A. 1921. *Forensic Chemistry*. 1st ed. London: Edward Arnold & Co.

———. 1931. *Forensic Chemistry*. 2nd ed. London: Edward Arnold & Co.

Macinnins, P. 2004. *Poisons: From Hemlock to Botox and the Killer Bean of Calabar*. New York: Arcade Publishing.

Moran, B.T. 2005. *Distilling Knowledge: Alchemy, Chemistry, and the Scientific Revolution*. Cambridge, MA: Harvard University Press.

Morris, R. 2003. *The Last Sorcerers: The Path From Alchemy to the Periodic Table*. Washington, DC: John Henry Press.

Murray, R.C., and J.C.F. Tedrow. 1975. "Chapter 1: History of the Science." In *Forensic Geology*. Rahway, NJ: Rutgers University Press.

Rafter, N.H. 1997. *Creating Born Criminals*. Chicago, IL: University of Illinois Press.

Read, J. 1995. *From Alchemy to Chemistry*. New York: Dover Publications. Original edition, 1957.

Salzberg, H.W. 1991. *From Caveman to Chemist: Circumstances and Achievements*. Washington, DC: American Chemical Society.

Sassoon, J. 2001. *Ancient Laws and Modern Problems*. Hong Kong: Midas Printing Group Ltd.

Shaler, R.C. 1997. "Forensic Biology: A Walk through History." In *More Chemistry and Crime: From Marsh Arsenic Test to DNA Profile*. Edited by S. M. Gerber and R. Saferstein. Washington, DC: American Chemical Society.

Somerset, A. 2003. *The Affair of the Poisons*. New York: St. Martin's Press.

Stoney, D.A., and P.M. Dougherty. 1997. "The Microscope in Forensic Science: Forensic Microscopy in the 1890s and the Development of the Comparison Microscope." In *More Chemistry and Crime: From Marsh Arsenic Test to DNA Profile*. Edited by S. M. Gerber and R. Saferstein. Washington, DC: American Chemical Society.

Szabadvary, F. 1966. "Chapter VII: Further Developments in Quantitative and Gravimetric Analysis." In *History of Analytical Chemistry*. Oxford, UK: Pergamon Press.

———. 1966. "Chapter XI: Optical Methods." In *History of Analytical Chemistry*. Oxford, UK: Pergamon Press.

———. 1966. *History of Analytical Chemistry*. Oxford, UK: Pergamon Press.

Taylor, A.S. 1856. *Medical Jurisprudence*. 4th American from the 5th and improved London ed. Philadelphia: Blanchard and Lea.

Thorwald, J. 1962. *Science and Secrets of Early Medicine*. New York: Harcourt, Brace & World, Inc.

———. 1964. *The Century of the Detective*. Translated by C. Winston and R. Winston. New York: Harcourt, Brace & World, Inc.

———. 1966. "Chapter I: At the Limits of Detectability: Forensic Serology." In *Crime and Science*. New York: Harcourt, Brace & World, Inc.

Tz'u, Sung. 1981. *The Washing Away of Wrongs*. Translated by B. McKnight. Ann Arbor, MI: The University of Michigan Press. Original edition, 1247.

Versteeg, R. 2002. *Law in the Ancient World*. Durham, NC: Carolina Academic Press.

Webster, C. 2005. *From Paracelsus to Newton: Magic and the Making of Modern Science*. Mineola, NY: Dover Press. Original edition, 1982.

Zollinger, H. 2003. "Chapter 1: Introduction." In *Color Chemistry: Syntheses, Properties, and Applications of Organic Dyes and Pigments*. Zurich, Switzerland: Wiley-VCH.

JOURNALS AND ARTICLES

Abraham, H.J. 1980. "Religion, Medicine, and the State: Reflections on Some Contemporary Issues." *A Journal of Church and State* 22(3): 423–436.

Abraham, M.H. 2004. "100 Years of Chromatography—Or Is It 171?" *Journal of Chromatography A* 1061(1): 113–114.

Adelson, L. 1989. "Forensic Pathology Then and Now. Retrospect and Reflections." *The American Journal of Forensic Medicine and Pathology* 10(3): 251–260.

"Advances in Optical Spectroscopy and Mass Spectrometry. A Tribute to David M. Hercules." 2002. *Analytical and Bioanalytical Chemistry* 373(7): 517–675.

Amundsen, D.W., and G.B. Ferngren. 1978. "The Forensic Role of Physicians in Ptolemaic and Roman Egypt." *Bulletin of the History of Medicine* 52(3): 336–353.

Antman, K.H. 2001. "Introduction: The History of Arsenic Trioxide in Cancer Therapy." *The Oncologist* 6(Suppl 2): 1–2.

Aronson, S.M. 2005. "Murder, Most Foul, in a Medical School Laboratory." *Medicine & Health Rhode Island* 88(3): 71.

Avis, S.P. 1998. "Death Investigation in Canada." *Journal of Forensic Sciences* 43(2): 377–379.

Báez, H., M.M. Castro, M.A. Benavente, P. Kintz, V. Cirimele, C. Camargo, and C. Thomas. 2000. "Drugs in Prehistory: Chemical Analysis of Ancient Human Hair." *Forensic Science International* 108(3): 173–179.

Bain, M., A. Bentley, and T. Squires. 1999. "Sir Henry Duncan Littlejohn—A Dynamic Figure in Forensic Medicine and Public Health in the Nineteenth Century." *Proceedings of the Royal College of Physicians of Edinburgh* 29(3): 248–252.

Ball, C., and R. Westhorpe. 2003. "Local Anaesthesia—Freud, Koller and Cocaine." *Anaesthesia and Intensive Care* 31(3): 249.

Barnum, D.W. 2003. "Some History of Nitrates." *Journal of Chemical Education* 80(12): 1393–1395.

Bartle, K.D., and P. Myers. 2002. "History of Gas Chromatography." *Trends in Analytical Chemistry* 21(9–10): 547–557.

Bartlett, P. 2001. "Legal Madness in the Nineteenth Century." *Social History of Medicine* 14(1): 107–131.

Bauer, G. 2004. "Austrian Forensic Medicine." *Forensic Science International* 144(2–3): 143–149.

Beck, C.M. 1994. "Classical Analysis: A Look at the Past, Present, and Future." *Analytical Chemistry* 66: 224A–239A.

Beck, J. 1992. "Luke May of Seattle—'America's Sherlock Holmes.'" *Journal of Forensic Sciences* 37(1): 349–355.

Benecke, M. 2001. "A Brief History of Forensic Entomology." *Forensic Science International* 120(1–2): 2–14.

Bergman, G. 2005. "Darwinian Criminal Theory: A Tragic Chapter in History." *Rivista di Biologia/Biology Forum* 98: 47–70.

Bodde, D. 1982. "Forensic Medicine in Pre-Imperial China." *Journal of the American Oriental Society* 102: 1–15.

Brain, P.F., and G.A. Coward. 1989. "A Review of the History, Actions, and Legitimate Uses of Cocaine." *Journal of Substance Abuse* 1(4): 431–451.

Breathnach, C.S. 1987. "Biographical Sketch: Orfila." *Irish Medical Journal* 80(3): 99.

Brittain, R.P. 1966. "The History of Legal Medicine: Charlemagne." *The Medico-Legal Journal* 34(3): 122–123.

———. 1966. "Origins of Legal Medicine. The Origin of Legal Medicine in France." *The Medico-Legal Journal* 34(4): 168–174.

———. 1967. "The Origin of Legal Medicine in France. Henri IV and Louis XIV." *The Medico-Legal Journal* 35(1): 25–28.

Brody, J.R., and S.E. Kern. 2004. "History and Principles of Conductive Media for Standard DNA Electrophoresis." *Analytical Biochemistry* 333(1): 1–13.

Brothwell, D., and M. Spigelman. 1993. "Drugs in Ancient Populations." *The Lancet* 341(8853): 1157.

Burchell, H.B. 1983. "Digitalis Poisoning: Historical and Forensic Aspects." *Journal of the American College of Cardiology* 1(2 Pt 1): 506–516.

Burnett, B., and P. Golubovs. 2000. "The First Mail Bomb?" *Journal of Forensic Sciences* 45(4): 935–936.

Burney, I.A. 1994. "Viewing Bodies: Medicine, Public Order, and English Inquest Practice." *Configurations* 2(1): 33–46.

———. 2002. "Testing Testimony: Toxicology and the Law of Evidence in Early Nineteenth-Century England." *Studies in History and Philosophy of Science* 33(2): 289–314.

Burns, D.T. 1990. "Highlights in the History of Quantitation in Chemistry." *Fresenius' Journal of Analytical Chemistry* 337: 205–212.

———. 2000. "Analytical Chemistry and the Law: Progress for Half a Millennium." *Fresenius' Journal of Analytical Chemistry* 368(6): 544–547.

Burns, T.D. 1991. "Highlights in the History of Quantitation in Chemistry." *Fresenius' Journal of Analytical Chemistry* 63(20): 993A–1008A.

Cameron, J.M. 1980. "Presidential Address to the British Academy of Forensic Sciences. The Medico-Legal Expert—Past, Present and Future." *Medicine, Science and the Law* 20(1): 3–13.

Camp, F.R., Jr. 1980. "Forensic Serology in the United States. I. Blood Grouping and Blood Transfusion—Historical Aspects." *The American Journal of Forensic Medicine and Pathology* 1(1): 47–55.

Campbell, W.A. 1978. "Some Early Chemical Analyses of Proprietary Medicines."
    Isis 69(247): 226–233.
———. 1981. "The History of the Chemical Detection of Poisons." *Medical History*
    25(2): 202–203.
Caplan, R.M. 1990. "How Fingerprints Came into Use for Personal Identification."
    Journal of the American Academy of Dermatology 23(1): 109–114.
Caraway, W.T. 1981. "Major Developments in Clinical Chemical Instrumentation."
    *Journal of Clinical Chemistry and Clinical Biochemistry/Zeitschrift fur Klinische
    Chemie und Klinische Biochemie* 19(7): 491–496.
Chapenoire, S., and M. Bénézech. 2003. "Forensic Medicine in Bordeaux in the
    16th Century." *The American Journal of Forensic Medicine and Pathology* 24(2):
    183–186.
Cho, A., and D. Normile. 2002. "Nobel Prize in Chemistry. Mastering Macro-
    molecules." *Science* 298(5593): 527–528.
Christen, A.G., and J.A. Cristen. 2003. "The 1850 Webster/Parkman Trial: Dr.
    Keeps Forensic Evidence." *Journal of the History of Dentistry* 51(1): 5–12.
Cohen, S. 1975. "Cocaine." *The Journal of the American Medical Association* 231(1):
    74–75.
Coley, N.G. 1991. "Alfred Swaine Taylor, MD, (1806–1880): Forensic Toxicologist."
    Medical History 35(4): 409–427.
Courtwright, D.T. 1978. "Opiate Addiction as a Consequence of the Civil War."
    Civil War History 24(2): 101–111.
Cox, T.M., N. Jack, S. Lofthouse, J. Watling, J. Haines, and M.J. Warren. 2005. "King
    George III and Porphyria: An Elemental Hypothesis and Investigation." *The
    Lancet* 366(9482): 332–335.
Cozanitis, D.A. 2004. "One Hundred Years of Barbiturates and Their Saint." *Journal
    of the Royal Society of Medicine* 97(12): 594–598.
Daldrup, T., and E. Klug. 2004. "100 Years of Toxicology in the German Society of
    Legal Medicine." *Forensic Science International* 144(2–3): 215–220.
Das, G. 1993. "Cocaine Abuse in North America: A Milestone in History." *Journal
    of Clinical Pharmacology* 33(4): 296–310.
Davenport-Hines, R., and D. Black. 1998. "Acid—The Secret History of LSD." *The
    Times Literary Supplement* (4974): 32.
Davis, B. 1985. "A History of Forensic Medicine." *The Medico-Legal Journal* 53(Pt 1):
    9–23.
De Renzi, S. 2002. "Witnesses of the Body: Medico-Legal Cases in Seventeenth-
    Century Rome." *Studies in History and Philosophy of Science* 33(2): 219–242.
Delly, J.G. 1999. "The Microchemical Bench." *Microscope* 47(1): 13–28.
Di Costanzo, J. 2002. "Gastrointestinal Diseases of Napoleon in Saint Helena:
    Causes of Death." *Science Progress* 85(Pt 4): 359–367.
Dingwall, H.M. 1993. "'General Practice' in Seventeenth-Century Edinburgh: Evi-
    dence from the Burcgh Court." *Social History of Medicine* 6(1): 125–142.
Dundee, J.W., and P.D. McIlroy. 1982. "The History of Barbiturates." *Anaesthesia*
    37(7): 726–734.
Eckert, W.G. 1970. "Forensic Sciences." *The New England Journal of Medicine* 283(25):
    1414.
———. 1977. "He Learned from the Dead to Help the Living." *The Journal of Legal
    Medicine* 5(10): 54–56.

———. 1980. "The Lindbergh Case. A Triumph in Forensic Investigation." *The American Journal of Forensic Medicine and Pathology* 1(2): 151–153.

———. 1980. "The St. Valentine's Day Massacre." *The American Journal of Forensic Medicine and Pathology* 1(1): 67–70.

———. 1981. "Advances in American Forensic Sciences. California's Role." *The American Journal of Forensic Medicine and Pathology* 2(2): 155–161.

———. 1981. "Forensic Cases of Note." *The American Journal of Forensic Medicine and Pathology* 2(2): 171–173.

———. 1981. "Historical Aspects of Poisoning and Toxicology." *The American Journal of Forensic Medicine and Pathology* 2(3): 261–264.

———. 1981. "The Medicolegal and Forensic Aspects of Fires." *The American Journal of Forensic Medicine and Pathology* 2(4): 347–357.

———. 1981. "Sir Bernard Spilsbury." *The American Journal of Forensic Medicine and Pathology* 2(2): 179–182.

———. 1981. "Unusual Findings in Medicolegal Cases." *The American Journal of Forensic Medicine and Pathology* 2(3): 265–270.

———. 1981. "The Whitechapel Murders: The Case of Jack the Ripper." *The American Journal of Forensic Medicine and Pathology* 2(1): 53–60.

———. 1982. "American Forensic Sciences 1776–1976." *The American Journal of Forensic Medicine and Pathology* 3(1): 57–62.

———. 1982. "Fatal Commercial Air Transport Crashes, 1924–1981. Review of History and Information on Fatal Crashes." *The American Journal of Forensic Medicine and Pathology* 3(1): 49–56.

———. 1982. "Identification of the Remains of John Paul Jones: A Look at Early Methods." *The American Journal of Forensic Medicine and Pathology* 3(2): 143–152.

———. 1982. "Physician Crimes and Criminals. The Historical and Forensic Aspects." *The American Journal of Forensic Medicine and Pathology* 3(3): 221–230.

———. 1982. "The Rockne Crash. American Commercial Air Crash Investigation in the Early Years." *The American Journal of Forensic Medicine and Pathology* 3(1): 17–27.

———. 1983. "Medicolegal Investigation in New York City. History and Activities 1918–1978." *The American Journal of Forensic Medicine and Pathology* 4(1): 33–54.

———. 1984. "The Writings of Sir Bernard Spilsbury: Part I." *The American Journal of Forensic Medicine and Pathology* 5(3): 231–238.

———. 1985. "The Writings of Sir Bernard Spilsbury: Part II." *The American Journal of Forensic Medicine and Pathology* 6(1): 3137.

———. 1987. "Charles Norris (1868–1935) and Thomas A. Gonzales (1878–1956), New York's Forensic Pioneers." *The American Journal of Forensic Medicine and Pathology* 8(4): 350–353.

———. 1988. "The Forensic or Medicolegal Autopsy. Friend or Foe?" *The American Journal of Forensic Medicine and Pathology* 9(3): 185–187.

———. 1989. "The Ripper Project. Modern Science Solving Mysteries of History." *The American Journal of Forensic Medicine and Pathology* 10(2): 164–171.

———. 1990. "Forensic Sciences and Medicine." *The American Journal of Forensic Medicine and Pathology* 11(4): 336.

———. 1990. "The Lockerbie Disaster and Other Aircraft Breakups in Midair." *The American Journal of Forensic Medicine and Pathology* 11(2): 93.

———. 1991. "Mass Deaths by Gas or Chemical Poisoning: A Historical Perspective." *The American Journal of Forensic Medicine and Pathology* 12(2): 119.

———. 1991. "Medicolegal Aspects of Tornadic Storms in Kansas, U.S.A." *The American Journal of Forensic Medicine and Pathology* 12(4): 281.

———. 1992. "Comparison of the Battles at the Little Bighorn and at Isandhlwana: Medicolegal and Forensic Aspects." *The American Journal of Forensic Medicine and Pathology* 13(1): 56–68.

———. 1992. "The Development of Forensic Medicine in the United Kingdom from the 18th Century." *The American Journal of Forensic Medicine and Pathology* 13(2): 124–131.

Eckert, W.G., and N. Garland. 1984. "The History of the Forensic Applications in Radiology." *The American Journal of Forensic Medicine and Pathology* 5(1): 53–56.

Eckert, W.G., and S. Kaye. 1983. "Alexander O. Gettler (1883–1983). A Centennial of His Birth." *The American Journal of Forensic Medicine and Pathology* 4(4): 297–301.

Eckert, W.G., T.T. Noguchi, and T.C. Chao. 1985. "Geographic Forensic Medicine and Forensic Sciences." *The American Journal of Forensic Medicine and Pathology* 6(4): 343–346.

Eckert, W.G., and W.R. Teixeira. 1985. "The Identification of Josef Mengele. A Triumph of International Cooperation." *The American Journal of Forensic Medicine and Pathology* 6(3): 188–191.

Engelhardt, H. 2004. "One Century of Liquid Chromatography. From Tswett's Columns to Modern High Speed and High Performance Separations." *Journal of Chromatography B, Analytical Technologies in the Biomedical and Life Sciences* 800 (1–2): 3–6.

Erzinçlioglu, Y.Z. 1983. "The Application of Entomology to Forensic Medicine." *Medicine, Science and the Law* 23(1): 57–63.

Ettre, L.S. 2000. "Starting a New Century." *Journal of Chromatographic Science* 38(3): 89–90.

———. 2002. "The Invention, Development, and Triumph of the Flame Ionization Detector." *LCGC North America* 20(1): 48–60.

———. 2003. "Comments on the Early History of Gas Chromatographic Methods for Oil Analysis." *Journal of Chromatography A* 993(12): 217–219; discussion 221.

Fee, E., and T.M. Brown. 2005. "'A Doctors' War': Expert Witnesses in Late 19th-Century America." *American Journal of Public Health* 95(Suppl 1): S28–S29.

Feenstra, O., and I. Seybold. 1989. "Roots of Medicine and Law in Ancient Mesopotamia." *Liege* 39(2): 335–338.

Felts, J.H. 2002. "Henry Ingersoll Bowditch and Oliver Wendell Holmes." *Perspectives in Biology and Medicine* 45(4): 539–548.

Ferguson, M.B., and M.A. Vance. 2000. "Payment Deferred: Strychnine Poisoning in Nicaragua 65 Years Ago." *Journal of Toxicology—Clinical Toxicology* 38(1): 71–77.

Ficarra, B.J. 1977. "History of Legal Medicine." *Legal Medicine Annual* 1976: 3–27.

Forbes, T.R. 1981. "Early Forensic Medicine in England: The Angus Murder Trial." *Journal of the History of Medicine and Allied Sciences* 36(3): 296–309.

Forrest, A.R. 2003. "Coroners—What Next for Death Investigation in England and Wales?" *Science & Justice* 43(3): 125–126.

Fredrick, J.F. 1964. "Gel Electrophoresis: Preface." *Annals of the New York Academy of Sciences* 121: 307–308.

Fresenius, W. 2000. "The Position of the Analyst as Expert: Yesterday and Today." *Fresenius' Journal of Analytical Chemistry* 368(6): 548–549.

Fritz, J.S. 2004. "Early Milestones in the Development of Ion-Exchange Chromatography: A Personal Account." *Journal of Chromatography A* 1039(1–2): 3–12.

Froede, R. 1972. "Drugs of Abuse: Legal and Illegal." *Human Pathology* 3(1): 23–36.

Fu, L.K. 2004. "Sung Tz'u (1186–1249) and Medical Jurisprudence in Ancient China." *Journal of Medical Biography* 12(2): 95–104.

Gallop, A.M. 2003. "Forensic Science Coming of Age." *Science & Justice* 43(1): 55–59.

Garland, A.N. 1987. "Forensic Medicine in Great Britain. I. The Beginning." *The American Journal of Forensic Medicine and Pathology* 8(3): 269–272.

Gibbs, H.D. 1926. "Phenol Tests I. Classification of the Tests and a Review of the Literature." *Chemistry Review* 3(3): 291–319.

Gilani, A.H., and A.U. Rahman. 2005. "Trends in Ethnopharmocology." *Journal of Ethnopharmacology* 100(1–2): 43–49.

Giusti, G.V. 1982. "Leone Lattes: Italy's Pioneer in Forensic Serology." *The American Journal of Forensic Medicine and Pathology* 3(1): 79–81.

Goddard, C.H. 1980. "A History of Firearms Identification to 1930." *The American Journal of Forensic Medicine and Pathology* 1(2): 155–168.

Golan, T. 2004. "The Emergence of the Silent Witness: The Legal and Medical Reception of X-rays in the USA." *Social Studies of Science* 34(4): 469–499.

Goldblatt, D. 1991. "Stiffs." *Seminars in Neurology* 11(3): 295–300.

Goode, A.W., and J.M. Cameron. 2000. "Looking to the Past for the Sake of the Future." *Medicine, Science and the Law* 40(1): 2–3.

Gordon, A.H. 1979. "Electrophoresis and Chromatography of Amino Acids and Proteins." *Annals of the New York Academy of Sciences* 325: 94–105.

Gorman, M. 1984. "Sir William Brooke O'Shaughnessy, F.R.S. (1809–1889), Anglo-Indian Forensic Chemist." *Notes and records of the Royal Society of London* 39(1): 51–64.

Goulding, R. 1978. "Poisoning as a Fine Art." *The Medico-Legal Journal* 46(1): 6–17.

Grant, J. 1976. "The past, present and future rôle of the private forensic science laboratory." *Journal—Forensic Science Society* 16(3): 197–200.

Green, S.T., and F.A. Green. 1986. "The Last Public Execution in Glasgow: The Case of Dr Edward Pritchard, M.D." *Scottish Medical Journal* 31(4): 256–260.

Gros, L. 2005. "Wilhelm Fresenius 1913–2004." *Analytical and Bioanalytical Chemistry* 382(8): 1730–1732.

Guillén Sans, R., and M. Guzmán Chozas. 1988. "Historical Aspects and Applications of Barbituric Acid Derivatives. A Review." *Die Pharmazie* 43(12): 827–829.

Guiochon, G. 2005. "Csaba Horváth and Preparative Liquid Chromatography." *Journal of Chromatography A* 1079(1–2): 7–23.

Guiochon, G., and L.A. Guiochon-Beaver. 2004. "Csaba Horváth (1930–2004)." *Journal of Separation Science* 27(15–16): 1247–1248.

Haglund, H. 1971. "Isoelectric Focusing in pH Gradients—A Technique for Fractionation and Characterization of Ampholytes." *Methods of Biochemical Analysis* 19: 1–104.

Hahn, S. 2003. "'A General Rule in the Post-Mortem Finding of suicides?' German Pathology and Forensic Medicine and the Suicide Problem 1900–1945." *Neuere Medizin- und Wissenschaftsgeschichte* 6: 105–120.

Hamilton, G.R., and T.E. Baskett. 2000. "History of Anesthesia—In the Arms of Morpheus: The Development of Morphine for Postoperative Pain Relief." *Canadian Journal of Anesthesia = Journal Canadien d'Anesthésie* 47(4): 367–375.

Handley, J., and C.M. Harris. 2001. "Great Ideas of a Decade." *Analytical Chemistry* 73(23): 660A–666A.

Hanzlick, R. 1997. "Death Registration: History, Methods, and Legal Issues." *Journal of Forensic Sciences* 42(2): 265–269.

Heilbron, J.L. 1966. "The Work of H.G.J. Moseley." *Isis* 57(3): 336–364.

Helpern, M. 1981. "History of the Methods of Detecting Murder." *The American Journal of Forensic Medicine and Pathology* 2(1): 61–65.

Hirschhorn, B. 1983. "Richard Spencer Childs (1882–1978). His Role in Modernization of Medicolegal Investigation in America." *The American Journal of Forensic Medicine and Pathology* 4(3): 245–254.

Hirt, M., and P. Kovác. 2005. "History of Forensic Medicine—The Second Part. The Autopsy in the Middle Age and the Renaissance." *Soudni Lekarstvi/Casopis Sekce Soudniho Lekarstvi Cs Lekarske Spolecnosti J Ev Purkyne* 50(3): 32–37.

"The History of Intravenous Anaesthesia." 1977. *Anaesthesia* 32(7): 662–663.

Hjertén, S. 1972. "Arne Tiselius 1902–1971." *Journal of Chromatography* 65(2): 345–348.

———. 1988. "The History of the Development of Electrophoresis in Uppsala." *Electrophoresis* 9(1): 3–15.

Hollister, L.E. 1983. "The Pre-Benzodiazepine Era." *Journal of Psychoactive Drugs* 15 (1–2): 9–13.

Hopen, T.J. 2004. "Dr. Walter C McCrone's Contribution to the Identification of Explosives." *Journal of Forensic Sciences* 49(2): 275–276.

Hosztafi, S. 1997. "The Discovery of Alkaloids." *Die Pharmazie* 52(7): 546–550.

Houck, M. 2006. "CSI: Reality." *Scientific American* 295(1): 84–89.

Hua, P., J.M. Cameron, and J.J. Tao. 1987. "Forensic Medicine in China: Its History to the Present Day." *Medicine, Science and the Law* 27(1): 2–12.

Hunter, G.M. 1980. "Murder by Morphine." *History of Medicine* 8(3): 39.

Jackson, C.O. 1976. "Before the Drug Culture Barbiturate/Amphetamine Abuse in American Society." *Clio Medica* 11(1): 47–58.

James, A.T. 1970. "The Development of Gas-Liquid Chromatography." *Biochemical Society Symposium* 30: 199–211.

James, B. 1998. "Murder and Mystery: Medical Science and the Crime Novel." *Transactions of the Medical Society of London* 115: 45–53.

Jeffreys, A.J., V. Wilson, and S.L. Thein. 1985. "Hypervariable 'Minisatellite' Regions in Human DNA." *Nature* 314 (March): 67–73.

Karch, S.B. 1999. "Cocaine: History, Use, Abuse." *Journal of the Royal Society of Medicine* 92(8): 393–397.

Kay, L.E. 1988. "Laboratory Technology and Biological Knowledge: The Tiselius Electrophoresis Apparatus, 1930–1945." *History and Philosophy of the Life Sciences* 10(1): 51–72.

Kaye, S. 1992. "The Rebirth and Blooming of Forensic Medicine, Milton Helpern Lecture." *The American Journal of Forensic Medicine and Pathology* 13(4): 299–304.

Keynes, M. 2004. "The Death of Napoleon." *Journal of the Royal Society of Medicine* 97(10): 507–508.

Kirk, P.L. 1963. "Criminalistics." *Science* 140: 367–370.

Knight, B. 1988. "The Evolution of Methods for Estimating the Time of Death from Body Temperature." *Forensic Science International* 36(1–2): 47–55.

Koeppler, N. 2003. "The Aspirin Story." *Scalpel and Tongs* (October–December): 9–11.

Krauland, W. 2004. "The History of the German Society of Forensic Medicine." *Forensic Science International* 144(2–3): 95–108.

Kyle, R.A., and M.A. Shampo. 2005. "Arne Tiselius—Father of Electrophoresis." *Mayo Clinic Proceedings* 80(3): 302.

Lambourne, G.T. 1978. "A Brief History of Fingerprints." *Journal—Forensic Science Society* 17(2–3): 95–8.

Larson, C.P. 1980. "The Imported Forensic Expert." *The American Journal of Forensic Medicine and Pathology* 1(3): 233–237.

Lattimer, J.K., and A. Laidlaw. 1996. "Good Samaritan Surgeon Wrongly Accused of Contributing to President Lincoln's Death: An Experimental Study of the President's Fatal Wound." *Journal of the American College of Surgeons* 182(5): 431–448.

Laughlin, G.L. 2004. "Dr. McCrone's Teaching Methods in Forensic Microscopy, Their Nature, History, and Durability." *Journal of Forensic Sciences* 49(2): 270–274.

Lawton. 1980. "The Limitations of Expert Scientific Evidence." *Journal—Forensic Science Society* 20(4): 237–242.

Lenihan, J. 1990–1992. "James Maxwell Adams, (1817–1899), Physician, Forensic Scientist and Engineer." *The Scottish Society of the History of Medicine. Report of Proceedings, Session 1990–1992* 45, p. 49.

Leonetti, G., M. Signoli, A.L. Pelissier, P. Champsaur, I. Hershkovitz, C. Brunet, and O. Dutour. 1997. "Evidence of Pin Implantation as a Means of Verifying Death during the Great Plague of Marseilles (1722)." *Journal of Forensic Sciences* 42(4): 744–748.

Lesney, M.S. A History of Analytical Instrumentation. From "Made to Measure," a supplement to *Analytical Chemistry* and *Today's Chemist at Work. Today's Chemist at Work*, Vol. 8, no. 3, pp. 40–97.

Lewin, R. 1989. "News & Comment: DNA Typing on the Witness Stand." *Science* 244: 1033–1035.

Lewis, A. 1968. "Historical Perspective." *British Journal of Addiction to Alcohol & Other Drugs* 63(3): 241–245.

Lewontin, R.C. 1991. "Twenty-five Years Ago in Genetics: Electrophoresis in the Development of Evolutionary Genetics: Milestone or Millstone?" *Genetics* 128(4): 657–662.

Lignitz, E. 2004. "The History of Forensic Medicine in Times of the Weimar Republic and National Socialism—An Approach." *Forensic Science International* 144(2–3): 113–124.

Lin, Xilei, D. Alber, and R. Henkelmann. 2004. "Elemental Contents in Napoleon's Hair Cut before and after His Death: Did Napoleon Die of Arsenic Poisoning?" *Analytical and Bioanalytical Chemistry* 379(2): 218–221.

Lord, Ross. 1996. "Medicine and Law." *Vesalius: Acta Internationales Historiae Medicinae* 2(1): 3–9.

Lowry, O.H. 1994. "The Evolution of Analytical Biochemistry (1933–1983). A Biased 50-Year Review." *The FASEB Journal* 8(2): 262–264.

Lu, G.D., and J. Needham. 1988. "A History of Forensic Medicine in China." *Medical History* 32(4): 357–400.

Lucas, D.M. 1997. "CAC Founder's Lecture: The Development of Forensic Science in Canada." *Science & Justice* 37(1): 47–54.

Lugli, A., A.K. Lugli, and M. Horcic. 2005. "Napoleon's Autopsy: New Perspectives." *Human Pathology* 36(4): 320–324.

Lykknes, A., and L. Kvittingen. 2003. "Arsenic: Not So Evil After All?" *Journal of Chemical Education* 80(5): 497–500.

Maltby, J.R. 1988. "Sherlock Holmes and Anaesthesia." *Canadian Journal of Anesthesia = Journal Canadien d'Anesthesie* 35(1): 58–62.

Mant, A.K. 1987. "Forensic Medicine in Great Britain. II. The Origins of the British Medicolegal System and Some Historic Cases." *The American Journal of Forensic Medicine and Pathology* 8(4): 354–361.

Mari, F., E. Bertol, V. Fineschi, and S.B. Karch. 2004. "Channelling the Emperor: What Really Killed Napoleon?" *Journal of the Royal Society of Medicine* 97(8): 397–399.

Martin, P.D., H. Schmitter, and P.M. Schneider. 2001. "A Brief History of the Formation of DNA Databases in Forensic Science within Europe." *Forensic Science International* 119(2): 225–231.

Matthew, H. 1975. "Barbiturates." *Clinical Toxicology* 8(5): 495–513.

Mellen, P.F. 1985. "Coroners' Inquests in Colonial Massachusetts." *Journal of the History of Medicine and Allied Sciences* 40(4): 462–472.

Mellen, P.F., and E.C. Bouvier. 1996. "Nineteenth-Century Massachusetts Coroner Inquests." *The American Journal of Forensic Medicine and Pathology* 17(3): 207–210.

Meyers, S., and E.S. Shanley. 1990. "Industrial Explosives—A Brief History of Their Development and Use." *Journal of Hazardous Materials* 23: 183–201.

Mitchell, E.K., J.T. Prior, N.T. Forbes, M.J. Hyland, S.M. Menchel, J.M. Uku, and F.T. Zugibe. 1991. "Historical Perspective and a Proposal for Forensic Medical Services in New York State." *New York State Journal of Medicine* 91(11): 497–500.

Montagne, M. 1993. "LSD at 50: Albert Hofmann and His Discovery." *Pharmacy in History* 35(2): 70–73.

Morling, N. 2004. "Forensic Genetics." *The Lancet* 364(Suppl 1): s10–s11.

Mund, M.T., and W. Bär. 2004. "Legal Medicine in Switzerland." *Forensic Science International* 144(2–3): 151–155.

Musto, D.F. 1989. "Why Did Sherlock Holmes Use Cocaine?" *Pharmacy in History* 31(2): 78–80.

———. 1991. "Opium, Cocaine and Marijuana in American History." *Scientific American* 265(1): 40.

———. 1998. "International Traffic in Coca through the Early 20th Century." *Drug and Alcohol Dependence* 49(2): 145–156.

Nichols, D.E. 2004. "Hallucinogens." *Pharmacology & Therapeutics* 101(2): 131–181.

Niwa, T. 1995. "Clinical Mass Spectrometry. Introduction." *Clinica Chimica Acta; International Journal of Clinical Chemistry* 241–242: 3–12.

Niyogi, S.K. 1980. "Historic Development of Forensic Toxicology in America up to 1978." *The American Journal of Forensic Medicine and Pathology* 1(3): 249–264.

Noguchi, T.T. 1986. "Medicolegal Investigations in Hollywood." *Journal of Forensic Sciences* 31(1): 376–385.

Nordling, C.O. 1998. "The Death of King Charles XII—The Forensic Verdict." *Forensic Science International* 96(2–3): 75–89.

Oatley, C.W. 2004. "The Early History of the Scanning Electron Microscope." *Advances in Imagine and Electon Physics* 133: 7–34.

"Obituary: Stuart Stanley Kind." 2003. *Science & Justice* 43(2): 65–69.

Oeppen, R.S. 2003. "Discovery of the First Local Anaesthetic—Carl Koller (1857–1944)." *The British Journal of Oral & Maxillofacial Surgery* 41(4): 243.

Olukoga, A.O., J. Bolodeoku, and D. Donaldson. 1997. "Laboratory Instrumentation in Clinical Biochemistry: An Historical Perspective." *Journal of the Royal Society of Medicine* 90(10): 570–577.

Onuigbo, W.I. 1985. "Expert Evidence. Historical Perspectives." *The American Journal of Forensic Medicine and Pathology* 6(2): 141–143.

Page, D. 2005. "Life in a Disaster Morgue." *Forensic Magazine* (December–January): 8–11.

Pappas, A.A., N.A. Massoll, and D.J. Cannon. 1999. "Toxicology: Past, Present, and Future." *Annals of Clinical and Laboratory Science* 29(4): 253–262.

Patzelt, D. 2004. "History of Forensic Serology and Molecular Genetics in the Sphere of Activity of the German Society for Forensic Medicine." *Forensic Science International* 144(2–3): 185–191.

Pavlova, L.B., and A.N. Shamin. 1992. "Bibliography on the History of Analytical Chemistry." *Journal of Analytical Chemistry* 47(1–2): 169.

Pearce, D.N. 1994. "Sherlock Holmes, Conan Doyle and Cocaine." *Journal of the History of the Neurosciences* 3(4): 227–232.

Peterson, J.L. 2004. "Dr. Walter McCrone's Contributions to Microscopy Workshops and the Certification of Criminalists." *Journal of Forensic Sciences* 49(2): 1.

Pilipenko, A.T. 1992. "History of Photometric Methods of Analysis." *Journal of Analytical Chemistry* 47(1): 70.

Pounder, D.J. 1984. "Death Investigation in Early Colonial South Australia, 1839–40." *Medicine, Science and the Law* 24(4): 273–282.

———. 1985. "Death Investigation in Colonial South Australia: The Early Years 1836–1839." *Pathology* 17(1): 129–134.

Preub, J., and B. Madea. 2004. "Portraits of Some Founders of the German Society of Legal Medicine." *Forensic Science International* 144(2–3): 109–112.

Püschel, K., H. Lach, E. Türk, and S. Pollak. 2004. "The Centenary of the German Association of Legal Medicine—From Its Foundation in 1904 to 21st Century Legal Medicine." *Forensic Science International* 144(2–3): 285–288.

Ragsdale, B.D. 1984. "Gunshot Wounds: A Historical Perspective." *Military Medicine* 149(6): 301–315.

Raszeja, S., and E. Chróscielewski. 1994. "Medicolegal Reconstruction of the Katyn Forest Massacre." *Forensic Science International* 68(1): 1–6.

Rible, H. 1973. "Historical and Theoretical Aspects of Isoelectric Focusing." *Annals of the New York Academy of Sciences* 209: 11–22.

Rilbe, H. 1995. "Some Reminiscences of the History of Electrophoresis." *Electrophoresis* 16(8): 1354–1359.

Rinsema, T.J. 1999. "One Hundred Years of Aspirin." *Medical History* 43(4): 502–507.

Rinsler, M.G. 1981. "Spectroscopy, Colorimetry, and Biological Chemistry in the Nineteenth Century." *Journal of Clinical Pathology* 34(3): 287–291.

Rogers, N.L., K. Field, R.C. Froede, and B. Towne. 2004. "The Belated Autopsy and Identification of an Eighteenth Century Naval Hero—The Saga of John Paul Jones." *Journal of Forensic Sciences* 49(5): 1036–1049.

Rollin, H. 2004. "The Attitude of the Legal Profession towards the Medical Profession." *The British Journal of Psychiatry: The Journal of Mental Science* 184: 273–274.

Romolo, F.S., and P. Margot. 2001. "Identification of Gunshot Residue: A Critical Review." *Forensic Science International* 119: 195–211.

Rosenfeld, L. 1985. "Alfred Swaine Taylor (1806–1880), Pioneer Toxicologist—And a Slight Case of Murder." *Clinical Chemistry* 31(7): 1235–1236.

Ross, J.E., and S.M. Tomkins. 1997. "The British Reception of Salvarsan." *Journal of the History of Medicine and Allied Sciences* 52(4): 398–424.

Rothbart, Daniel, and Ladislav Kohout. 2003. "Part III—Representation and Instrumentation—Justifying Instrumental Techniques of Analytical Chemistry." *Annals of the New York Academy of Sciences* 988: 250–257.

Sachs, H. 1997. "History of Hair Analysis." *Forensic Science International* 84(1–3): 7–16.

Salgado, M.S. 1988. "Forensic Medicine in the Indo-Pacific Region: History and Current Practice of Forensic Medicine." *Forensic Science International* 36(1–2): 3–10.

Schneider, R.G. 1987. "Life among the Hemoglobins." *Acta Haematologica* 78(2–3): 75–79.

Schneider, W.H. 1983. "Chance and Social Setting in the Application of the Discovery of Blood Groups." *Bulletin of the History of Medicine* 57(4): 545–562.

Schroeder, O., Jr. 1980. "Toxicology and Law." *Legal Medicine* 91–110.

Scrutator. 2002. "Let's Talk of Graves, of Worms and Epitaphs." *The New Zealand Medical Journal* 115(1155): 266.

Settle, F.A. 2002. "Analytical Chemistry and the Manhattan Project." *Analytical Chemistry* 74(1): 37A–43A.

Shampo, M.A., and R.A. Kyle. 1982. "Robert Boyle." *The Journal of the American Medical Association* 247(4): 516.

Shapiro, B.J. 2002. "Testimony in Seventeenth-Century English Natural Philosophy: Legal Origins and Early Development." *Studies in History and Philosophy of Science* 33(2): 243–263.

Simon, J. 2002. "Analysis and the Hierarchy of Nature in Eighteenth-Century Chemistry." *British Journal for the History of Science* 35(124 Pt. 1): 1–16.

Smith, D.E., and Richard B. Seymour. 1994. "LSD: History and Toxicity." *Psychiatric Annals* 24(3): 145.

Sneader, W. 1998. "The Discovery of Heroin." *The Lancet* 352(9141): 1697–1699.

Snyder, L.J. 2004. "Sherlock Holmes: Scientific Detective." *Endeavour* 28(3): 104–108.

Snyder, L.R. 2000. "HPLC: Past and Present." *Analytical Chemistry* 72(11): 412A–420A.

Somogyi, E. 1985. "The History of Forensic Medicine in Hungary." *The American Journal of Forensic Medicine and Pathology* 6(2): 145–147.

"The Stationary Phase and Chromatographic Retention. Festschrift in Honor of J.J. Kirkland." 2004. *Journal of Chromatography A* 1060(1–2): 1–252.

Stewart, T.D. 1978. "George A. Dorsey's Role in the Luetgert Case: A Significant Episode in the History of Forensic Anthropology." *Journal of Forensic Sciences* 23(4): 786–791.

Stoney, D.A. 2004. "A Selection of Some of Dr. McCrone's High and Low Profile Cases in the Forensic Analysis of Art." *Journal of Forensic Sciences* 49(2): 1.

Sturner, W.Q. 1998. "The Wit and Wisdom of Milton Helpern: A Glimpse in Time." *The American Journal of Forensic Medicine and Pathology* 19(3): 288–290.

Summers, R.D. 1978. "History of the Police Surgeon." *The Practitioner* 221(1323): 383–387.

Summers, W.C. 1999. "The Chinese Nail Murders: Forensic Medicine in Imperial China." *The Yale Journal of Biology and Medicine* 72(6): 409–419.

Svec, F. 2004. "Csaba Horváth's Contribution to the Theory and Practice of Capillary Electrochromatography." *Journal of Separation Science* 27(15–16): 1255–1272.

Swann, J.P. 1985. "Paul Ehrlich and the Introduction of Salvarsan." *Medical Heritage* 1(2): 137–138.

Synge, R.L. 1970. "A Retrospect on Liquid Chromatography." *Biochemical Society Symposium* 30: 175–182.

Tabakman, M. 1980. "Forensic Medical Service in the U.S.S.R." *The American Journal of Forensic Medicine and Pathology* 1(3): 271–276.

Taborda, J.G., and J. Arboleda-Flórez. 1999. "Forensic Medicine in the Next Century: Some Ethical Challenges." *International Journal of Offender Therapy and Comparative Criminology* 43(2): 188–201.

Tedeschi, L.G. 1981. "The Massachusetts Medico-Legal Society. The Early Years." *The American Journal of Forensic Medicine and Pathology* 2(3): 257–260.

Tewari, R.K., and K.V. Ravikumar. 2000. "History and Development of Forensic Science in India." *Journal of Postgraduate Medicine* 46(4): 303–308.

Touchstone, J.C. 1993. "History of Chromatography." *Journal of Liquid Chromatography* 16(8): 1647–1665.

Tsunenari, S., and H. Suyama. 1986. "Forensic Medicine in Japan." *The American Journal of Forensic Medicine and Pathology* 7(3): 219–223.

Vanezis, P. 2004. "Forensic Medicine: Past, Present, and Future." *The Lancet* 364(Suppl 1): s8–s9.

Vesterberg, O. 1989. "History of Electrophoretic Methods." *Journal of Chromatography* 480: 3–19.

———. 1993. "A Short History of Electrophoretic Methods." *Electrophoresis* 14(12): 1243–1249.

Vlasov, Y.G. 1992. "Chemical Sensors: History of Design and Development Trends." *Journal of Analytical Chemistry* 47(1): 80.

Vycudilik, W. 2000. "Historical Development of Expertise in Forensic Chemical Analysis. General Survey, Illustrated by Case Studies from the Viennese Institute." *Fresenius' Journal of Analytical Chemistry* 368(6): 550–552.

Wadee, S.A. 1994. "Forensic Pathology—A Different Perspective: Investigative Medicolegal Systems in the United States." *Medicine and Law* 13(5–6): 519–530.

Wagner, H.J. 2004. "On the Prehistory of the German Society of Legal Medicine." *Forensic Science International* 144(2–3): 89–93.

Walls, H.J. 1976. "The Forensic Science Service in Great Britain: A Short History." *Journal—Forensic Science Society* 16(4): 273–278.

Way, E.L. 1982. "History of Opiate Use in the Orient and the United States." *Annals of the New York Academy of Sciences* 398: 12–23.

Weider, B., and J.H. Fournier. 1999. "Activation Analyses of Authenticated Hairs of Napoleon Bonaparte Confirm Arsenic Poisoning." *The American Journal of Forensic Medicine and Pathology* 20(4): 378–383.

Wells, C. 1978. "Palaeopathology—Modern Medical Evidence from Ancient Human Remains." *The Medico-Legal Journal* 46(2): 35–46.

Whelan, W.J. 1995. "The Advent of Paper Chromatography." *The FASEB Journal* 9(2): 287–288.

Wiener, A.S. 1972. "Forensic Blood Group Genetics. Critical Historical Review." *New York State Journal of Medicine* 72(7): 810–815.

"Wilhelm Fresenius Memorial Issue." 2005. *Analytical and Bioanalytical Chemistry* 382(8): 1727–1998.

Woolridge, E.D. 1977. "Legal Aspects of Forensic Medicine and Dentistry." *Dental Clinics of North America* 21(1): 19–32.

Wright, R.K., and L.G. Tate. 1980. "Forensic Pathology. Last Stronghold of the Autopsy." *The American Journal of Forensic Medicine and Pathology* 1(1): 57–60.

Wyman, A.R., and R. White. 1980. "A Highly Polymorphic Locus in Human DNA." *Proceedings of the National Academies of Science* 77(11): 6754–6758.

Yashin, Ya I. 1994. "The Ninety-Year History of Chromatography (1903–1993)." *Journal of Analytical Chemistry* 49(10): 939.

OTHER REFERENCES

Amirani, A. 1996. "Sir Alec Jeffreys on DNA Profiling and Minisatellites" [cited October 19, 2005]. Available at http://www.mindfully.org/GE/DNA-Profiling-Minisatellites-Jeffreys1996.htm.

"The FBI Laboratory: An Investigation into Laboratory Practices and Alleged Misconduct in Explosives-Related and Other Cases (April 1997)." 2007. Office of the Inspector General, US Department of Justice. Available on-line: URL: http://www.usdoj.gov/oig/special/index.htm. Accessed February 23, 2008.

Lucas, D.M. 2003. "Highlights in the Forensic Science Odyssey: The First Ten Thousand Years." Paper read at American Society of Crime Laboratory Directors, October 28, 2003.

Moenssens, A.A. 1962. "The Origin of Legal Photography." Forensic-Evidence.com. Available online. URL: http://forensic-evidence.com/site/EVID/LegalPhotog.html. Accessed February 23, 2008.

Newton, G. 2004. "Discovering DNA Fingerprinting." The Wellcome Trust [cited October 19, 2005]. Available at http://www.wellcome.ac.uk/en/genome/genesandbody/hg07f005.html.

"Paul Erhlich: The Nobel Prize in Physiology or Medicine. Biography." In *Nobel Lectures, Physiology or Medicine 1901–1921*. Amsterdam: Elsevier Publishing Company. Available at http://nobelprize.org/medicine/laureates/1908/ehrlich-bio.html.

Smith, C.S. "Nearly 100, LSD's Father Ponders His Problem Child." *The New York Times*, January 7, 2006.

Index

ABOUT THE AUTHOR

DR. SUZANNE BELL is an assistant professor of chemistry with the Bennett Department of Chemistry at West Virginia University (WVU) in Morgantown. Her large international research group includes undergraduate, master's, and doctoral students working in forensic chemistry and forensic toxicology. Prior to joining the faculty at WVU, she was a professor at Eastern Washington University (EWU) where she worked with the Washington State Patrol to establish a forensic chemistry degree. She is a fellow of the American Academy of Forensic Sciences, a Diplomate of the American Board of Criminalistics certified in drug analysis, and a member of the Society of Forensic Toxicologists and the American Chemical Society.

A graduate of Northern Arizona University with a dual major in chemistry and police science, she went on to the University of New Haven where she earned an M.S. in forensic science in 1983. She worked for several years as a forensic chemist with the New Mexico State Police Crime Laboratory in Santa Fe before venturing north to the Los Alamos National Laboratory, where she spent eight years as an environmental analytical chemist. After going back to university, she obtained a Ph.D. in chemistry from New Mexico State University in 1991. She accepted the position at EWU after a postdoctoral appointment.

Her other books include *Forensic Chemistry* (2006), a textbook and lab manual; *Dictionary of Forensic Science*; and *Encyclopedia of Forensic Science*. In 2008, she released the second edition of the *Encyclopedia* and in 2009, a series for young adults entitled *Essentials of Forensic Science* will be published.